Spiritual Concepts for a New Age

Spiritual Concepts for a New Age

Connie Johnson

Balboa Press books may be ordered through booksellers or by contacting:

Balboa Press
A Division of Hay House
1663 Liberty Drive
Bloomington, IN 47403
www.balboapress.com
1-(877) 407-4847

Because of the dynamic nature of the Internet, any web addresses or links contained in this book may have changed since publication and may no longer be valid. The views expressed in this work are solely those of the author and do not necessarily reflect the views of the publisher, and the publisher hereby disclaims any responsibility for them.

ISBN: 978-1-4525-4628-5 (sc)
ISBN: 978-1-4525-4629-2 (hc)
ISBN: 978-1-4525-4630-8 (e)

Library of Congress Control Number: 2012901833

The author of this book does not dispense medical advice or prescribe the use of any technique as a form of treatment for physical, emotional, or medical problems without the advice of a physician, either directly or indirectly. The intent of the author is only to offer information of a general nature to help you in your quest for emotional and spiritual well-being. In the event you use any of the information in this book for yourself, which is your constitutional right, the author and the publisher assume no responsibility for your actions.

Any people depicted in stock imagery provided by Thinkstock are models, and such images are being used for illustrative purposes only.
Certain stock imagery © Thinkstock.

Printed in the United States of America

Balboa Press rev. date: 04/06/2012

To
Kristina and Benjamin
with deepest gratitude for lifetimes of shared blessings

Contents

Preface
Acknowledgments

Section One: Universal Laws—Metaphysics in the Physical World

Introduction: What Is a New Age?
- Unifying Principles of a New Age
- Criticisms of New Age Thinking
- The Ten-Foot-Pole Department

Chapter 1: Universal Law
- What Is Universal Law?
- Living within Universal Law: Love Your Neighbor as Yourself
- Reflections of Universal Law: "The Bum in the Ditch"
- Universal Law and Jesus
- Universal Law and the Gnostics
- Contributing Factors: The Rise of the Church and the Fall of Gnosticism
- Universal Law and Science

Chapter 2: Personal Energies and Healing
- Chakras and Auras: Our Personal Energies
- Healing Our Chakras and Auras
- Healing Our Personal Energies in the Context of Our Relationships
- Healing Our Energies with the Assistance of Another
- Other Alternative Healing Methods
- Disease as a Metaphor
- Environmental Energy Healing
- The Emerald Tablet

Chapter 3: Unseen Energies: Higher or Different Vibrations
- Source Energy: The Universal Mind
- Free Will
- Spiritual Helpers: The Higher Vibrating Energy of Angels and Guides
- Spiritual Assistance from a Different Vibration
- A Special Vibration: Loved Ones Who Have Crossed

Preface

What is a New Age? In the late 1960s, the rock group 5th Dimension popularized the song "Age of Aquarius," or "Let the Sunshine In." The message of the song was this: when we move into the Age of Aquarius, harmony, trust, and understanding will thrive; we should let the light come into our lives.

During the time that this song was popular, we were involved in a war that many opposed and we were rapidly losing faith in our national leaders. This was a refreshing message indeed. We could, if we let the sunshine in, suffer no more deceit or ridicule but rather experience mystic revelation. It was seductive and heady stuff, and an assorted and diverse group of people set out to discover what was meant by the Age of Aquarius: the New Age.

Since that time, many of us have continued to explore this world, and we have moved inevitably and intentionally into the philosophies, the values, and the beliefs of the New Age. I am one of those many, and I am a social worker and a psychic reader.

What is a psychic? Simply defined, a psychic is a person who uses paranormal abilities to access and acquire information. The word *paranormal* comes from the Greek and means, essentially, beyond or beside the rule. A reader "reads" this information. A psychic reader is a person who uses abilities that are not currently described in the known physical world of classical mechanics to read, understand, interpret, and convert information. (There is, however, another world of physics, and this is quantum physics. I believe that much of what is to be found beyond or beside the rule may be discovered here.)

In the past several years, I have often been asked if there is a book that defines the philosophy and the terminology of the New Age or psychic world in a manner that is concise and understandable. I could not find the book that I wanted and so decided to write it.

Acknowledgments

The biggest of all thanks go to my children, their spouses, and my grandchildren for their patience, support, encouragement, and above all, their love.

Thanks also to my seven best friends (in order of appearance):
Liz: BFF since fifth grade, first editor, and teacher extraordinaire
CinDee: who has allowed me to channel for her since we were in college
Stacey: an exceptionally creative sister traveler
Terry: who happily reinforced my eccentric ideas with her own similar ideas
Deb: who has resolutely listened and supported me
Linda: who encouraged me to expand my place in the metaphysical world
Fay: a sweet survivor and courageous woman

Thanks to Carolyn Rae Curtin for her photos
Thanks to Terry for her expertise on Runes, Enneagram, and Graphology
Thanks to Kristin Erlandsen for her help with Feng Shui
Thanks to Lissa for sharing her love of Faeries

Teachers to whom I owe a great deal:
Mary Wagner: Latin/English Literature teacher, GFHS
Hannah Hogsven: English/English Literature teacher, GFHS
Orel B. Vangen: Music and Band teacher, GFHS
Nathaniel I. Hart: Writing/Composition professor, UMM
Fred Peterson: Art History professor, UMM
So much food for the Soul. I bow to you.

Metaphysical practitioners and teachers who have helped me on my journey:
K.G. (also known as Kathy Knutson) from Sunsight Bookstore
Moon Rabbit, astrologer
Bobby Sullivan, psychic and ghost buster
Jenny Canfield, psychic and healer

Section One: Universal Laws—Metaphysics in the Physical World

Introduction: What Is a New Age?
- Unifying Principles of a New Age
- Criticisms of New Age Thinking
- The Ten-Foot-Pole Department

Introduction: What Is a New Age?

I am writing from my own perspective, that of a social worker and a psychic. Many who are in the world of the New Age will disagree with some of what I write, and that is to be expected, as there is no central, unifying belief. Indeed, many who are in the world of the New Age will be offended by the term "New Age." As with so many other groups who are outside of the social norm, identifying names become passé, and so we change the names and reject the old names, all in an effort to improve our image and give ourselves more social credibility.

Defining New Age philosophy is a formidable task. It is an eclectic and individual expression that takes its beliefs and values from many other spiritual expressions. New Age thinking is influenced by Hinduism, Buddhism, Taoism, as well as by Christianity, Gnosticism, Judaism, and Islam. It is also influenced by pagan religions and by the Gaia philosophy. New Age belief also incorporates scientific concepts since science often offers explanations for that which we have already embraced spiritually.

Unifying Principles of the New Age

In the New Age world, there is no single or specific person, place, or document that can offer an explanation of the New Age philosophy. Different viewpoints and beliefs have been embraced, rearranged, and discarded as each of us evolved in our own manner. There are, however, certain unifying principles. Here are some of them:

➤ There is no central belief system or doctrine; each individual's journey is deeply personal, and there are many paths up the mountain. Spirituality and our relationship to God is an individual and private journey. No one other person, group, or institution can define our spiritual relationship to the Universe. Others can assist, enlighten, inform, and educate, but they cannot find God for us. Spiritual reality is a transcendental reality; it is subjective and deeply personal.

➤ There is Universal Truth, and all reality is God. All things created by God and in the Universe are precious to God and are to be honored.

➤ God is variously thought of as "God," "Universal Energy," "Universal Source Energy," "the Source," "the Universe," "the Cosmic Mind," "One," "the Universal Mind," and/or "Universal Truth".

➤ Everything is energy, including God, people, animals, plants, thoughts, and feelings. There is limited need to create God in man's image, as God is abstract and energetic.

➤ Energy vibrates and at different rates. Source Energy or God is the highest vibration.

➤ Life has a purpose. Every thing and every experience is connected through Universal Source Energy (God) and there is Universal synchronicity; there are no accidents and no coincidence as everything happens for a reason.

➤ Consciousness persists after death.

➤ Negative expressions or imbalanced issues within the self and/or in relationships are destined to be repeated until a positive and balanced expression is achieved. This is the process of reincarnation.

➤ Personal experience, including intuition and other psychic experience, is valued; therefore relativity and subjectivity are acknowledged and embraced.

➤ Love is the unifying force, and our ultimate goal is to raise our personal vibration through love and through trust in the Universe.

➤ "Positive" emotions, such as love, compassion, and gratitude, are on one end of the emotional continuum, while "negative" emotions, such as anger, fear, and revenge, are on the opposite end of the continuum. Indulging in negative emotion is not conducive to good health.

➤ Spiritual, emotional, and physical healing can be enhanced and increased through alternate methodologies such as Reiki, Qi Gong, yoga, acupuncture, herbal therapy, aromatherapy, affirmations, positive thinking, etc.

➤ The total person is more than the sum of the individual parts, and health is achieved when mind, body, and spirit work together and in harmony.

➤ Information about the world around us and ourselves can be accessed through methodologies, such as numerology, astrology, tarot, and through various and other psychic avenues.

➤ We are full participants in the creation of our reality, and our thoughts and emotions are significant to our creation; therefore, love and gratitude are essential.

➤ All life is choosing.

➤ We have free will.

Criticisms of New Age Thinking

New Age philosophies have certainly been criticized and ridiculed. There are cynics and detractors who have a good deal to say about it. Here are just some of the issues that have been expressed:

➤ There is no central authority, no uniform set of beliefs or values, and no unifying policy. There are no buildings, temples, cathedrals, or mosques in which to gather and find persons of like mind. There is no one person who will tell us what is the right way or the wrong way to believe, think, feel, or to act. One could say that people who embrace New Age philosophy, to a certain extent, get to make it up as they go along. And this is somewhat true.

However, there are beliefs and values that, although they do not define the microcosm of the New Age world, do define the macrocosm. There is an acknowledged Universal Truth: there is a highest of all vibrations that many call God. God is love, and it is our responsibility, our mission, to reach for God and for love. The purpose of each journey through each lifetime is to help us raise our vibration so that we get closer and closer to God, or the Source vibration.

➤ Some have said that the belief in reincarnation gives us all a second chance so there is no motivation to behave well in the current lifetime. In fact, we get many chances. However, the concept of reincarnation should, can, and does motivate people to behave in life. If imbalance is created, if we harm others, the Earth, or ourselves, we come back again and again until we achieve balance. And so, if one feels stuck in a harmful, unconstructive situation, wouldn't one also be motivated to do the utmost to move out of it, knowing that the experience must be repeated, in some way or another, until balance is achieved?

➤ Many find the New Age idea that God is not solely in charge of our lives, our decisions, and even the Earth offensive and, I am sure for some, frightening. We are all cocreators with God and, therefore, bear substantial and significant responsibility for our choices and behaviors for ourselves, for our choices and behaviors within the context of our relationships, for our choices and behaviors toward and within our institutions, and for our choices and behaviors regarding the Earth itself. God, the Universe, Source Energy, the Cosmic Mind, whatever it is that you chose to call this highest of vibrations, is not a finished product. The Universe is ever expanding, and we are part of that expansion. We are cocreators with God, and so every day we must ask ourselves, "What am I creating?"

The Ten-Foot-Pole Department

If we are interested in entering the world of the New Age and in exploring our spiritual relationship to ourselves, to others, and to God through this avenue, there are issues of which we should be aware. This is especially true if we are seeking out such things as intuitive or psychic readings, energy healings, group meditations, or channeling. The New Age world is an unregulated world. This gives us the freedom to find our personal path to God, but it also opens the door for exploitation and manipulation. The good and the bad news is that there is no one to tell us how to think, what to do, or what choices to make, but there is also no one to protect us. We must be responsible for our choices, our decisions, our lives, and ourselves. If we make a good choice, we own it, but we do so as well if we make a bad choice.

We must keep an open and observant mind regarding human practitioners. While there is occasional fraudulence, most of those working

4

within these concepts are making an honest and sincere effort to bring accuracy into their endeavor. Information received from Spirit is correct. The practitioner's interpretation, however, may be imperfect and/or incomplete as he or she is filtering it through his or her own earthly experience.

"I would not touch it with a ten foot pole". This cliché means that we do not wish to go anywhere near that person, group, situation or concept. We may find it distasteful, offensive, or perhaps even dangerous. In any case, we intend to avoid it. The following is my personal ten-foot-pole list:

➤ Renunciation of your current spiritual expression need not be a prerequisite to adopting New Age philosophies or practicing within them.

➤ If you find a concept distressing or unnerving and believe that you cannot agree with it, do not embrace it. If it is right for you, you will find your way to it in your own time. Trust yourself.

➤ Never work with anyone with whom you are not comfortable. If you are being intimidated, manipulated, or coerced in any manner, if you observe negative techniques, if the work goes against your personal beliefs, or if things are presented with secrecy and are not explained to your satisfaction, do not work with that person or group.

➤ Avoid any form of manipulation, including the attempt to manipulate other people's thoughts, lives, or belief systems; do not do it and do not allow it. Again, it if makes you uncomfortable, you may not want to participate.

➤ Do what you want to do, but do not harm anyone, and this includes yourself. Never attempt to create something at the expense of someone else.

➤ Never ever threaten another person, Soul, or a Spiritual Guardian.

Never seek revenge—revenge is anti-healing in all directions. If you are learning about meditation, channeling, energy healing, or anything of this nature, *especially* do not use this psychic or energetic avenue to seek revenge. Any act of revenge will generate karma. However, using revenge in work of a spiritual nature will significantly increase that karma.

➤ When you attempt to create a negative experience for someone else, you also create one for yourself, as that which you send out comes back to you. We harvest what we plant. Creating with a mind to the positive, compassionate, generous, and balanced is always a good idea.

➤ Don't make "deals" with other Souls or with your Spiritual Guardians. You can ask for what you want, need, or desire without offering yourself or that which you value as a sacrifice.

➤ Always ask that what you are bringing into your life be for your highest good. Do not try to control it; let it come.

➤ When manifesting, use the words "I intend to receive," or "I gift myself," or "I draw into my life," or any other phrase that expresses your desire in a positive manner. Never use negative words or negative concepts; do not state what you don't want, rather state what you want. For example:

Do not say, "I don't want to be poor," but rather say, "Prosperity abounds for me."

Express gratitude for what you already have.

Chapter 1: Universal Law

- What Is Universal Law?
  - ❖ Four Universal Laws of Energy
    - ○ Law of Energy
    - ○ Law of Energetic Interconnection
    - ○ Law of Vibration
    - ○ Law of Energy in Rate, Rhythm, and Harmony
  - ❖ Two Universal Laws of Creation
    - ○ Law of Dichotomy or Opposition (Duality)
    - ○ Law of Generation
  - ❖ Two Universal Laws of Power
    - ○ Law of Transformation
    - ○ Law of Transmutation
  - ❖ Two Universal Laws of Manifestation
    - ○ Law of Attraction
    - ○ Law of Abundance
  - ❖ Three Universal Laws of Evolution
    - ○ Law of Evolution
    - ○ Law of Reincarnation
    - ○ Law of Karma
  - ❖ The Universal Law of Completion
    - ○ Law of Silence
- Living within the Law: Love Your Neighbor as Yourself
- Reflections on Universal Law: "The Bum in the Ditch"
- Universal Law and Jesus
- Universal Law and the Gnostics
  - ○ Wisdom and Truth Revealed: The Laws of Power, Evolution, and Completion
  - ○ Jesus, an Energetic Spiritual Presence: The Laws of Energy
  - ○ Mystical Visions and Revelations: The Laws of Energy
  - ○ A Personal Path to God: The Laws of Power and Manifestation
  - ○ Gender Roles: The Laws of Creation
  - ○ Mary Magdalene: The Laws of Creation
  - ○ The Creation Story Revisited: The Laws of Creation
  - ○ Resurrection and Reincarnation: The Laws of Evolution
- Contributing Factors: The Rise of the Church and the Fall of Gnosticism
- Universal Law and Science

What Is Universal Law?

Universal Law is a collection or series of spiritual laws that govern the Universe. People in numerous diverse spiritual expressions have presented these laws in a variety of formats, in part or in whole. There is no single unified or centralized body of work that is "universal law." There are, however, certain commonalities within these laws that cross spiritual cultures and communities. Often the words to express the Law are different, but the concept is the same.

Countless people have recently been introduced to and have become interested in the Laws of Attraction and Abundance. These two Laws clearly indicate that each of us has power to affect the course of our lives. And indeed we can make changes. In fact, we *are* the power in our lives. But there is more to Universal Law than just the Laws to which our society has recently been giving so much attention.

Universal Law largely has its origins in Eastern philosophical thought. We can also find Universal Law at work in the New Testament of the Bible. We must give our attention to the concept and not the language, however, as different wording is used in the language of the Bible. Additionally, there is a body of work by the early Christian Gnostics that incorporates Universal Law into their texts. Universal Law is increasingly supported by science.

I first became acquainted with Universal Law in the mid 1980s when I attended a workshop given by Naunie Batchelder, and much of what she taught has remained the groundwork or basis of how I understand Universal Law. There are various more (or less) complicated explanations of the Law, and it is my intention to present Universal Law as clearly, concisely, and understandably as possible. These are the laws that, for me, organize the New Age concepts with which I work, and that are now being offered to you. For ease in understanding, I have divided fourteen Laws into six categories:

- ➢ Energy
- ➢ Creation
- ➢ Power
- ➢ Manifestation
- ➢ Evolution
- ➢ Completion

The Four Universal Laws of Energy

Law of Energy
This law says that everything is energy; this includes all things that come into form, or manifest physically. We are energy as is everything around

8

us. Energy that comes into form is visible to us as mass. Energy is always changing, moving into physical form or mass, and then coming back as pure energy; it is always transforming and transmuting. Much of the energy around us and in the Universe is not visible to the physical eye. Any form of energy can manifest into another form. Within our world, the total energy always remains the same—it cannot be lost or destroyed.

Law of Energetic Interconnection

All energy is from Source Energy and is a part of Source Energy. This energy forms a great Universal tapestry where all energetic vibration is interwoven or interlaced. As a result, everything in the Universe connects, relates to, or interacts with us in some way, just as we connect, relate to, or interact with it. This includes all life and everything of the earth: people, animals, plants, the waters, the soils, the air, and the rocks and crystals. It includes the energy generated by our thoughts, feelings, and actions. It includes all that exists in the Universe. All energy is interconnected, and we are all parts of a complex whole.

Law of Vibration

This law simply says that all energy moves or vibrates, and that nothing in the Universe rests. This includes the energies that we see as matter or form: people, animals, plants, crystals, and the earth itself. It also involves or incorporates all of the unseen energies. Our thoughts are energy, and each thought has its own vibration. When we think, we transmit a vibrational indicator into the Universe, so what we think matters. Vibration can be increased and decreased. Vibration that is sent out for good—for our personal good, for the good of someone or something else, for the "higher good"—increases in vibration as it moves through the Universe. This higher vibration is returned with the blessings of those higher frequencies. The same is true for vibrations that are meant to harm—those that are vengeful, greedy, or selfish, and that attempt to take power over another. These vibrations will return with a lower frequency and will bring struggles and challenges. That which we send out comes back to us.

Law of Energy in Rhythm, Rate, and Harmony

This law says that all energy moves in its own rhythm and at its own rate. Rhythm and rate characterize the existence of all that is in the Universe. People, animals, plants, rocks, and the earth itself all vibrate in different rhythms and at different rates. There is a diurnal and a nocturnal rhythm that establishes day and night. There are rates and rhythms that determine seasons and the movement of the sea and the planets. People have cardiac, respiratory, and circadian rates and rhythms. Celestial beings move in their own rates and rhythms and in frequencies so high that they are not

9

discernible to us. Every distinct and separate thing moves at its own rate, in its own rhythm, and in its particular time and space. And every single disparate piece works in harmony with every other single disparate piece, creating a great interrelated whole and reflecting the regularity and the rhythm of the Universe.

The Two Universal Laws of Creation

Law of Dichotomy or Opposition (Duality)

This is the law of contradiction or opposition within the whole. It states that everything is whole and within that whole a duality exists: yin and yang. For instance, female and male, receptivity and aggression, dark and light, passivity and activity, or stagnation and movement are all opposites within a whole. The whole is incomplete and cannot exist without the dichotomous parts. The contrasting parts complete the whole, and neither part negates the whole or can be excluded. Opposites within the whole ensure that the whole stays in motion. This, in turn, ensures the growth that is necessary to create balance.

Law of Generation

This is the creative triangle. It takes two opposing or contrasting energies plus a third point from which to create or manifest. For instance, in a physical expression, a man and a woman use the creative energy of sexual union to bring another person onto the planet. Intentions, thoughts, emotions, and behaviors are all third points out of which we can transform or transmute energy. Without sorrow, we would not know joy; without division, we would not know integration.

The Two Universal Laws of Power

Law of Transformation

This law says that we can transform that which is undesirable by concentrating on that which is desirable. Every situation is whole in and of itself, and within that whole, there is negative and there is positive. The third point out of which we transform the situation is our own intention. For instance, we wish to have increased joy in our lives; joy is the positive aspect of the circumstance, whereas despondency is the negative aspect. We must intentionally turn our attention to that which gives us joy and remove our focus from that which brings despair.

Law of Transmutation

This law says that the only authentic power is the power of transmutation; that is, taking something that is of a lower vibration and changing it into something with a higher vibration. When we are using power appropriately and in a balanced manner, the energy circulates in the pattern of a number eight as it goes from lower to higher. It pulls from the lower vibration and brings it into the higher vibration. If we use power inappropriately, we lose the top half of the eight and end up with only the bottom half, and so we go round and round in circles, never moving into the next higher evolution. Our first responsibility is to raise our own vibration.

The Two Universal Laws of Manifestation

Law of Attraction

We create our own reality. Everything exists in a state of pure potential until something or someone acts upon it, observes it, or interacts with it. What we imagine, we create. The more we direct our attention to what we want, the more we attract it; the more we direct our attention to what we do not want, the more we attract it. The more joy we feel, the more joy we create and attract. The more despair we feel, the more despair we attract and create. Our thoughts and emotions are energy and are acknowledged by and are a part of the Universe; what we think and what we feel help us to create our reality. We manifest our own reality.

Law of Abundance

The Universe was designed so that everything each person needs is available to him or her. We are meant to live in a state of abundance. Abundance refers to our material world, but it also pertains to our emotional, social, intellectual, and spiritual world. Abundance simply means that there is a plentiful supply. In its purest state, abundance is about everything that we need to propel ourselves into a higher vibration. This law is frequently misunderstood, and when people are initially working within this law, there is the tendency to want to bring only ease, comfort, good health, and plentiful material resources into their life. And, of course, there is the ability to make vast improvement in all of these areas. However, we are also working within other laws. If, on a Soul level, we have decided that we need a particular or specific experience to raise our vibration, we may not permit alterations to the current plan. We may not allow certain things to enter our life or allow certain things to leave it. This is our choice on a Soul level. This does not mean that we cannot improve the situation or that we cannot bring ourselves support and comfort, for we certainly can do so.

Law of Evolution

All things are evolving toward God. In the human experience, our
Souls drive our growth, but the move to evolve is true for all things.
Everything, including us, is pushing to evolve to the next level, pulling up
from the previous level in a process of progressive complexity. Our goal is to
vibrate at higher and higher levels as we "reach" for God. In the human
experience, we are pushing ourselves to move from the lower vibrations
(such as anger, fear, greed, jealousy, and hatred) to the higher vibrations (such
as love, joy, trust, compassion, and completion). Evolution always exists and
is dynamic in all expressions of life.

Law of Reincarnation

This law is interwoven with the Law of Evolution—each Soul goes
through the process of reincarnation as we move to increase our vibration
and to reach for God. Reincarnation means simply that we are born, live a
life, die, spend time in the world of Spirit, and then are born again, repeating
this process over and over. This law tells us that our Souls are never lost but
are energy and are constantly cycling. Each time we incarnate, we are
(allegorically) separating the grain from the chaff until we are "finished" and
can move into a different experience. When we decide to incarnate, we
choose the components of the upcoming life experience. We choose our
names, our birthdates and times, and our birthplaces. We choose the major
players in the coming life experience, and we choose the major events. Of
course, free will operates as well, and we can always alter the story. It is likely
that we will commit to the relevant relationships and experiences, however, as
our choices are based on our push for the higher vibration.

Law of Karma

How we act, think, and behave matters; the results of our thoughts,
feelings, and actions create karma. Karma is the law of cause and effect.
Karmic law is unbreakable. This is the Buddhist wheel of
action/reaction/action/reaction. As we reap, so shall we sow. "Bad" karma
means that we have created an imbalance. We may have failed to give
ourselves proper care and respect; we may not have accorded dignity to those
with whom we are in relationships; we may have negatively disturbed life in
God's Universe. "Good" karma means that we have corrected an imbalance.
We have transformed the situation and may receive energy that positively
supports us in our journey in the human experience. People create karma at
different rates and at different speeds. When we choose to reincarnate, we
also choose which karmic issues we will address in the lifetime. We choose
the people (with their consent, of course), we choose the situations, events,

and places. Each of us creates and have created our own karma, and each of us has chosen when and how we will deal with it. It is easy to start blaming when are living the effect and don't remember the cause. *We* are the cause of our karma, and whatever our response is to anything, we start another karmic chain.

The Universal Law of Completion

Law of Silence

This law is the law of completion and therefore the law of initiation. It is the law that speaks to achievement and therefore to the conclusion of an experience, a situation, a relationship, or a worldview and then makes way for the new. Again, this law is very connected to the Law of Evolution. It says that we are what we have become, and we show it; we do not need to talk about it, or proselytize, or preach; we reflect it in our very being. It is the law that declares that we are who we are, we have evolved to this vibration, and we will not change that by announcing that we are something else. *Esse Quam Videri*: "to be, rather than to seem to be." It is what it is; I am who I am.

Living within the Law: Love Your Neighbor as Yourself

We live within Universal Law whether we are aware of it or not. But how does living within the essence of the Law pertain to our daily lives? The Law informs us that we are energy as is everything else, seen and unseen. All energy connects to all other energy, and so what we say, what we feel, and how we behave is important as it reverberates with all other energy. Conversely, what others say, think, feel, or do affects us as well.

Our primary purpose in each life is to raise the vibration of our own energy. We do this by focusing on the higher frequencies of love, compassion, generosity, and gratefulness. We move our attention away from the lower frequencies and that which is born of hatred, fear, revenge, and thanklessness.

We are all reaching for and evolving toward Source Energy, or God. This energy exemplifies or embodies the qualities, traits, and behaviors that have their origins in the higher frequencies. Therefore, as much as we are able, we must reflect these qualities in ourselves. We have the power to create within our life, and we can (and should) do so with a constructive and beneficial intention. We must accord ourselves dignity and respect, just as we must do so for those around us.

When we have created harmful or imbalanced circumstances (karmic situations) with ourselves, others, or any Universal energy or creation, we must rectify the situation. We may do so at once and in this lifetime or we

13

may do so at a later time and in a different incarnation. But we must set it right, eventually. When we have remedied the situation, we are blessed with the gift of encouragement, consideration, and support from those with whom the energy is balanced. We gift them as well.

Each time we balance imbalanced energy, we raise our vibration and move from a lower frequency to a higher frequency. We have become something new, and we open the door for further increase and development. We give ourselves opportunity for expansion in each lifetime through the process of reincarnation and karma.

Reflections on Universal Law: "The Bum in the Ditch"

Our primary purpose is to enact power in our own lives, to transform and transmute our own energies, and to evolve into the next higher vibration. We must be exceedingly careful when we are bringing our power into the life of another. When we bring ourselves into others' lives, we must do so with knowledge, balance, and above all, with love. This is particularly so when we believe that we must take an action that is objectionable to others involved in the circumstance. It is only then that power will work as it should and transmute from lower to higher. This is what the saying "loving a thing to its next higher level" means.

We do not, however, know the complexities of the karmic issues of any person, place, or situation. If we interfere in a karmic journey, if we attempt to use our power to rescue someone or something that needs the karmic journey, we may be at best wasting our time in a fruitless endeavor or at worst doing harm.

I was introduced to the following allegory thirty years ago, and it has been of immeasurable assistance to me in my own life's journey. The metaphorical "bum in the ditch" is any person (or place or situation) asking for our intervention or assistance. The asking is not necessarily a verbal request but can be a presentation of victimization in a multitude of expressions.

When encountering the bum in the ditch, we must ask ourselves the following:

➢ Is the bum there for us to serve? This is always our first concern. We will know soon enough if the bum is there for us to serve by the thoughts, feelings, and actions of the bum. Is the bum accepting the issue and attempting to change the energy? Or is the bum off-loading that issue onto us or someone else, who may also be a bum?

➢ Does the bum need the ditch? This is possibly part of the karmic journey and has been chosen prior to the current incarnation.

> Does the bum want the ditch? The bum may not want to relinquish the thoughts, feelings, or behaviors that to us appear painful and unhealthy. There may be a reward or an incentive for continuing the actions that we find intolerable. Is the bum getting attention for the drama? Does the bum transfer responsibility for something to someone else by continuing the action?

Each of us can only create within our own lives. If the bum does not wish to alter the life, situation, or circumstance, in the end there is little we can do about it.

Universal Law and Jesus

There is only one reference to Jesus as a young person, and that is Luke's account of his visit to a temple when he was twelve years old. Except for this narrative, the time period between Jesus' infancy, and the beginnings of his adult ministry, are undocumented. Certain religious scholars speculate that Jesus spent his "lost years" in the East, where he acquainted himself with the Eastern philosophical and spiritual teachings. This is an interesting conjecture and may indeed be so, but if Jesus is an aspect of the highest energies that we call God (and it is my personal opinion that he is), he was surely aware of Universal Law even without traveling east.

For the first several centuries following Jesus' death, there was a philosophical or doctrinal struggle between orthodox Christianity (the traditional Christian church) and Gnostic Christianity. The Gnostic Gospels often differ dramatically in their interpretation of Jesus, who he was and what he taught.

The New Testament in the Christian Bible is, for most people, the only source of information about Jesus and his teachings. But the New Testament and what has been given to us as the approved or sanctioned teachings of Jesus has been carefully chosen and edited.

The gospels of Matthew, Mark, Luke, and John were reputedly written by the apostles Matthew, Mark, Luke, and John. Traditional Christians rely on the information given in these books, and there is general agreement that these Gospels contain the heart of Jesus' teachings. Various Biblical scholars, however, challenge the belief that contemporaries of Jesus (the apostles Matthew, Mark, Luke, and John) actually wrote the New Testament gospels. In fact, we know virtually nothing about who really wrote these books. In addition, a number of Biblical scholars believe that the apocalyptic visions attributed to Jesus in the New Testament gospels of Matthew, Mark, and Luke were not a part of his teachings but were assigned to him by those who wrote those particular gospels. Indeed, they may have been added after the initial writings. Apocalyptic writings, such as are found in these gospels, are uncommon elsewhere.

The traditional Christian church holds the position that the apostles (four of whom were Matthew, Mark, Luke, and John) define the teachings of Jesus. Authorities within the church (priests, popes, ministers) believe that they receive their mandate from the apostles and consider themselves to be the only legitimate spokespersons for Jesus. When this hierarchy was created, the stated intention was to correctly interpret and then deliver Jesus' message. This gave the men within the hierarchy the power to be the managers of Jesus' teachings.

Even within the New Testament gospels, however, we can see the Laws at work. The following themes are taken from the gospels of Matthew, Mark, and Luke. These three gospels are called the Synoptic Gospels because they are very similar in perspective and content.

➢ Jesus invites us to trust God, (Source Energy, the Universal Mind). He asks that we not be afraid of the truth, but that we receive the Word with joy. "Word" frequently refers to Jesus, or the Spiritual Energy of Jesus, or the teachings of Jesus.

➢ He encourages us to embrace mercy, justice, faith, love, and generosity. He instructs us in the greatest commandment—that we first love God and then love our neighbor as we love ourselves. Jesus asks us to reach for the higher vibrations.

➢ He bids us to administer fair treatment to the sick, the wounded, and the poor. Again, he asks us to reach for the higher vibrations.

➢ He asks that we turn away from revenge, avarice, greed, deceit, envy, pride, self-indulgence, hypocrisy, and slander. He asks that we turn away from the lower vibrations and the harm that they will bring should we embrace them.

➢ He recognizes that living a spiritual life is difficult but directs us to actually live righteously and not just talk about it.

➢ He warns us against false prophets and instructs us that we will know them not by their words but by their actions. This reflects the Law of Silence—we are who we are, and we show it.

➢ He advises us that the disciple should be like the teacher.

The gospel of John stands alone, as John takes particular positions and develops specific themes that the other Gospels do not. It has been suggested by certain scholars that the gospel of John may be the only gnostic writing that has made it into the New Testament:

➢ In the third chapter, John tells us that God so greatly loved the world, that he sent Jesus to us. Those who embrace Jesus, who believe in him, will live eternally. Many scholars interpret this statement to mean that each of us must find our way to God; no one can save us but ourselves.

> In the third chapter he also says that we will not see God's kingdom unless we are born again, and that no one can enter God's realm unless we are born of Spirit and water. This may refer to baptism with water, it may refer to Spiritual rebirth, but it may also refer to reincarnation.

Universal Law and the Gnostics

Gnostics were mystics who believe that spiritual salvation was found through knowledge. The early Gnostic Christian community flourished in the first several centuries after the death of Jesus. They created a tremendous body of written work regarding Jesus and his teachings. None of it has been included in the New Testament (except perhaps the gospel according to John) and, indeed, much of it has been destroyed. Fortunately, some of the early Gnostic Christian work was recovered in Nag Hammadi, Egypt, in 1945.

The early Christian Gnostics believed that much of humanity stumbled through life in a deep sleep of spiritual ignorance. *Gnosis* (from the Greek word for knowledge) involved awakening from this bleak unawareness and attaining enlightenment and illumination. The early Christian Gnostics believed that the path to spiritual wisdom was through the liberation of the mind and the acquisition of knowledge.

Knowledge could be gained through a process of knowing oneself. On the deepest level, knowing oneself was the gateway to knowing human nature, human destiny, and God. Gnostics embraced the principle that insight could be gained through intuition and through mystic visions and revelations. The acquisition of knowledge and wisdom was a deeply personal process; there was no need for intervention or mediation by religious authority.

There is ample evidence that the Gnostics were well traveled and well read. The foundation of their philosophy was grounded in the tenets of Judaism, just as was the philosophy of the Orthodox Christians. Greek and Roman religious teachings, as well as spiritual doctrine from the smaller, local religions, also influenced their thinking. In addition, the Gnostics incorporated Eastern spiritual beliefs, including astrology, into their worldview.

The Gnostic Gospels are composed in a similar manner to other written spiritual or religious work, including the Bible. They incorporate abundant allegories, metaphors, symbolisms, and parables. When reading these gospels, it is often apparent that the Gnostics, at least many of them, had a good working knowledge of Universal Law. They may have phrased and framed it in a manner different from how we do so in the twenty-first century, but Universal Law permeates the Gnostic Gospels.

Gnostic teaching frequently departed from traditional church teaching. Following is a brief synopsis of some of those teachings.

Wisdom and Truth Revealed: The Laws of Power, Evolution, and Completion

In the Valentinian *Gospel of Truth* (written in the mid second century), the writer states that Jesus came to Earth to bring knowledge and enlightenment; this was his true purpose. Acquiring knowledge does not cause destruction (as in the story of Adam and Eve), but rather it brings joy to us as well as to God. The *Gospel of Truth* also tells us that Jesus is a quiet guide; a sage who came to us to teach wisdom. We can embrace his teachings if we desire to do so. It is our choice.

The *Songs of Solomon* declare that God is not stagnant but increases in wisdom and understanding and multiplies his knowledge. It is through divine grace that this knowledge is shared with us. *The Prayer of Thanksgiving* glorifies knowledge and the mind. It embraces joy and asserts that our divine selves are realized through knowledge. *The Gospel of Thomas* has a cautionary tone, telling us that if we do not know ourselves, we are destined to live an impoverished life.

Jesus, an Energetic Spiritual Presence: The Laws of Energy

In the *Commentary on the Gospel of John*, Herakleon interprets what John the Baptizer is saying in John 1:26 when he declares: "Among you stands one whom you do not know." According to Herakleon, Jesus is an energetic vibration, and the spiritual Jesus is already revealed to us. His energy is present in the world now, and he is in the midst of us.

Mystical Visions and Revelations: The Laws of Energy

In *The Secret Book of John*, a Pharisee asks John where his dead teacher is. John tells him that he has returned to the place from whence he came. The Pharisee censures John and tells him that he has been deceived. They have a brief conversation, and John retreats to a barren mountain for a bit of meditative contemplation. There John has a vision—the world shakes, heaven opens, and a light shines on creation. God tells John to pay attention as truth is about to be revealed so that John can understand it. Jesus tells John the true story of the creation of our world. In the Conclusion of *The Secret Book of John*, we are told that all that was communicated to him was communicated in mystery. When the message was delivered, the messenger disappeared.

In *Letter of Peter to Philip*, Jesus speaks to his disciples (long after he has been crucified and killed). When he is done speaking, he is taken again to heaven amid thunder and lightning. In *The Vision of the Foreigner*, Allogenes the Foreigner receives information in a revelation that is delivered by luminaries.

A differentiation is made between "primary revelation," which is visual or clairvoyant, and "revelation," which is verbal or clairaudient.

A Personal Path to God: The Laws of Power and Manifestation

In *The Secret Book of James*, Jesus tells us that each of us must choose whether or not we are going to abide by his teachings. We do not receive Universal grace because of someone else but must individually and independently have faith and behave in a loving manner.

The *Letter of Peter to Philip* was written during a time when Christianity was in its infancy and was struggling to survive. In this writing, Peter advises the disciples to resist authority because authority denies the inner person. In other words, those who take power over us do not have our Soul's best interest in mind; their agenda is different from that, and so we must look to our own Soul's growth. Instead, Jesus asks the disciples to focus on teaching the people as Jesus has instructed them to do. They are not to be afraid because Jesus is always with them, just as he was with them when he was embodied and living among them.

Gender Roles: The Laws of Creation

As in most religious traditions, Christianity has not had a flawless history when it comes to the worth and significance of women. In the Gnostic community, however, the energies of the yin and the yang as they pertained to female and male were often honored in an improved manner. For instance, in the second century, many of the Gnostic Valentinian leaders and teachers were women. The Gnostic Christian community frequently welcomed women into positions and roles that were denied them in the traditional Christian community.

Letter to Flora is a Valentinian gnostic work written by Ptolemy. Flora may be an actual person; Ptolemy leads us to believe that she is his sister, and that he is instructing her on the Laws of Moses. If she is indeed his sister, we can assume that she is an educated woman. However, Ptolemy may be speaking metaphorically, and Flora may reference the church.

In any event, Ptolemy has chosen to share valuable teaching either with a woman or in a woman's name. There are no works addressed to women or written by women in the New Testament. In the New Testament, Paul's treatment of women is often harsh. Ptolemy's approach achieves a balance between the yin and the yang, the female and the male, that is not found in the New Testament. Both men are using the Laws of Dichotomy and Generation albeit quite differently.

Thunder Perfect Mind is a beautiful text that speaks to the Universal Laws of Creation. Perhaps the voice represents Sophia, the aspect of the One that personifies Wisdom, but the voice is beyond doubt uncompromisingly female. *Thunder* repeatedly identifies the dichotomies that are paradoxically necessary for creation. She declares that she is virgin and whore, strength and fear, war and peace, wisdom and ignorance; she is cherished and respected everywhere, and she is detested and debased everywhere. *Thunder* clearly describes the duality that exists within the wholeness and asks that we recognize it, honor it, and take it into ourselves. Only by doing so can we create within ourselves and in the world in a healthy and balanced manner.

Mary Magdalene: The Laws of Creation

The *Gospel of Philip* tells us that Mary Magdalene was Jesus' companion, that he loved her more than the disciples, and that he kissed her often. In the *Gospel of Mary*, the disciples Peter and Andrew doubt that Jesus would speak privately to Mary and give her secret information. Levi (probably the disciple, Matthew) defends Mary and asks Peter and Andrew if it is wise to reject the Savior's measurement of her worthiness.

The Creation Story Revisited: The Laws of Creation

In their search for gnosis, the Gnostics had a central question: If God is good, how did evil come into the world? To answer the question, they reinterpreted the creation myth of the Old Testament. Their explanation of the genesis of the Universe differs significantly from the Orthodox Jewish teachings, as well as from the teaching of the traditional church.

The Gnostics believed in the highest of all vibrations—a vibration so elevated that it was illimitable and inconceivable. This vibration was the One, the Universal Mind, Source Energy, or God. The Universal Mind always existed and will exist forever. This energy created other energies and created them in pairs. Sophia (as Wisdom) and Christ (as Truth) was one of those pairs.

Sophia generated a thought, and because she had supreme power, her thought was not idle. She generated this thought independently, however, without the consideration or consent of either God or her partner. Therefore, what she brought forth was imperfect and misshapen. What she brought forth was Jehovah.

Jehovah was deficient and damaged. Sophia was ashamed, so she placed Jehovah on a throne and hid him in the clouds. He was not aware that there were other higher energies. Jehovah began creating; he created our solar system, our material world, and a host of angels. Jehovah did not know the derivation of his own force, and so he was mindless. His mindlessness and creating within it brought forth wickedness. He created without knowledge and by himself.

Sophia repents, and all of heaven intercedes on her behalf. The Universal Mind sends Jesus to Earth to restore the fullness (the Gnostics repeatedly use the word *fullness* to describe the highest realm of the Universal Mind). She created without honoring the dichotomy within the whole, and so her creation was inadequate, imperfect, and incomplete, as was Jehovah's creation.

Resurrection and Reincarnation: The Laws of Evolution

The traditional church teaches that Jesus' resurrection was a literal event; Jesus was human, he died, his body was raised from the dead, and restored to life. The early Christian Gnostics also addressed the resurrection, but their interpretation of it diverges from the traditional interpretation. They believed that the resurrection referred to a spiritual transcendence.

The early Christian Gnostic texts, as well as the Old and New Testaments of the Bible, contain metaphor and symbolism; they both include an abundance of obscure imagery. The Gnostic texts and the traditional Christian texts can be variously and diversely understood, and we can find the suggestion of reincarnation in both. The Gnostic texts, however, allude to reincarnation over and over again.

In the *Treatise on the Resurrection*, we are told that the resurrection is an on-going process and has already begun. When we are born, we take on a body, but when we die we live on, even though the body perishes. We do not give up the Soul when we die. Death is a transformation, and we transition into something new.

The *Gospel of Thomas* says that we came from the Light, and we will return to it. Thomas' students ask him when will the dead arise and when will the new world arrive. He tells them that it is happening now. Later, he states that they have had images that came into being prior to the image that they have currently assumed. Still later, he tells them that the Father's kingdom will not come because they are watching for it but rather that it is already spread out across the earth.

The *Songs of Solomon* informs us that God has taken the dead, given them bodies, and then the energy of life. *Poimandres* recounts the descent of the Soul to Earth and then the return to God, who is light and life. Our bodies are mortal, but our Souls are immortal, and it is our Souls that must make the journey through many spheres in a process that ultimately renders evil powerless. When wickedness is obliterated and balance and harmony are restored, we can enter the highest sphere where we can be with God and become Godlike.

The *Song of the Pearl* is a narrative poem about a prince who was sent into the world by his father (Truth) and his mother (Wisdom) to retrieve a pearl. They wrapped him in a glorious robe and wrote knowledgeable words in his heart to that he would be protected and remember his mission. When he got here, however, he put on the garments of those around him and fell into a deep sleep of ignorance; he forgot his mission. His parents sent emissaries to remind him of his mission. He awoke and remembered his duty, yet he longed to return to the world from which he had come. He recovered the pearl, cast off the filthy robes of the world, and began the journey home. He regained the glorious robe, which was gnosis, and returned home.

The *Song of the Pearl* may have multiple meanings, but surely it is an allegorical story about reincarnation. When the prince sets out, he knows he has a purpose; he is to collect a thing of great value. He gets caught up in the wiles of the world, however, and loses his way. He forgets that his purpose is to evolve, to embrace a higher vibration. The Spiritual World sends reminders, and he eventually awakens and resumes the journey. When he fulfills his purpose, which is to gain knowledge and to raise his vibration, he returns home to the Spiritual World.

Contributing Factors: The Rise of the Church and the Fall of Gnosticism

The Gnostics were driven to acquire wisdom and enlightenment. Although there were certain similarities in worldview among them, they had no unifying philosophy, as did the traditional Christian church. Also unlike the traditional church with its powerful hierarchy of authorities, they operated out of loosely organized groups.

In 325, Constantine adopted the teachings of the traditional Christian church and became the first Christian emperor of the Roman Empire. Through his conversion, the church gained influential political power. In 367, the Archbishop of Alexandria, Athanasius, ordered all apocryphal books with heretical tendencies destroyed. According to Archbishop Athanasius, the Gnostics were heretics. Their literature was apocryphal (invented and untrue), and so it was largely obliterated. Fortunately, a small number of the Gnostic manuscripts were hidden and saved. It is believed that the monks of Saint Pachomius in Upper Egypt are responsible for preserving those found in Nag Hammadi.

Universal Law and Science

People in many ancient cultures described various aspects of Universal Law. Those who described these concepts had no way of proving them to be true; they relied on knowledge that was passed down to them and on faith. However, science is now giving us new language and additional ways to imagine or to visualize the concepts of Universal Law. Although much work has been done scientifically, much remains to be done. The Universe belongs to God, God created the Universe, God is the Universe, and so whatever science has to offer us is of value.

The origin of our Universe has long fascinated all cultures, and there are countless creation myths. The scientific community currently embraces the theory that our Universe was created in a big bang. Between ten to twenty billion years ago, the Universe erupted in a gigantic explosion, a singular event that released all space and all matter. About a billion years after this big bang, gravity—the force of attraction between all bodies that have mass—began to pull that mass together, and galaxies, stars, and planets began to form.

Our galaxy in which our sun and planets reside is the Milky Way. Within our galaxy alone there are one hundred to five hundred billion stars, one of which is our sun; other galaxies are believed to have millions to trillions of stars. The Hubble Space Telescope is able to see about ten thousand galaxies, but scientists posit hundreds of billions of galaxies in our Universe. Earth is infinitesimal in the context of the Universe.

The Universe is unimaginably vast, and all manner of things happen out there of which we have minimal understanding. The Big Bang Theory is an explanation for how our Universe came into existence, and at this point in time and based on physics and mathematical formulas, it seems that it is accurate. Simply stated, the Big Bang Theory says that our Universe emerged from a state of extremely high temperature and infinite density in an explosive expansion.

Did our Universe come from a black hole from a dead star in another space and time? A black hole is formed when a star can no longer sustain itself and is overcome by the force of its own gravity. The star essentially eats itself, and nothing is left but a hole in the space/time fabric. As the black hole is approached, there arrives a critical distance from which nothing can escape; this is called the event horizon. The actual hole of the hole is called a singularity, and this is where matter is crushed to infinite density. It is at the singularity where the known laws of physics break down and space and time cease to exist as we know them. Singularities are hidden so we cannot observe what happens there.

Could our Universe have come from a black hole that was created from another space and time? A black hole is a singularity of infinite density that has pulled in all matter and energy. The most current speculation is that our Universe emerged thirteen billion years ago from a singular state of extremely high temperature and infinite density in an explosive expansion that released all space and matter. No doubt we will not have the answer to that question in our lifetimes.

How God creates is the business of God, and it is human arrogance to limit the imagination of this highest of all vibrations. It is a supercilious conceit to confine this being within our limited belief systems, mine included.

However the creation of the Universe was accomplished, I believe it was done with purpose. It is mystery, and it is ours to explore.

Chapter 2: Personal Energies and Healing

- Chakras and Auras: Our Personal Energies
  - ❖ Chakras
  - ❖ Auras
- Healing Our Chakras and Auras
  - ❖ Meditation
  - ❖ Color
  - ❖ Affirmations
- Healing Our Personal Energies in the Context of Our Relationships
  - ❖ Boundaries
  - o The Connection Continuum
  - o Etheric Cording
  - o Cutting the Etheric Cord
- Healing Our Energies with the Assistance of Another
  - ❖ Body Work, Massage, and Somatic Therapy
  - ❖ Acupuncture
  - ❖ Acupressure
  - ❖ Reflexology
  - ❖ Reiki
  - ❖ Qi Gong
  - ❖ Yoga
- Other Alternative Healing Methods
  - ❖ Homeopathy
  - ❖ Aromatherapy
  - ❖ Herbal Medicine
- Disease as a Metaphor
  - ❖ Why Do We Bring Accident and Illness into Our Lives?
  - ❖ Symbolic Meanings of Bodily Complaints
  - ❖ The Symbolic Correspondences and Our Body
- Environmental Energy Healing
  - o Feng Shui
  - o The Emerald Tablet

Everything is energy. Everything that comes into form or manifests physically is energy. We are energy as is everything around us. Energy that comes into form is visible to us; our bodies are energy that has come into form. Much of the energy around us and in the Universe, however, is not visible to us using the physical eye. We all have personal energies that vibrate at particular rates and rhythms; they are vital to our health and well-being and play a role in our connection to others.

Our chakras and our aura are a part of our energetic vibration and are our personal energies. We all have them. They vibrate at different rates and rhythms depending on our interaction with the circumstances of our lives. We can raise our vibration by giving attention to these energies and what they correspondingly represent.

Chakras and Auras: Our Personal Energies

Chakras

Chakras are personal energies. They are energy vortices, or wheels, inside the body that receive and moderate universal life force energies, or chi. Each chakra acts as a kind of valve or regulator and controls the flow of energy through our system. The universal life force (chi) enters the body through the chakra at the top of the head and travels down the spinal column to the other chakras. When we are living in harmony with the Universe, these vortices, or valves or chakras, are open and allow an abundant flow of chi energy. When we are living imbalanced lives—lives that are not in harmony with Universal energies—our chakras become closed off and function poorly. They do not allow for a generous flow of the chi that is so necessary to our well-being.

How we choose to perceive the conditions in our lives is reflected in the functioning of our chakras. How we choose to respond to our circumstances affects the flow of chi through them. When we try to control that which is not ours to control, when we approach the world and ourselves with anger, fear, jealousy, greed, and the like, we impair the proper functioning of our chakras. We open our chakras to a healthy flow of chi, the Universal life force energy, when we trust the Universe, "let go and let God," and when we are grateful and loving.

Although there are hundreds of chakras, seven of them are considered to be of central importance. All areas of human experience, both conscious and unconscious, can be divided into seven areas of awareness and correspond to these seven chakras. I am including an eighth chakra, as I consider it to be significant in our search for spiritual awareness. Each chakra has a name, a specific function, color or colors association, and location.

➤ The root chakra is associated with the color red; it is located at the perineum. This chakra governs all issues regarding our physical security, safety, and survival. It helps us regulate our instincts, particularly our fight, flight, or freeze responses. It is our courage and our confidence in the face of adversity of any kind. The root chakra corresponds to our sexual selves.

➤ The sacral chakra is associated with the color orange; it is located at the sacrum, just above the root chakra. This chakra governs all issues regarding our basic emotional needs, our desire for physical pleasures, and our cravings. It helps us regulate emotional balance so that we integrate our emotional selves with our intellectual, physical, and spiritual selves. It also helps us regulate our physical desires so that we can provide ourselves with healthy pleasures without creating addictive patterns. The sacral chakra represents our bodies and how we look; it also represents our reproductive processes.

➤ The solar plexus chakra is associated with the color yellow; it is located in the solar plexus region of the body. This chakra governs issues of power and control. It helps us regulate our concerns about owning and using our own power appropriately and effectively. It helps us regulate our concerns and fears about others taking unacceptable power and inappropriate control over us. It is the "pit" in our stomach. It is our personal empowerment and helps us move from the lower vibrations of fear and anger to the higher vibrations of trust and compassion. The solar plexus chakra represents our digestive issues.

➤ The heart chakra is associated with the colors green and pink; it is located in the center of the chest. This chakra governs all issues concerning love and relationships. It helps us regulate our personal boundaries and our healthy or unhealthy attachments to people. It helps us balance the positive emotional vibrations, such as compassion, forgiveness, and grace, with the negative emotional vibrations, such as condemnation, blame, and rejection. The heart chakra represents our circulatory issues.

➤ The throat chakra is associated with the colors turquoise or light blue; it is located at the top of the throat. This chakra governs all issues involving communication, self-expression, and how we impart our information. It helps us regulate any of our concerns with speaking, writing, singing, teaching, and channeling. It is the desire and the ability to speak our truth and to require that our needs be met. The throat chakra represents our throat, neck, and mouth.

➤ The third-eye chakra is associated with the colors violet, indigo, or purple; it is located in the middle of the forehead. This chakra governs all issues regarding intelligence and intuition, and our ability to clearly see the past, the present, and the future. It helps us regulate and embrace visual consciousness and embodies our ability to trust inner guidance. The third eye chakra represents our eyes and our brains.

➤ The crown chakra is associated with the colors deep purple or white; it is located at the crown of the head (where the "soft spot" of a newborn is found). It governs Divine guidance and our spirituality; it plays a crucial role in our consciousness and our spiritual awareness. The crown chakra governs karma. It embodies Universal Consciousness and helps us regulate our meditative and contemplative abilities and our reach for Source Energy and the higher vibrations.

➤ The stellar gateway chakra is associated with the colors gold or silver; it is located above the head. This is the link between the self and the Universe and is the gateway through which we channel Divine Guidance.

Auras

The aura, or etheric body, is an envelope of colorful, luminous energy that radiates around any natural or innate body, including human beings, animals, and plants. Each person, animal, or plant has an aura whose color is characteristic to that being. Depictions of Jesus frequently show his aura, which is generally seen as white, silver, or gold.

The aura is often seen in gradual layers, or gradations that blend into each other. A particular color might be closer to the body but can blend into a different color farther out from the body. The color blends can be different in different areas of the body. For instance, the inner color may be in blues, but as we go to the outer layers, the colors may change to greens. Or the head area may be in purples, while the torso or trunk of the body may be in yellows.

Our body is truly our temple, and our aura will reflect the health of the body as well as our emotional, mental, and spiritual health. As our health changes, we can expect a corresponding change in our aura colors. We can clean and strengthen our aura by giving attention to our health: physical, mental, emotional, or spiritual.

The part of the aura that is closest to the physical body represents the body itself; it reflects by color change any change or compromise to the physical health of the individual. One can always clean and strengthen this part of the aura by attention to bodily issues: diet, exercise, sunshine, and fresh air. The next layer represents emotional health; the next represents mental health; the last layer represents spiritual health.

Our aura will interact with the auras of others around us. If we feel adversely affected when around people who are depressed or ill, it is because our aura and the aura of the other person are interacting. This does not mean that we need to be ill or depressed, but it does mean that we might want to pay attention to what belongs to whom. The imbalanced energy of another person can imbalance our energy, and knowing this can help us guard against it.

Auras are said to extend out from the body from four feet to up to six or even eight feet. The more our aura comes into contact with the aura of another person, the more likely we are to experience their energy. If they are joyful and loving, we will encounter and perhaps feel that energy; if they are despondent or angry, we may unintentionally participate in that energy.

How do we see auras? There are computers with special programs that can actually take a picture of our aura. This is probably the easiest and quickest way to see an aura. Many people see auras, and children often see them with little difficulty, especially in the first few years of life. Some people are able to see them with the physical eye by looking to the side of or "around" the person, animal, or plant, using an unfocused eye. Some people see them with the third eye (see Chapter Seven); third-eye seeing is clairvoyant seeing and is an inner seeing or experience. Physical-eye seeing, as well as third-eye seeing, takes practice.

Chakras and auras work together. If the flow of chi through the chakras is balanced and healthy, the aura will reflect health and will present with vibrant, clear color. If the flow of energy is unbalanced or unhealthy, this too will be evident in the aura.

Healing Our Chakras and Auras

We are all ultimately in charge of our own health, whether it is physical and in the body, mental or emotional and in the mind, or spiritual and at a Soul level. Healing can only occur with our participation and permission.

We live in the human experience and have challenges and difficulties for a reason. Anything that is being healed has purposefully been brought into the life. As a result, it is unlikely that healing will be complete in the first undertaking; most often, it will take many attempts, a great deal of effort, and time.

Even so, it is our responsibility to address our healing issues and to move ourselves into a higher vibration. Our job is to live in awareness. It is important that we make it our intention to address our healing needs and to then give it our ongoing attention.

It is detrimental and disadvantageous to bring rage, blame, accusation, or denial into any healing situation. Instead, we want to embrace a calm acceptance and eventually move into gratitude, joy, love, and peace as the process progresses. The higher vibrating emotions support the flow of chi, the universal life force, while the lower vibrating emotions block it.

Much of the work that is to be accomplished in the healing process is work that we are able to do for ourselves. Meditation, for instance, is a tool that is especially useful in personal healing. Meditation allows us to connect to our subconscious self and gives us an opportunity to address the energies within us. The use of color and affirmations in combination with meditation can be a powerful ally in healing.

Meditation

Meditation allows a connection to a higher level of consciousness. During a meditation, we are intentionally directing our attention to calming the mind and altering our state of awareness. The purpose of meditation is to connect to our inner self. Meditation is a time to stop the mind and give it a chance to take a new direction. It helps us to examine ourselves as whole and complete. Meditation is extremely useful when we are addressing our own healing needs. (For a comprehensive explanation of meditation, see Chapter Seven.)

Meditation is frequently used for personal healing. Once you are in a meditative state, a state of deep relaxation, begin to visualize your chakras one at a time, starting with the root chakra. Visualize that chakra in its given color, and clean it up. Move from a muddier color to a color that is jewel-like and sparkling, rotating, or spinning freely, and just a bit translucent. Raise its rate and rhythm to a comfortable level.

Concentrate on each chakra until you feel that you have made a good effort to balance, heal, and restore it before you move on to the next chakra. Reflect on the meaning of each chakra and how your life will improve when you are functioning in all directions of good health in this particular area. Think of your body, mind, emotions, and your Soul. As you clean and clear your chakras, so too do you clean and clear your aura.

Colors

Colors have meanings, and many colors are associated with auras and chakras. Colors can show us where we have balance and where we have imbalance. Color is frequently used in the restoration and healing of personal energies and certainly with the clearing and balancing of the chakras. Colors other than those of the chakras have been included, as all color has meaning. Color may have a deeply personal meaning to each of us and may be different from what I have described here. We must trust ourselves to know what works for us.

We can use color and meditation to heal more than our chakras. For instance, if we are facing a difficult situation and need the courage to persevere, we may visualize ourselves surrounded by red (for courage and protection). Or, if we are in a disagreement with a loved one, we may visualize our loved one and ourselves surrounded by pink (for love) and green (for healing). If we have a cold or flu, we might visualize ourselves surrounded by green (for healing) and orange (for vitality and vigor).

Color Meanings:

➢ *Red:* This is the color of strength, passion, and will; it can be a powerful grounding color. Red can represent an exceptionally straightforward, hardworking person who lives through the five senses. It is the densest of the colors, and the color of emotional friction. As a result, it can indicate nervousness, anxiety, anger, or foul temper.

➢ *Orange:* This is the color of vitality, vigor, warmth, and creativity. It suggests energy and a sense of adventure. As a result, it can be the color of a person who delights in stimulating, adrenaline-producing endeavors. A golden, clear orange indicates self control, while a muddy orange indicates stress related to addictions or appetites.

➢ *Yellow:* This is the color of shared experience and indicates optimism and social ability. It is the color of mental aptitude, intelligence, awakenings, and inspiration. A golden yellow means that a person has appropriate personal power in their life, whereas a muddy yellow may mean that a person holds back and does not bring personal authority and strength into their life.

➢ *Green:* This is the color of nature and is a healing color. This color often means growth, balance, and healthy change. It is the color of love and compassion. A dark, muddy green can mean that a person is uncertain about a love relationship or is jealous. In our culture, green is also the color of money.

➢ *Blue:* This is the color of calm, caring sensitivity. This color often means a person knows what is wanted in the personal life and is achieving it. Blue is the color of expanded intuition and the ability to use it. A muddy blue may indicate depression, moodiness, or a flagrant and blatant display of emotions.

➢ *Indigo:* Indigo is the color of the seeker. This is generally someone who is interested in spiritual truth and is intuitive and sensitive. Muddier shades of indigo may indicate that a person has challenges and obstacles in their journey or at least the perception of challenges and obstacles.

➢ *Violet:* This is the wisest and most sensitive of colors and is also the color of the seeker who is interested in spiritual truth. These are the people who some describe as having their head in the clouds. Violet indicates psychic ability.

➢ *Pink:* This is the color of unconditional love and compassion. Pink also indicates a love of the arts and of all things creative. A muddier pink can indicate immaturity.

➢ *Brown:* This color generally indicates a person who is grounded to earth's concerns and is structured and analytical. It can also mean, when seen in the chakra, that a person's energy is blocked in some manner.

➢ *Black:* This is the color of protection. It is a transformative color that captures light and pulls energies toward it. It may also indicate that something is being hidden; black spots may mean negative or imbalanced habits, or secrets.

➤ *White:* This is the color of purity and truth. It is the pure state of light and suggests transformation and transcendence.

➤ *Silver spots, lights, or twinkles:* This generally indicates a person of great creativity and may indicate the creation of "new" life or pregnancy.

➤ *Silver and Gold:* These colors are generally associated with Divine Life Force Energy and are frequently seen as the aura in depictions of God, Jesus, angels, and other beings that are considered divine.

Affirmations

Affirmations can also be a useful tool in healing and balancing energies. The word *affirmation* comes from the word *affirm*, which means to state as a fact, or to make a factual statement. Every word we say and every thought we think is an affirmation of our personal truth.

Some of our personal truths are working to our advantage and help keep us healthy and balanced. Some of our personal truths do just the opposite and invite into our lives that which we say we do not want. For instance, if we believe that we are good at our job and that we have the time and the energy to devote to it, it is likely that we can and will do this. If we believe that we can easily balance our job needs with our family needs, it is likely that we can and will do so.

However, if we believe, for example, that we are overweight and no matter what we do we cannot be other than that, it is likely that we will be overweight. And if we think that we do not deserve to be in a loving and harmonious relationship, we will attract to us people who bring discord and suffering.

When creating affirmations, we are making the effort to rewrite our personal stories ourselves. We are constructing a new reality and embracing possibilities that we may not have heretofore acknowledged. It is therefore essential that affirmations are positive.

Affirmations are frequently used in personal healing. When composing positive affirmations, start by thinking about that which you would like to improve. What do you want? What would you like to enhance or increase or develop or create? Do not say what you do not want, but say what you want.

For example, don't say, "I don't want to be poor," but say, "I attract abundance in all areas and in all directions." If there are negative things that you feel must be addressed, use the word *release*. So you might say, "I release all thoughts of poverty and scarcity and bring abundance and prosperity into my life."

Always be grateful for what you already have. You might say, "I am grateful for the wonderful blessings that are a part of my world; I release all thoughts of poverty and scarcity and bring abundance and prosperity into my life."

Some examples of positive affirmations:

➤ *Health:* every cell in my body vibrates with vitality, harmony, and health; my body is my temple, and I am perfect.

➤ *Happiness:* my heart shines on every aspect of my life, and I am filled with wonder; I release all fear and invite health and happiness into my life.

➤ *Love:* I am a beautiful person and love flows effortlessly through me; I open myself to love and to joy. I feel love all around and echoing within me; love comes to me in many ways.

➤ *Self-Esteem:* I rejoice in myself, and I am perfect in every way; I am filled with energy and enthusiasm, and I create the best in life; brilliance shines from my heart and my Soul.

➤ *Strength:* I am confident and deal with every issue perfectly; I take total, beautiful control of my life, and harmony, joy, beauty, and safety surround my loved ones and me.

Our experiences and awareness, our development and evolution correspond to our chakras. Giving our chakras attention, clearing and balancing them, promotes well-being and good health. If we are having special issues in specific areas, it is particularly beneficial to clear and balance the chakra that corresponds to the issue.

We can clear and balance our chakras simply by giving it our attention and making it our intention to do so. Direct the attention to calming the mind and entering a meditative state of awareness. Visualize the chakra as a pure, vibrant, translucent ball of color. Allow it to spin or rotate freely; raise its rate and rhythm to a comfortable level. Repeat an appropriate affirmation.

Crystals of compatible color can be used to assist the visualization. Crystals also lend their personal energy to our endeavor, so choose the crystal carefully. (See Chapter Nine for information on crystals.) Crystals can be held or placed in the location of the chakra.

Clearing and balancing a chakra may not bring immediate relief but will eventually help raise the vibration in the area that corresponds to that chakra. Clearing and balancing all of the chakras contributes to overall health. It supports a free flow of chi; it also keeps our attention on the issues that need resolution and evolution. Cleaning and strengthening our chakras advantageously affects the health of our aura.

Healing Our Personal Energies in the Context of Our Relationships

We can improve our relationships by attending to our personal energies. We cannot do much with other people's energies without their consent, but we can look to our own vibration. We are all separate entities that are energetically interwoven with all other separate entities, including other people.

We have boundaries, however, that indicate where our energies stop and other energies, including other people, begin. The more we are aware of those boundaries and can make informed decisions regarding our connection to others, the more health and well-being we can actualize.

Boundaries: Separateness, Connection, and Etheric Cording

Boundaries

Each of us is a distinct and separate individual surrounded by a personal aura. Our aura represents the outer edge of our "self"; it is the boundary that distinguishes where we stop and another begins. Boundaries represent the distinctions and divisions between our individual selves and another person. Ideally, we both stay within our boundaries as we connect and relate to each other; we take our separate self and connect or relate to another separate self. We maintain ourselves as distinct, separate, and individual.

Our boundaries exist so that we can regulate the levels, or degrees of separation or connectedness, between us and another person. A healthy relationship with another person involves a connection to that person while also maintaining separateness from that person. Although this may seem paradoxical or contradictory, this separateness while connecting is essential to the health of the individuals and the relationship.

The Connection Continuum

Connection occurs on a continuum. On one end of the spectrum are the blockades to any meaningful connection. In this instance, boundaries can be impenetrable walls that are designed to keep people out. They prohibit intimacy, familiarity, or closeness. This can be a very controlled approach to connecting to another person and allows minimal openness or vulnerability. People who erect barriers of this intensity often feel helpless or defenseless in the face of other people's energy and so are protecting themselves by erecting their own energetic fortress.

On the other end of the continuum, boundaries can be so permeable that they almost dissolve altogether and merging occurs. Merging is not connecting but is being swallowed up, or absorbed, by another; it is losing the self in another self so that two selves, or parts of two selves, become indistinguishable.

Merging is almost never beneficial or healthy except in very exclusive, limited situations. For instance, the merging that takes place between a parent and an infant is essential to the baby's emotional health.

However, as the baby grows older, this merging should evolve into something else. As the child grows, the parent must construct a different boundary and shift toward a connection to the child that allows that child to be a distinct and individual person. The parent must gracefully allow the child a personal expression in that unique journey that belongs to the child and the child alone.

Additionally, people merge during the sexual act, and if the relationship is loving and healthy, this is desirable. Minimally, sex creates a temporary merging through a psychological, emotional, and physical bond. However, there is always the risk that one or both parties will want to stay emotionally and psychologically merged when physical sexual union is complete. This is not desirable or healthy.

Merging is not etheric cording but can quickly lead to etheric cording. For example, when the sexual act is complete, individuals must again return to their separate selves. Additionally, if the parent is not able to become more separate as an infant becomes a toddler and a child, an etheric cord will likely be created. This does not mean that a healthy connection cannot be maintained, but we must all ultimately reside again within our own boundaries.

Etheric Cording

An etheric cord is an energetic attachment or tie that represents an imbalance; it is a connection that does not promote health or growth. Our aura can be attached, or we can attach our aura, to another person or object, situation, or experience, place, or time. Etheric cording is always a deleterious, detrimental, or damaging attachment, without exception. Etheric cords frequently occur when intense emotions are involved. This might include emotions, such as anger, fear, jealousy, obsession, or greed, but it might also include skewed or distorted expressions of love, compassion, gratitude, or joy.

An etheric cord is created when love is confused with codependence and there is an unwholesome interest in the affairs of another person. An etheric cord is indicated when there is a refusal to move on from a relationship in which one felt misused in some manner. There is warning of a potent and detrimental cording if there is a decision made that someone has to pay for a perceived personal injustice—particularly when there is a significant commitment to delivering punishment and revenge.

There might be an obsessive fondness for money, the big house, or the fancy car, and an etheric cord might be created for the experience of wealth or for the goods. There might have been a move to another abode or another state but with a fixation about association to the previous place, and the attendant refusal to live in the present space and in the present moment. This too is an indication of an etheric cord.

One of the most powerful etheric cords and one of the most difficult to break can be created during a sexual experience. Even when the sexual union is chosen and beneficial, it is difficult to keep the experience and the other person in the realm of a healthy bond and away from merging. If the sexual experience contains confusion or conflict, the experience goes beyond merging and almost always an etheric cord is created. If aggression and violence are a part of the experience, the survivor of that experience will initially be corded to the event.

One of the most complex and challenging cords one might be called upon to address is the etheric cord to a past life experience. There is generally considerable confusion about why this particular issue exists. If it doesn't make sense in the current life, however, it may well be corded to a previous life. An example of past life cording might be an inexplicable, incomprehensible, debilitating fear of a particular person. Feelings of panic regarding this individual have no apparent basis in the current life; nothing evident has ever occurred that would contribute to the fear. However, great lengths are taken to avoid this person, and the life is compromised as a result. No doubt this is an issue that has its roots in a previous life.

Heightened awareness of these situations, personal energy, time, and work are required to break these cords. This is not an easy or effortless process, but at some point, one must preserve the health by cutting that etheric cord and beginning the process of living differently.

Cutting the Etheric Cord

Etheric cords are never beneficial or healthy. Even when we care about the person to whom we are corded, we cannot help them by being corded to them. The breaking of the etheric cord does not mean that we must break the connection entirely and stop loving them.

Breaking the cord, however, releases that person to his or her own journey. All of us have challenges and struggles, and we have a responsibility to walk our own paths and live the lives we have created. At times, we are called upon to love another from a distance so that we can allow that person their journey. This might be difficult for them and for us, but we must do it. Etheric cords can harm us. They are depleting, confusing, and exhausting; they weaken our aura, imbalance our chakras, and restrict the flow of life force energy.

To release cording, we must have the courage to examine our lives and ourselves with purposefulness and honesty, taking inventory of our emotions, behaviors, and habits. We must understand that we are responsible for our own Soul's growth, and that each person on the planet is also mandated with this responsibility. We must understand that in order to live a balanced life, we must address not only our physical needs but also our emotional, mental, social, and spiritual needs.

We can cut the cord through intention; direct our attention to calming the mind and entering a meditative state of awareness. We then visualize ourselves and the person or object, place, or time that is bringing difficulty or concern and see ourselves cutting the cord that binds us. If desired, we can visualize ourselves wrapped in a protective (red), healing (green), or compassionate (pink) color. Concentrate on the wonderful feelings we will have when we free ourselves from the burden of the cording. Use an appropriate affirmation.

We must give our attention to the positive, beneficial, and constructive thoughts and feelings that we will have when we are able to move away from the unhealthy bond. It is not helpful or advantageous to mire ourselves in the negative energy that is attached to the situation.

Etheric cord cutting can be done with the assistance of another, and this is frequently indicated if the cording is powerful and intense. The person from whom we are getting assistance cannot cut the cord—we do—but the imagery and physical representation of the act of cutting may give the process clarity and a concentration of strength that benefit the process.

Healing Our Energies with the Assistance of Another

There are other methods of energy healing that are best supported by the assistance of another person. Healing can only occur with our participation and permission. This is true for the healing work that we do personally for ourselves, but it is also true for any mainstream or alternative healing that is administered to you by someone else.

Energy healing has been used for hundreds, even thousands, of years and can be exceedingly useful in balancing not only physical energy but also mental, emotional, and spiritual energy. Chi permeates the body, flowing through and around it. When the flow of chi energy is imbalanced, disease of body, mind, or spirit may result. Regulating the flow and rhythm of the chi energy can improve, increase, and even restore good health.

There are many practitioners who have studied, trained, and prepared themselves for work in the various modalities. There is generally limited oversight by any regulatory body in the "alternative" healing community, however, and healers might claim to be knowledgeable in their art when they possess incomplete or inadequate knowledge. I am most certainly an advocate of energy healing as an assist to the healing process, and I am not an advocate of regulation. However, "buyers beware." Be sure that you get references, and carefully examine your practitioner's experience and training.

Recorded below are several of the most common or popular modalities. This list is intended to be an example of what is available and, on a very basic level, illustrate how the selected methods work. One or more of them might be appropriate for you. Trust yourself to know what you need, and then do your research regarding the chosen method.

➢ *Body Work, Massage, and Somatic Therapy*: Bodywork is a touch therapy that involves manipulating and re-patterning or moving the body in such a way as to bring about structural change. An example of bodywork is craniosacral therapy, in which the spine and the skull are gently manipulated so as to increase the flow of cerebrospinal fluid and thereby promote healing; it also affects structural change in the body. Massage is touch therapy that involves the manipulation of soft tissue, muscles, and connective tissue. Somatic therapy is a term that is used when a "whole body" or body, mind, and spirit approach is incorporated into the body work or massage philosophy. All of these therapies address the physical needs of the body and can help with back pain, joint inflexibility, atrophied or overused muscles, migraine headaches, and the like. Bodywork, massage, and somatic therapy can also help with sleep, decrease anxiety, improve concentration, and reduce fatigue. People who regularly receive these kinds of therapies often report an increased sense of awareness or clearer perception after having this healing work done.

➢ *Acupuncture*: This is from an ancient Chinese healing system that identifies certain meridians in the body that correspond to the body's internal organs. When the chi or life force energy is interrupted, the result is disease. Needles are inserted into meridian points and then stimulated so that the chi can be restored to its normal flow. Acupuncture is a whole-person approach and addresses the body, mind, emotions, and spirit. Acupuncture is professionally taught and is more widely regulated than most of the other alternative healing modalities. However, there are differing levels of training, and the wise consumer will investigate where the training and practice has occurred and how extensive it has been.

➢ *Acupressure*: This is, again, an ancient Chinese healing system that uses meridian points to unblock the flow of chi energy. Acupressure deals with the whole person so that the body, mind, emotions, and spirit are included and addressed. Pressure is applied to selected points in the body to relieve pain, stress, or tension and to restore a healthy flow of chi in the body.

➢ *Reflexology*: This is a healing system that has been described in the ancient texts of the Chinese, Egyptians, and Indians. Reflexology involves the feet. Specific zones in the foot have been found to correspond to specific organs, glands, and muscles in the body. Our feet may have injurious or harmful crystalline deposits under the skin; massage and pressure break down these deposits. This helps the lymphatic system remove toxins from our bodies. Simultaneously, the zones of our feet correspond to specific nerves throughout the body, and the stimulation of the feet also helps restore a healthy flow of chi in the body.

➢ *Reiki*: Reiki comes from the Japanese words *rei*, which means "God's wisdom," and *ki*, which means "chi," or "universal life force." It is believed to have originated in Tibet thousands of years ago and was rediscovered by a Japanese Buddhist monk in the 1800s. Reiki addresses the restoration of the proper and healthy flow of chi, or life force energy, throughout the body so that physical, mental, emotional, and spiritual health is improved. Over time, each person's system develops blockages that weaken the flow of the life force energy. The Reiki practitioner uses thoughts, personal energy fields, and hands to help remove the blockages and restore the flow of the chi. Reiki is based on the belief that each of us is responsible for our own health and well-being; we must want to be healed and participate in the process. It emphasizes a healing attitude that is without fear and worry and is filled with gratitude.

➢ *Qi Gong*: Qi Gong is loosely translated as "working with life force energy." It is an ancient system of breathing techniques, meditation, exercises, and postures that are designed to promote the flow of chi in the body. Again, it addresses the physical and spiritual body, as well as mental and emotional functioning.

➢ *Yoga*: Yoga is an Indian spiritual philosophy that seeks to join body, mind, and soul in an effort to attain universal consciousness. The word *yoga* comes from a Sanskrit word that, loosely translated, means the "joining of the individual soul with the cosmos." Yoga is a system of breathing techniques, exercises, postures, and meditation that is designed to improve physical, mental, emotional, and spiritual functioning.

Other Alternative Healing Methods

Whatever is imbalanced in the thoughts, emotions, or spirit is reflected in the body. Traditional medicine offers valuable diagnostic and treatment options. There are other alternative healing approaches that involve the energies found in certain materials or substances, that can be used as an adjunct to traditional medicine, or by themselves. Consultation with a practitioner of conventional medicine may be indicated.

Homeopathy

Homeopathy is a holistic and alternative medicine that concerns itself with the vibration of the chi, or life force energy. The philosophy in homeopathic medicine is that "like cures like." The homeopathic remedies or treatments that are administered to a client or patient are comprised of a highly diluted preparation of a substance that causes similar symptoms to that which is being treated. The minimum dose of this substance is thought to correct an imbalanced vibration and restore the proper flow of the chi, thereby achieving improved health in the whole person.

Aromatherapy

Aromatherapy is a holistic approach to the care of the body through scents. These scents stimulate the brain, the nervous system, and the olfactory nerves, and trigger certain therapeutic effects. Aromatherapy is the controlled use of volatile plant materials, known as essential oils, for the purpose of promoting physical, mental, emotional, and spiritual health and well-being. For instance:
  ➢ *Bay Laurel*: colds and flu
  ➢ *Clary Sage:* anxiety
  ➢ *Lavender*: depression
  ➢ *Chamomile*: digestive distress
  ➢ *Eucalyptus*: expectorant for coughs

Herbal Medicine

Many plants have medicinal and therapeutic properties. They can address not only physical ailments but also improve mental functioning and help stabilize the emotions. Herbal healing can be extraordinarily helpful; nevertheless, some caution is required. For every effect, there is a side effect. For instance, comfrey may assist with joint pain, but it also treats diarrhea, and so if one doesn't have diarrhea, one might become constipated. Additionally, some people may be allergic to certain herbs. And finally, proper preparation of the herbal remedy is crucial, as improper preparation may render the herb useless.

Again, incomplete or inadequate knowledge can cause harm, so be sure that you get references, and carefully examine your practitioner's experience and training. If treating yourself, be sure that you do adequate research. Use your resources. There are many books available that can help you with your inquiries and practitioners with whom you can consult.

Some of the more common herbal remedies include the following:
  ➢ *Anxiety*: Valerian Root
  ➢ *Burns*: Aloe Vera
  ➢ *Colds*: Echinacea
  ➢ *Colds and Coughs*: Pennyroyal
  ➢ *Constipation*: Senna
  ➢ *Cuts and Scrapes*: Tea Tree Oil
  ➢ *Depression*: St. John's Wort
  ➢ *Fever*: Willow or White Oak Bark

40

- *High Blood Pressure:* Garlic or Celery Seed
- *Indigestion:* Chamomile or Peppermint
- *Insomnia:* Evening Primrose
- *Menopause:* Black Cohosh
- *Mental Functioning:* Ginkgo
- *Motion Sickness:* Ginger
- *Pain Reliever:* Slippery Elm Bark
- *Toothache:* Clove or Willow

And remember, whether we want it to be or not, food is medicine.

Disease as a Metaphor

A metaphor is a figure of speech in which a term or phrase is used that is meant to indicate a resemblance. It is an analogy between two ideas or two things. It is not a literal translation but a suggestion and is meant to show how two things that are not necessarily alike in most ways, are similar in an important way. For instance, "she was a rat," or "he is a couch potato," or "it's raining buckets."

As part of our culture, we have been taught to believe that we have no participation in, or influence over, illness, accident, or pain; that these are things that just happen to us. This is not so. We bring illness, accident, and pain into our lives in various ways, and our thought patterns, emotional responses, physical habits, and beliefs about ourselves and the world around us all contribute to imbalances that manifest as disease or pain. This manifestation can take place in the physical body but also in the spiritual, mental, or emotional body.

For example, you have a sore neck. Perhaps you have injured yourself in a physical activity. Additionally, however, you might also be acting in an inflexible manner in your opinions and, as a result, have alienated someone close to you. You are being a "stiff-necked fool," in the words of this person. The injury to your neck symbolizes or signifies that your problem is more than just a sore neck—it has an emotional, mental, or spiritual component as well. Your body, mind, emotions, and spirit are all working together and in harmony, and you have injured that particular part of your body to help you understand your other issues.

With insight, awareness, and effort, we can influence this situation and move from *dis*ease to ease. We may not be able to effect a cure entirely, depending on the root cause of the problem and how deeply entrenched we are in the issue, but we can ease the situation.

Why Do We Bring Accident or Illness into Our Lives?

➢ We may bring illness, disease, accident, or pain into the current life from a past life situation. This is a karmic situation and probably the most difficult to influence, particularly if we do not know the origin of our difficulty. We could bring the issue in because, on a Soul level, it reminds us of a karmic imbalance and it is our desire that we address the matter in the current life. We could bring the issue in as some kind of a test or challenge that, when overcome or dealt with in a balanced manner, will enlighten us in some way. We may bring it in because it was traumatic in a past life and our Soul continues to work on releasing the condition or the situation.

➢ Suggestions about our environment and ourselves can influence us. If we are repeatedly told something, and come to believe it, we can manifest it in our physical, emotional, and spiritual body. For instance, if we are told that getting our feet wet causes cold and flu, and we believe it, we invite cold and flu whenever we get our feet wet. If we are told that breaking a mirror causes seven years of bad luck, and then we break a mirror, we may invite accident or misfortune into our life. If someone tells us that they can and will put a curse on us and cause us to have pain, and we decide to believe that, we may manifest pain in our body. (Be aware that no one can have this kind of power over us without our full cooperation, and should we fall victim to a "spell," it is because we have colluded with the spell caster.)

➢ We all have intellectual, emotional, and psychological issues in our lives. If we refuse to deal with them, they may demand to be addressed on a physical level. Physical distresses can be symbols, or metaphors, for our intellectual, emotional, and psychological issues. If we change our thinking and feelings, we can influence the physical manifestation that is occurring in the body.

Many of our colloquial expressions reflect the mind and emotion, body and spirit connection. Whether we are consciously aware of it or not, we are on other levels aware of the interconnectedness, and our speech reveals it. Terms like "I felt left out in the cold," "he didn't have my back," she pisses me off," "he made my blood boil," "I couldn't stomach it," and "I couldn't stick my neck out" are all examples.

Symbolic Meanings of Bodily Complaints

The following exemplify metaphoric or symbolic physical issues or complaints and the attendant intellectual, psychological, or emotional correspondence:

➢ *Addictions*: guilt and a desire to forget the accompanying issues; running from your beliefs and feelings about yourself; fear about living your life

➤ *Anxiety*: not trusting the evolution and progress of your life; holding fear, being afraid of joy; expecting the "other boot to drop"

➤ *Asthma*: feeling stifled or smothered, especially in important relationships; suppressing emotion

➤ *Balance* (loss of): erratic and unbalanced thinking; not being centered and grounded

➤ *Bladder problems*: not releasing emotions—they come out in the form of burning urine; being "pissed off"

➤ *Car sickness*: fear of being trapped or held captive, or (conversely) fear of moving forward

➤ *Cholesterol*: blocking your path; creating obstacles to receiving love and joy

➤ *Colds*: mental disarray—too much happening at once; feeling left out—"out in the cold"

➤ *Constipation*: refusing to release outdated information and emotions; ungenerous attitudes toward others

➤ *Diarrhea*: not getting the value out of life experiences, or letting go too soon; meaninglessness in the life

➤ *Diabetes*: lack of sweetness and joy in life; fear of accepting joy and sweetness, or fear of losing it

➤ *Fatigue*: lack of excitement for what one is doing; boredom

➤ *Fevers*: burning anger

➤ *Headache*: listening to another when you do not want to or should not; listening to your own self-criticism; unexpressed anger

➤ *Heart problems*: material possessions are more important than love, relationships; lack of compassion—"they get what they deserve" attitude

➤ *Hemorrhoids*: sitting on something dreadful; afraid to move on or let go; fear of failure

➤ *High blood pressure*: fears about your ability to deal with the pressures of your life; anger and the desire to compel another to do what you want

➤ *Hives*: giving small things exaggerated importance

➤ *Indigestion*: experiencing life too hurriedly—biting off more than you can chew; worried attitude—cannot stomach it

➤ *Influenza*: feelings of powerlessness in response to mass negative beliefs

➤ *Insomnia*: fear about what you achieved today or need to do tomorrow; who sleeps with you?

➤ *Jaw problems*: unexpressed anger and a desire for revenge

➤ *Kidney problems*: shame; unwillingness to let go of old, negative feelings and move on

➢ *Liver problems*: justification for finding fault with others and for blaming them; unceasing complaining and failure to take personal responsibility

➢ *Menstrual problems*: inability to embrace femininity and take pride in it

➢ *Nail biting*: eating away at yourself (often due to beliefs about yourself); self denial; not protecting your personal space

➢ *Nausea*: fear of embracing an idea or experience; cannot stomach an idea or experience

➢ *Neck problems*: unbending stubbornness or rigid beliefs; unwilling to take a chance or "stick your neck out"

➢ *Numbness*: mental and emotional "deadness"; withholding good treatment to another

➢ *Overeating*: fear of emotions and the need to deaden or conceal them; self-protection and the idea that big is powerful; substituting eating for other pleasures

➢ *Paralysis*: escaping a person or situation; fear of your own actions

➢ *Pneumonia*: giving up; desperately tired of your life and what you are making of it

➢ *Skin problems*: desire to protect yourself and your identity; buried junk, just under the surface; out of sight out of mind

➢ *Smoking*: clouding an issue or numbing insecure feelings; mental and emotional escape

➢ *Stomachaches*: inflexible, refusal to digest new ideas; cynicism; cannot "stomach" it

➢ *Teeth problems*: biting off more than you can chew; inability to break down ideas and think and decide

➢ *Throat problems*: misuse of speech—critical, gossiping, and being judgmental; not speaking up when indicated

➢ *Thyroid problems*: humiliation; sense of entitlement that has not been fulfilled

➢ *Urinary problems*: "pissed off"

➢ *Yeast infections*: a feeling that sex is dirty and an inclination toward compulsive cleanliness

The Symbolic Correspondences and Our Body

Parts of our bodies represent bodily issues, but they also represent certain aspects of our mental, emotional, and spiritual selves. Understanding this metaphorical relationship can help us with personal healing as well.

➢ *Arms* represent how you hold and carry the experiences, relationships, and situations of your life. Are you holding something that is burdensome and needs to be let go? Are you carrying our own weight?

➤ *Backs* represent physical, emotional, mental, and spiritual support. Are you getting the support that you need? Who "has your back"? Or are you not getting the support that you need? Is your "back against a wall"? Do you need someone to "get off your back"?

➤ *Bones* represent structure. What structure, what foundation are you providing for yourself in your life? How are the external structures, such as family, educational institutions, or church, supporting you?

➤ *Brains* represent your internal "command center." It is your "hard drive" and directs and regulates the functioning of your body, mind, and emotions. Are you planning and executing those plans so that you can achieve what you wish to achieve?

➤ *Breasts* represent nurture. Who is nurturing you? Are you properly nurturing yourself, and are you providing nurture to those around you who need it? Are you over-nurturing, or nurturing in places where you should leave well enough alone?

➤ *Ears* represent listening. Are you listening to gossip or to verbally dismissive or abusive messages about yourself or those around you? Are you listening to philosophies or ideas that are pessimistic, harmful, unconstructive, or depressing?

➤ *Eyes* represent the ability to see clearly. Do you see how your past has lead you to here or how your present will lead you into your future? Are you seeing abundance around you, or are you focusing on inadequacies?

➤ *Feet* represent how your follow your personal path in life. Are you following your path as you define it? Are you following someone else's definition of your path?

➤ *Fingers* represent the detail of your life, and each finger has its own definition. Are you paying attention to the details? Are you over-involved in the details and failing to see the big picture?

▪ *Thumbs* represent your rational, analytical skills and the detail that you bring or do not bring to your cognitive thinking.

▪ *Index fingers* represent the self and your confidence or fear about being able to take care of good old number one.

▪ *Middle fingers* represent sexuality, but they also represent anger, rage, or temper. Sex or anger can be represented here; however, sex and anger combined can also be represented.

▪ *Ring fingers* represent your unions with other significant people in your life. Are you loving appropriately and being loved appropriately? Are you causing grief to yourself, to others, or are others causing you grief?

▪ *Little fingers* represent your family and how you feel you fit into your family but also how your family fits into society as a whole. The little finger also represents pretense.

➤ *Hands* represent how you handle your experiences. Do you hang on too long, do you let go too quickly? Are you grasping at events and situations, or is your grip on your life experience feeble?

➤ *Hearts* represent love and your relationships. Are you giving and receiving love, compassion, and understanding? Hearts also represent security. Are you accepted and understood by those you love, or are you denounced, criticized, or attacked?

➤ *Joints* represent the ease and flexibility with which you change or accept change. Are you holding onto an experience or situation that should be released?

➤ *Knees* represent self-importance or pride and, conversely, humility. Are you remaining inflexible in your attitude in the face of new information or changing circumstance? Or are you humbling yourself, just a bit, and perhaps admitting that you do not have all the answers and that you are ready to move on?

➤ *Legs* represent how you move into life. Are you hesitant, afraid to take hold of life and live it? Or are you propelling yourself into life with little thought, preparation, or plan?

➤ *Lungs* represent the ability to self-actualize in a safe environment; it is "the freedom to be me" safely. Lungs are about the "breath of life" and your ability to access what you need, as much as you need, and in a sheltered atmosphere. Is someone smothering you with their needs, wants, and desires and discounting or disregarding yours? When can you breathe a sigh of relief?

➤ *Mouths* represent your ability to express yourself, but they also represent your dietary choices. Are you speaking your truth? Are you gossiping, threatening, or rambling on in meaningless speech? Is your diet balanced and nourishing?

➤ *Necks* represent flexibility and the ability to see what is around you. Are you observing the happenings, situations, and occasions of your life? Are you seeing the people around you? Are you approaching what is around you with adaptability and acceptance? Or are you being "stiff-necked"?

➤ *Nerves* represent how you are receiving or accepting information. Are you able to hear and understand what is being said to you? Are you denying your truth or someone else's truth?

➤ *Ovaries* represent a woman's creativity; they are the point of creation. Are you creating a peaceful, harmonious experience? Or are you creating an experience full of acrimonious dissent and discord? Are you failing to create at all?

➤ *Prostates and testes* represent the masculine principle. Are you accepting yourself as a man? Or are you listening to cultural bias and definition and allowing it to undermine your understanding of yourself as fully male?

➢ *Shoulders* represent what you carry. Are you burdened with more than your share and unable or unwilling to ask for help? Are you carrying despair, or hope? What are you carrying?

➢ *Spines* represent the ability to cope with life. Are you inflexible, stubbornly insisting that you get your own way? Or are you so flexible that you never get what you need or want?

➢ *Stomachs* represent the ability to digest ideas, experiences, and situations. Are you releasing your experiences before you have gotten the lessons that you need to get from them? Are you hanging onto outdated ideas?

➢ *Throats* represent how you express yourself. Are you speaking your truth? Are you gossiping? Are you obscuring information or concealing facts about some situation?

➢ *Uterus'* represent creativity, again, and are the heart of a woman's creative self. So again, are you creating a peaceful, harmonious experience? Or are you creating an experience full of acrimonious dissent and discord? Are you failing to create at all? What are you creating?

➢ *Wrists* represent the ease with which you move from experience to experience. Are you gracefully accepting the ebb and flow of your life?

Healing may hurt—there is often pain when something or someone grows. Long-standing habits or philosophies may need to be excised, and old wounding may need to be reopened and revisited. The achievement of true health often takes courage, but it is necessary if we desire wholeness in mind, body, and spirit.

Environmental Energy Healing

Feng Shui

Feng shui is an ancient Chinese system of aesthetics that addresses the vital life force, or the chi, that flows around the body and surrounds each of us in our personal environments. Balancing the rhythm and flow of environmental energy can promote vigor and vitality by blocking negative energies or by avoiding them altogether.

Feng shui means "wind and water." It is an ancient art that helps us create peace and harmony in our personal environments—our homes, office spaces, and work areas. It is also used, or can be used, for larger spaces, such as buildings, landscapes, and communities. Feng shui is based on the principle that our environments reflect our selves, and that we are interconnected with everything on all levels and in all directions. Tranquility and repose in the environment will encourage tranquility and repose in the self, just as discord and debris in the environment will encourage the same in the self.

There are many schools of feng shui, but the one with which I am most familiar was founded by His Holiness Grandmaster Lin Yun. It is the Black Sect method of feng shui. Black Sect Feng Shui is based on the bagua.

The bagua is an energy map that addresses nine areas of life. Health is in the center of the energy map, and the other areas radiate from the center. Each area is associated with color, direction, and one of the five elements: earth, water, wood, metal, or fire. The eight areas that surround and enclose the center are the following:

➢ Fame and Reputation
➢ Relationships, Partnerships, and Marriage
➢ Children and Creativity
➢ Benefactors or Helpful People and Travel
➢ Career
➢ Knowledge and Spirituality
➢ Family
➢ Wealth

There are various schools of thought regarding feng shui, and each method determines the areas of our homes differently. The Compass method, for instance, relies on direction - north, south, east and west. The Black Sect School tends to be more adaptable to Western thought. In the United States, and in much of the Western world, we do not situate our homes or towns using a consistent direction; as a result, other methods would require more adjustment than does the Black Sect method.

The Emerald Tablet

The Emerald Tablet is a text that is said to reveal the secret of primal, elemental substance and its transmutation. The origin of the Emerald Tablet is unknown, but Hermes Trismegistus is most often credited with either writing it or translating it and handing it down. Hermes Trismegistus is an early Christian Gnostic.

The Emerald Tablet has survived and been passed down in many translations; the content of these translations appear neither to have been altered nor edited. One of the tenets of the Emerald Tablet is, "What is from above is also from below, and what is from below is also from above; the work of wonders is from one substance." It is from here that we get our sayings, "As above, so below" and "As within, so without."

The Emerald Tablet tells us that all things are connected, and the microcosm and the macrocosm reflect each other. It helps us understand how our environment reflects us and we reflect our environment. The areas in the bagua correspond to and reflect our environment. They work in harmony with each other.

For those who are interested in the Emerald Tablet, this is what it says:

> ➤ What is told is accurate and authentic.
> ➤ That which is below corresponds to that which is above, and that which is above corresponds to that which is below. All things come from the one thing, the primordial substance.
> ➤ Everything sprang from this substance in a single projection; how wonderful is this transmutation; this is the first principle of the Universe.
> ➤ Its father is the sun, and its mother is the moon; the wind carried it, and the earth nourished it.
> ➤ It is the origin of everything.
> ➤ It is the sanctification of the Universe; in it all things are perfect.
> ➤ It is the energy that became Earth; separate earthly concerns from heavenly energy, through wisdom and care, then concentrate on the higher energies.
> ➤ The energy rises from earth to heaven and descends again to earth, containing the energy of both. Now you can obtain the glorious energy of the Universe, and all will be made clear to you.
> ➤ Universal energy is the source of all power and prevails over everything in the heavens and on the earth.
> ➤ The microcosm was formed just as the macrocosm was formed; as above, so below; as within, so without. This is the universal blueprint and is relevant to all.
> ➤ This is wisdom.
> ➤ Hermes the Thrice Great was blessed with this wisdom.
> ➤ He has preserved this information for others to obtain.

Chapter 3: Unseen Energies: Higher or Different Vibrations

- Source Energy: The Universal Mind
  - ❖ Defining the Indefinable: The Universal Mind
  - ❖ Our Personal Relationship with God: The Universal Mind
- Free Will
- Spiritual Helpers: The Higher Vibrating Energies of Angels and Guides
  - ❖ What Is an Angel?
    - ○ An Angelic Presence
    - ○ Guardian Angels
    - ○ Archangels
  - ❖ What Is a Guide?
    - ○ A Guiding Presence
    - ○ Naming Our Guides
    - ○ Our Guides Role after Our Current Incarnation
    - ○ Guides Providing Special Assistance: Bringers
- Spiritual Assistance from a Different Vibration: Star Beings and Faeries
  - ❖ Star Beings
    - ○ A Star Being Presence
  - ❖ Faeries
    - ○ Gaia Guardians
    - ○ Faeries and Humans: Ego and Judgment
    - ○ A Faerie Presence
- A Special Vibration: Loved Ones Who Have Crossed
  - ▪ Our Soul Families
    - ○ Sedona
    - ○ Caleb
    - ○ Rory
- Ghosts
  - ❖ Ghosts: Where Are They?
    - ○ A Ghostly Presence: A Haunting
    - ○ Ghost Sending
    - ○ The Sea of Faces
    - ○ Ghostly Energy
- Clearing Ghosts and Other Negative Energies
- Experiencing Higher and Lower Vibrations

Everything is energy. All energy vibrates in its own frequency, at its own rate, and in its own rhythm. Energy that becomes matter is evident to us, and we can see what form it has taken. Much of the energy in the Universe and around us, however, is not visible to us using the physical eye.

There are energies that vibrate higher than we do as humans. Several of these energies have such high frequencies, rates, and rhythms that they are unfathomable to us. The highest of all vibrations, Source Energy, vibrates so highly that is it utterly incomprehensible to us. Many spiritual and religious traditions inform us that we cannot know the name of God much less see that energy. Angels and spiritual guardians also vibrate at a higher rate and rhythm than we.

Other energies have very different frequencies, rates, and rhythms and are inscrutable in their own way. Star Beings and Faeries vibrate in a manner dissimilar to us, and their energies too are veiled. Their rates, rhythms, and frequencies may be higher, but we do not necessarily know. We do know that there is an essential and fundamental divergence from our own energies.

Loved ones who have crossed have energy similar to our own but a bit fainter. Ghosts are people who have died and have not crossed; their energy is slower and denser than ours.

Source Energy: The Universal Mind

No matter how we define or perceive Source Energy, it is this God energy that has the highest rate and rhythm of all the energies in existence. The Christian and Islamic religious traditions are founded in Judaism. Judaism has taught us that we cannot look into the face of God and live. God's energy is illimitable, inconceivable, incomprehensible, infinite, and unceasing. It is unknowable and beyond our intellectual grasp. It is mystery.

God is Source Energy. God is the Universal Mind. The early Christian Gnostics called this energy The One. It is pure light, and no one can gaze upon it. It is immeasurable, unfathomable, unutterable, and unnamable. It is immaculate and is the invisible virgin spirit. Everything exists within The One.

Defining the Indefinable: The Universal Mind

Nonetheless, it is part of human nature to want to put this energy into a framework that is understandable to us. We want to tame God and to make God look like us. We want to define God, so we make up rules and create hierarchies so that our rules can be properly interpreted. We decide that some of us get a direct line to God and some get no line at all. Some get to ascend to higher awareness, while others are consigned to uncertain depths.

And most often we decide that our definition is the correct definition. There is a path up the mountain to God, and we are the only ones who know what it is. Taking ownership of God in this way is both divisive and dangerous. It is religious tribalism and will eventually and inevitably result in violence.

Our Personal Relationship with God: The Universal Mind

Every single one of us has God within us; this is our Soul. Our Souls are divine energy that came from Source Energy, and as with Source Energy, they cannot be destroyed and have no end. Our Souls are pure, radiant energy that is an eternal aspect of the Universal Mind.

Source Energy is never stagnant but is in motion and ever expanding and creating. It is through our Souls that we cocreate with Source Energy; reincarnation is a vital part of this process. We are evolving toward God. Our yearning, desire, and purpose is to vibrate at higher and higher levels as we reach for God. We are reaching for the universal wisdom that is the Universal Mind.

As we go through each human journey or experience, we push ourselves to move from a lower vibration to a higher vibration. On a Soul level, we are pushing for a Christ-like vibration as we reach for the perfect love and the perfect trust that is God.

Free Will

On a Soul level, we are pushing for a Christ-like vibration. But we live in the human experience and can be sidetracked by the clamoring of our bodies, minds, and emotions. We may allow our desires to dictate our experiences or we may give weight to the opinions of others and alter our course. Although our Souls push for the higher vibration, we have free will and can allow distractions in the human experience to influence our decisions and direction.

Free will means that we have the right to choose. Our lives, decisions, and choices are in our care and under our control; no outside force makes us do what we do. All life is choosing, and we choose; we can change direction and write our story differently if we choose. But we do come into each human experience with an agenda, and so it is often unlikely that we will change the personal narrative of the current lifetime at least within the major life events. But we can change if we so desire, and we certainly can change a great deal within almost any given situation.

Although Spiritual Guardians, such as Angels and Guides, may know what we need to promote our growth and foster our well-being, they will not intervene without invitation and permission. They will not interfere even when they see us heading in a direction that may not be in our best interest, particularly if we are headstrong in our determination to go in that direction. We need to invite Angels and Guides into our lives and be open to communication from them. Our Guides and Angels suggest things to us, but they do not direct us. Our choices, decisions, life path, journey, and karma belong to us and to us alone.

Spiritual Helpers: The Higher Vibrating Energies of Angels and Guides

Angels and Guides are vibrational energies that exist in the spiritual realm. They may manifest to us as embodied beings, but in their natural state, they are energy. Energy vibrates at different rates and rhythms.

In the world of Spirit, a higher vibration does not mean higher worth. Higher vibration means that there is an acquired wisdom. The higher the vibration, the closer the being (ourselves included) is to Source Energy. We reach higher vibration by an increase in awareness, enlightenment, and understanding.

Higher Vibration Energies are more evolved, wiser beings; they have been on the journey of evolution for a very long time and have had a multitude of experiences that we can only begin to imagine. Angels vibrate higher than Guides. Some Angels vibrate higher than other Angels, and some Guides vibrate higher than other Guides.

When we have contact with higher vibrating entities when we channel, we are sensing a vibrational energy. Therefore, people in different spiritual and psychic communities may use different terminologies and language to describe that energy.

What Is an Angel?

Angels are nonhuman celestial beings; they are not human beings and were never human beings. They are sentient beings that may have had an evolutionary journey similar to our own. But if so, it was in another time and space.

The word *angel* means "messenger of God." Angels are beings of love and are reliable, constant, and benevolent spiritual helpers. They are highly vibrating energies that live next to us on a different energy level. They do not have corporeal bodies but will present to us as embodied. We tend to see them the way we think we should see them (probably for the sake of our own comfort).

If we are still and meditative, we can often feel their energetic presence. Many people can see Angels, especially children. Children often lose this ability however as they get older. We can open ourselves to the experience of seeing Angels if we so desire (see Chapter Seven). Angels frequently present as transparent or semi opaque; they glow in different colors, according to their particular energies.

Because Angels vibrate so much higher and faster than humans, they generally do not show themselves to us unless we specifically ask. Many people find the experience of actually seeing Angels alarming or even frightening, so out of respect to us, they tend to remain invisible. However, if we feel ready, we can always request that they show themselves to us in some manner.

An Angelic Presence

When I started channeling in the early 1980s, I was comfortable working with my Guides and tended to ignore the issue of Angels. Several years ago, however, I was up in my little camper all by myself reading about Angels and decided that I was ready for that energetic experience. Before I went to bed, I expressed that readiness to the Universe.

About 4:00 a.m., I woke up and saw a glowing light by my bed. This light was bright, and yet it was soft and did not affect the darkness around it; it did not light up the space. I did not correlate my statement to the Universe with this light and kept blinking my eyes in an attempt to focus. After perhaps thirty seconds, it left. I was completely unafraid and went back to sleep soon after. Only in the morning did I realize that I had had an Angelic visitation (for which I said, "Thank you").

Several months later, I was driving down the freeway in the early evening well before dusk. It was a beautiful autumn day, and I had all the windows wide open. A glowing ball of light flew beside my car for almost a mile before it faded. Since that time, I have been blessed with a fuller awareness of the Angelic presence around me.

Guardian Angels

Guardian Angels are our personal Angels, and we all have them. They are our protectors and guides and are with us from birth to death. If we want them to, they will shield us from harm and will guard and safeguard us. If we are entering into potential danger, they will often give a warning either through our emotions or our intuition. (We have free will, however, so if we wish to rush into the experience, they rarely actively prohibit it.)

People who have had a near-death experience frequently have more than one Guardian Angel. This is to aid them in their adjustment following their decision to remain on Earth. In addition, people may ask for divine intervention, either for themselves or for others; here again we may see additional Guardian Angels.

Archangels

Archangels are the highest vibrating of all the Angels. Although they do not technically have a gender, they do have characteristically female or male energies. We can ask for the assistance of any or all of the Archangels at any time. Due to the high, fast vibration, they can be anywhere at any time. Again, this is mystery to us, but if we desire their assistance, we can call them to us.

Below is a list of some of the better-known Archangels:

➤ *Michael* is considered to be the most powerful of all the Archangels. His name means "he who is like God." He protects us and helps us release fears and doubts. He is the patron Angel of police officers. His traditional color is deep purple.

➤ *Gabriel* means "messenger of God." He is the patron Angel of writers and teachers. Gabriel is also the patron Angel of children. His traditional color is dark yellow.

➤ *Raphael* means "he who heals." He is the patron Angel of healers as well as travelers. His traditional color is bright green.

➤ *Ariel* means "lioness of God." She helps us with our physical needs and our material world. She is the patron Angel of the earth and its creatures. Her traditional color is pink.

➤ *Azrael* means "whom God helps." He is the patron Angel of departed Souls. He consoles those who are grieving and helps those who have crossed enter the world of Spirit. His traditional color is beige.

➤ *Chamuel* means "he who seeks God." He is the patron Angel of World Peace. He helps us with personal peace as well and eases our anxieties. His traditional color is pale green.

➤ *Haniel* means "the grace of God." She is the patron Angel of women and helps with conception and childbirth. She is also the patron Angel of clairvoyance, or clear seeing. Her traditional color is pale blue.

➤ *Jeremiel* means "mercy of God." He helps us review our lives after we have crossed over. He also helps us take stock of our lives during the current experience so that we are able to make plans for positive change. His traditional color is violet.

➤ *Jophiel* means "beauty of God." She helps us heal our chaotic, negative thoughts and behaviors. She also helps us to bring beauty and harmony into our lives and homes. Her traditional color is fuchsia.

➤ *Raguel* means "friend of God." He helps heal misunderstanding and brings harmony into our relationships. His traditional color is aqua.

➤ *Raziel* means "secrets of God." He is said to sit so close to God that he hears all the secrets of the Universe. He helps heal spiritual blocks and issues from past lives. His traditional colors are all of the colors of the rainbow.

> *Uriel* means "God is light." He is the patron Angel of wisdom and philosophy, and he illuminates our minds. His traditional color is pale yellow.

> *Zadkiel* means "righteousness of God." He is the patron Angel of all who forgive. He is the Angel of mercy and benevolence and also helps with mental functions and memory. His traditional color is dark blue.

> *Metatron* and *Sandalphon* are the only two Archangels whose names do not end in "el" and who were human before becoming Archangels. Metatron was the prophet Enoch, and Sandalphon was the prophet Elijah. Enoch was a scribe on earth and was given a similar position when he became Metatron. He records everything that happens on earth; he also keeps the akashic record, which is a record of all of the lives, past and present, of all Souls who have inhabited earth. Elijah is the prophet who ascended to heaven in a fiery chariot. As Sandalphon, he carries our prayers to God and assists musicians. Metatron and Sandalphon are twins.

What Is a Guide?

Guides are Spiritual Guardians who are with us from birth to death. They are always present and are continually communicating to us through our intuition, feelings, hearts, and minds. They are here to assist, support, and, as the name indicates, guide us.

Guides are a lower vibrating energy than are Angels and, unlike Angels, have frequently lived human lives. We have often known them from previous incarnations and may incarnate with them again in some future time. Although they vibrate at a lower rate and rhythm than do Angels, they have a significantly higher vibration than we do and can therefore act as our Guides.

We all have more than one Guide, and each Guide may have a somewhat specific function. For instance, one of our Guides may be with us for purposes of comfort and healing. Another Guide may be with us to encourage growth in spiritual areas, while still another may be there to help us manifest that which we need on the physical plane. One Guide may be primary at certain times of our life, while another may be prominent at a different time, depending on what we need.

A Guiding Presence

I am aware of three of my Guides; I may have more of them, but I know of three. Of those three, I have an active relationship with only two of them. I am aware of the third, but I do not understand his purpose. I am convinced that he has a purpose, and that he communicates with me, but I just do not know how or why yet.

Ina is the first Guide who made her presence known to me. No doubt we have had many incarnations together, but I am only aware of the details of one of them. She has given me the gift of that information because it has been and is pertinent to my current life. In the life that she has shown me, she was a Medicine Woman, a healer and a mentor, and I was her student.

I became aware of Ina about thirty years ago. During that time, I was experiencing significant upheaval in my life, and her healing presence was of considerable benefit to me. I "see" her as a small, brown woman, wrinkled by the sun. Being in her energy gives me peace and contentment; she is safe and comforting. It was through Ina that I learned of and began experimenting with the various alternative approaches to health. It was under her influence that I began to understand the profound importance of synthesizing physical, social, emotional, intellectual, and spiritual health.

Ina was primary in my life for many, many years. She remains present but has now taken a less prominent role. During that time thirty years ago, another Guide stepped forward. I found him intimidating, however, and asked that he wait, as I did not think I was ready for him just yet. Perhaps he was simply introducing himself, as he did indeed remain in the background.

The second Guide is now front and center, however. For the last ten years, I have referred to him as "the Big Guy," as he would not give me a name nor would he give me details of any of our incarnations. He is much more forceful and vociferous than was Ina. He has been quite clear that giving me the information that I requested would be "irrelevant and distracting" and has called me "a lazy psychic." He is here for my spiritual growth and development, awakening, and enlightenment. He is pushy and demanding; he pushes me in the direction that I have clearly indicated I wish to go.

I have always seen the Big Guy as enormous—bigger than life and surely bigger than he ever was *in* life. He has only ever given me snippets of the past lives that we have shared, but it appears that he was always the teacher, and I was always the student. He shows himself to me in many different costumes, cultures, and colors. I am no longer intimidated when I am in his energetic presence but feel alive, open, and grateful. Very recently, he has been so kind as to give me his name, Julian.

The third Guide flits around my conscious awareness. He may have been prominent in the past and as a part of my childhood and may be foremost in my future. I believe he has a biblical name, perhaps Joel or David. He is around me, but I know virtually nothing about him.

Naming Our Guides

Guides give us names because we want them; it helps us relate to our Guide and makes that Guide real for us. However, sometimes they do not or will not give us a name. And sometimes they give us a name that is far removed from our own time or culture; we cannot pronounce it nor can we relate to it. This information is as important as the name itself, however. We may not have a name, but we have a better understanding of who we are and from whence we came.

We like to think of our Guides as solemn beings who take our issues under considerable consideration, and indeed they are and do. But they are Guides, so they help us see things. Sometimes they help us see that we are taking ourselves too seriously. There have been times when I am reading for another person and that person insists on getting a name for a Guide, and the Guide kindly replies, "Tell her she can call me Marvin."

Who wants a Guide named Marvin? We like to think of our Guides as mystical, magical, and splendorous. We want them to have names like Celestina, Running Bear, Gawain, Altair, Cato, or Jonathan. Perhaps our Guides are being humorous when they give us ordinary or mundane names. And perhaps they are asking us to move away from our worldly obsession with names and simply live in the energy that is our Guides and ourselves.

At times, we may talk to an imaginary person and will name that person; children are especially good at this. (The word *imaginary* comes from the word *imagine*, which means to form a mental image of something that is not perceived by the bodily senses.) If the imaginary person has high, light energy, certainly it is a Guide, and we have named that Guide. Listen to yourself when you name things. If you are chatting with yourself in your thoughts and you name a name, ponder it. You may very well be calling on a Guide.

We can call our Guides anything we want. They do not care. If a name comes to us and we feel good about it, that is the name to embrace.

Our Guides' Role after our Current Incarnation

Our Guides remain with us as least for a short time after we die and have crossed over. They guide us to the Light and stay with us as we grow accustomed to our death. They continue to guide us by helping us examine and understand the life that we have just left. What issues and relationships, what karma has been successfully addressed, healed, and balanced? What needs our further attention?

We scrutinize every aspect of the life we have just left. We examine our relationships with others, jobs we held, groups in which we participated, philosophies we believed, and philosophies we lived. While we are doing this, we also explore our akashic record to determine what further personal business needs our attention.

It has historically and generally been thought that we are in the World of Spirit or "Home" for approximately fifty to sixty years before we reincarnate. However, at this time, many Souls are returning more rapidly.

When we get ready to incarnate, our Guides help us choose when and where we will be born and what we will call ourselves. Through astrology, numerology, and cardology, we can then obtain information about ourselves—our purposes, strengths, weaknesses, destinies, and karmic issues.

With the help of our Guides and with the cooperation and consent of other Souls, we also choose who (what other Souls) will be in the new life. We choose what issues we will address with those Souls, which of them will be our supports and which of them will provide our challenges. We choose other concerns that we will address: what jobs we will have, and what our group associations will be. We decide what philosophies will challenge us and which ones will support us. We also choose which Guides we will bring into the next life.

What happens with our Guides if we choose not to cross? This isn't really clear, but there are no reports of ghosts being accompanied by their personal Guides. Instead, those who do not cross to the Light and remain grounded on the planet require special assistance.

Guides Providing Special Assistance: Bringers

There are special Guides, called Bringers, whose function is to guide troubled Souls to the Light after death. If a person is under the influence of alcohol or drugs, if there is a serious mental illness, or if the person has suffered traumatic brain injury prior to death, that person may be confused about what has occurred. If an individual thinks that the life has ended suddenly and unexpectedly, there may be uncertainty regarding what has happened.

When circumstances such as these occur, there may be a continued attachment to the body, to the personality, and to the life that has just ended. There is an aimless and bewildered drifting on the part of the Soul. It is the Bringer's job to return the drifting Soul to the World of Spirit—to the Light. If there is profound disorientation and confusion at the time of dying, our Guides and the Bringers, knowing our incipient confusion, may actually lift our Souls from our bodies.

A drifting or wandering Soul is not the same as a ghost; rather, it is a Soul in confusion that is temporarily drifting. With the assistance of Guides and Bringers, the wandering Soul is quickly united with the Light and is brought Home.

People with a dementia that occurs later in life generally have vivid memories of their earlier lives. When they die, they generally cross quickly and without the assistance of Bringers. Those suffering from dementia may not remember the living, but they accept the assistance of their own Guides; they remember loved ones who have crossed. They readily accept the presence, love, and comfort from those who have gone before them and are there to bring them Home.

Spiritual Assistance from a Different Vibration: Star Beings and Faeries

Star Beings

It is ignorant to suppose that a Universe as large as ours contains only the energies that we here on Earth have discovered and defined. As stated previously, there are one hundred to five hundred billion stars in our galaxy alone, and there are likely hundreds of billions of galaxies in our Universe. Earth is indeed infinitesimal in the context of the Universe.

Star Beings are energetic vibrations that live in other parts of the Universe. They are not human and were likely never human, at least not as we define it. That is not to say that they have not had an evolutionary journey similar to our own, but very likely, that journey was in another part of the Universe.

We do not know the provenance of these Star Beings; they are mystery, and that is perfectly all right. They are not Angels, and they are not Guides. Many Star Beings make their presence known, however, and so people become interested in the idea of "aliens." As a general rule, Star Beings are less interested in us than we are in them and only visit with us if they have a job to do. They come to us as energetic vibrations, but just as some people see or feel the presence of their Angels and Guides, so too do some people see or feel the presence of the Star Beings.

The Star Beings that are able to be in contact with us are highly vibrating, highly evolved energy. Not all life from "outer space" is able to make the energetic and vibrational journey, and no doubt some are not willing or it is not their purpose. The Star Beings that visit us are not to be confused with other beings that may be evolving in other places in the Universe. Rather, they are beings similar to our Guides; they have completed a good portion of their journey and so have attained a high vibration. They come to us to help us raise our own vibration. They are not here to guide or to protect but to help us grow.

A Star Being Presence

I have had limited conscious contact with Star Beings, but I do know several people who have. One is a friend who has intense and graphic dreams that she is being visited by Star Beings. Her dreams are not threatening or frightening in any way; rather, she feels that spiritual information is being shared with her in a format and manner in which she can accept it. Another friend is a healer and psychic. As she participates in healing work with her clients, she will inform them of other issues if they present themselves. During one such healing, she was startled to become aware of an energetic presence of which she had no experience. She was reluctant to bring it up but did tentatively broach the subject. Her client was unsurprised and said that she did indeed have an "alien" who was part of her spiritual helper team.

Faeries

According to Paracelsus (1493–1541), Faeries occupy a space between our human space and the space of the Spirits. They are corporeal as are humans and have human habits, such as eating, sleeping, and procreating, but they have the rapid motion associated with Spirits. They are able to travel between our space and their space with relative ease.

Gaia Guardians

Faeries are elementals, or Nature's "Angels." They are not Angels and do not have the higher vibration that Angels have. They live "next" to us on a different vibrational energy level and do not occupy the same vibrational space that human beings do. As with Angels, however, if we are still and meditative, we can often feel their energetic presence. With Faeries, though, it is helpful to be in nature, with an animal, tending to a plant, or connecting with Earth in some way.

In Greek mythology, Gaia is the goddess of the earth. She is primordial, and is the original, the first protector of our planet. As long as the earth has existed, Gaia has been its guardian. New Age philosophy uses the term Gaia to refer to the earth, itself. Faeries are an aspect of Gaia.

Faeries have a tutelary interest in things of the earth and, as such, are guardians and protectors of all things created for and naturally existing on our planet. As elementals, they have an abiding interest in that which naturally supports and transforms our planet: fire, water, earth, and air. They see Earth as a living organism and are the true Gaia philosophers.

Faeries have an ambivalent attitude toward humanity; they have limited interest in the personal desires of human beings, especially if those individuals are upsetting or disrupting the homeostasis of Earth. Loss of the rainforests, clear cutting forests in general, climate change, species extinction, and all things that harm Earth's balance are abhorrent to the Faerie. Anything that disrupts the harmonies in the ecosystem offends the Faerie. Poisonous herbicides and pesticides, for instance, do not only destroy that for which they were intended, but poisonous run-off enters the lakes and rivers and damages other life as well.

On the other hand, all things that support Earth and the natural world please the Faeries, and, if we are inclined to have some kind of contact with them, this is our avenue. Rescuing an animal, planting an organic garden, cleaning up a river, going for a walk, hugging a tree—these are all things that satisfy a Faerie.

Faeries, like human beings, have an ego and a distinct sense of themselves as individuals. Angels, on the other hand, are egoless and see themselves as parts of a great interrelated whole. As a result, Angels are nonjudgmental in the truest sense of the word. Because of our egos and our senses of ourselves as distinct individuals, humans and Faeries are creatures of judgment; on some level, we judge everything we see, every experience we have, and every person we meet.

Accordingly, Faeries watch and judge what we humans do. They have an enduring reverence for life and are partial to actions that sustain and strengthen the earth, her natural occurrences, and her native inhabitants. Faeries are acutely aware of the garbage that clutters the earth, how it is made, where it comes from, and how it chokes our atmosphere, waters, and lands. They judge us based on our use and reuse of anything that comes from or affects our world, and so they are offended by waste and satisfied by careful use and reuse.

Additionally, they are profoundly aware of how we take our food. Plants and animals must die to feed us, but are we respectful and grateful? Do we thank that which gave its life for us, do we take only what we need, and do we eat what we take? Do we know the source of our food and understand the violence that may have occurred so that we can eat? Faeries are the true stewards of the earth; they understand that they do not have dominion over Earth but rather are custodians and defenders of our planet and all the blessings that flow from it.

When Faeries observe disrespect and destruction in the natural world, they may respond to us by disrupting our lives with their pranks and trickery. When people behave in an unscrupulous, harmful, or vicious manner to each other or to themselves, Faeries may counter with mischief, interfering and disturbing the offenders.

Faeries do not like negative human behaviors. They are not fond of that which is superficial but favor that which is genuine and true. Boorish and offensive behavior toward others, selfishness, lack of compassion and generosity, and violence and brutality are all human behaviors that are repugnant to the Faerie.

When activity is transpiring around them that supports and honors life or behaviors that are respectful, genuine, and sincere, they are likely to be gracious, helpful, playful, and merry. Much has been written historically about Faerie malice and our need to protect ourselves from them. Indeed, when we disrespect the natural world, they may respond with what we would perceive to be wickedness. However, they are perfectly willing to assist us if we ask them as long as we respect their world (which is also our world!).

I have limited contact with Faeries. However, one weekend, some of us in my family decided to spend a girls weekend at our campers. Three generations were represented, and the women in the middle generation—those in their twenties and thirties—were particularly in touch with the Faeries that weekend. A Faerie, Mikel, presented himself to one of the women, and we were put on notice that this was to be a weekend of laughter and fun. If we got too serious, small mishaps and mischief would occur. And this is indeed what happened. It was a very fun weekend, and a big thanks to Mikel, who kept us on track.

A Special Vibration: Loved Ones Who Have Crossed

Loved ones who have crossed are just that—loved ones who have crossed. Although many people refer to them as Angels, they are not Angels. Angels are nonhuman celestial energy. However, if it is comforting to think of loved ones who have crossed as angels, perhaps "love angels" is an appropriate term.

Loved ones can and do communicate with us after death. Often we can feel their energetic presence if we ask them to come and are still and silent. They come to us in dreams; many times, we remember those dreams, but more often we do not. Nonetheless, they are communicating with us through our dreams, and our inner, subconscious selves are aware of the messages.

Once our loved ones have crossed, they are pure energy. They may present themselves to us just as we remember them, or they may present themselves as they were in happier days, before the illness or the accident. Sometimes when they are present, they drain other energies in the home, particularly electricity. If shortly after the death, there is an issue with light bulbs, appliances, battery-operated devices, or similar items, it is likely that a loved one is visiting.

They remain interested in us. We are after all their loved ones as well. They can see and hear us in a way that we can no longer see or hear them. Their interest may be more intense in the period immediately following their death.

As time passes, however, they become more concerned with their own Soul's journey and less involved with ours. If, however, we feel that we continue to need them, they will continue to be available in some way. And, of course, when we decide that it is time to cross to the Light and go Home, they are there to encourage and reassure.

Our Soul Families

We incarnate in massive Soul groups (as will be discussed in the following chapter). The people in our group, whether or not we know them in the current lifetime, have a continued energetic presence in each of our lifetimes. We have repeated incarnations with the Souls in our group, but even when they are not with us in life, energetically they are with us.

Souls that are in our family are the Souls that are the most essential or significant to us and have been so over time (as we understand time). In a sense, they are the ones who love us best and who bring us crucial support but also important challenges. They love us, we love them, and we all want to increase our vibration. Our friends are the next level out and bring us notable support (and challenges) but are not quite as significant to us as are the family Souls. Important others are part of our Soul group and play various roles in our lives, including bringing us support or challenges. These Soul relationships are reciprocal, and so we bring to our family, friends, and important others love, support, and challenge just as they bring it to us.

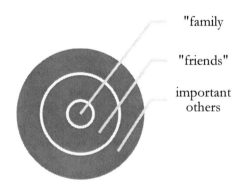

"family

"friends"

important others

Souls in our family Soul group may not necessarily be in our earthly family in each lifetime, just as our friend Soul group may not be earthly friends. We may bring in Souls from the important others to be fathers or mothers, grandparents, siblings, or children. Someone in our Soul family may be an earthly friend or employer or teacher in various lifetimes. We do not automatically bring in Soul family as earthly family, or

Soul friends as earthly friends, or Soul important others as earthly important others in each lifetime.

For instance, someone in our Soul family group may agree to be a teacher; we may know that teacher briefly, but the lessons that are taught are significant to a lifetime of increasing vibration. Or we may agree to be a parent to someone in our group of important others so that we can share vital information and energy with that person and help them raise their vibration.

The following are examples from my own experience. I am convinced that the energies of many other loved ones who have crossed are with these children, and this is simply the energy that I have identified:

➢ *Sedona*: Prior to Sedona's birth, her grandmother began to have vivid memories of her own grandfather, Sedona's great-great grandfather. Great-great grandfather Don had crossed when the grandmother herself was just a little girl of five, and so these memories, although bringing comfort to the grandmother, were also confusing to her. She had after all barely known the man. Family legend had it, however, that Don was a kind, generous man who had an inventive imagination. Memories of Don became even more pronounced after Sedona was born, and indeed, Sedona's round little baby face reminded the grandmother of Don in pictures she had of herself sitting on Don's lap when the grandmother was just a toddler. Don's presence was very much around Sedona, even though he died fifty years prior to her birth, was barely known to the grandmother, and was not known at all to Sedona's mother. After discussing this phenomenon with friends, the grandmother began to accept that Don was in some way acting in a guardianship role with Sedona. Indeed, one of the friends noticed that Don's name was imbedded in Se*don*a's name. Sedona's numerological life path is six, and so she must learn to take care of herself within the context of other people. She is also a Leo and has a dramatic, brash liveliness. Don is here to lend his gentle, loving energy to her current journey to help her calm herself and to love herself while learning to make room in her life and in her interest for other people. As Sedona grows, it becomes more and more apparent that she, too, has a phenomenally inventive imagination.

➢ *Caleb*: Caleb is a little boy who took his own, sweet time coming to earth, and his mother began planning his entrance long before he actually decided to enter. There were times when her longing for Caleb turned to despondency, and she thought she would not see this little man soon. During this time, she attended a group meditation where she was directed to ask for the presence of a loved one who had crossed. Much to her surprise, her paternal grandmother Clara, whom she had never met and who had crossed when her own father was in elementary school, was the Soul who became present to her. Although the mother had never met Clara, she became very emotional, sad, and grieved over her absence. Shortly thereafter, Mom was taking a shower and thinking strong thoughts about Clara. When she got out of the shower, in the fog on the mirror, there was a little drawing of a pregnant stick figure. As Mom was the only one home at this time, she was a little "freaked out," as she says. However, shortly thereafter, she realized she was pregnant with Caleb. Clara continues to lend her energy to Caleb's growth and well-being.

➢ *Rory*: Rory's great-grandfather, Otto, crossed several years prior to Rory's birth. While on earth, Otto had experienced many hardships and reversals. As a result, he had become emotionally distant, and so his children and his grandchildren knew his physical presence, but his psychological and emotional presence was diminished. As one of the grandchildren said, "He was just not there for us." With the advent of Rory's birth, Otto made his energetic presence known; he is here now to be at hand not just for Rory but also for his own grandson, Rory's father, Sam. His presence has a strong reciprocal quality to it. He is here to promote and encourage emotional connectedness within Rory's family; he is also here to heal himself within the loving relationships of that family. Otto is in attendance now to help others and to heal himself, to guide others and to learn from them. Additionally, while on earth, Otto did not always have the courage of his convictions; although he believed in fair treatment for all, he did not consistently behave in a manner that supported his belief. Rory's numerological life path is nine, which is a humanitarian number and is concerned with altruism, compassion, selflessness, and forgiveness. Sam is an Aquarius and, as might be expected, has a fervent desire to help the world. Otto is also with Rory's family to heal, learn, and raise his vibration in the areas of humanitarianism and forgiveness.

Ghosts

When our bodies die and our Souls return to the world of Spirit, they remain vibrant, energetic, and dynamic. If the choice is made to remain on the earthly plane, however, and the Soul refuses to enter the Light and the world of Spirit, the Soul begins to lose its vibrancy. It does not disappear, but its energy becomes slow, sluggish, and dense. These are the energies that we call ghosts.

Souls that resist their bodies' death and become ghosts on the earth are sometimes Souls who have had significant trauma in the life that they have just left. They might have abused someone who has previously died or even murdered someone and so are afraid of meeting that person again. They may have been abused and believe that they can avoid confronting the person and the issue if they remain behind.

Ghost Souls may have been alcoholics or drug addicts; they could have been heavily medicated when death occurred. They might have had mental health issues. They might have died suddenly or traumatically. As a result, they may have been confused by the body's death and resisted the efforts of their Guides and the Bringers to help them to the Light.

They may have religious beliefs that have frightened them into believing that safety lies in remaining a ghost. They may have died by suicide and believe that the life of the Soul will be terminated just as the life of the body has been. They may have been taught that this life is their only chance and believe that they have important, unfinished business. Because they have not entered the World of Spirit, they do not remember that they have other lifetimes in which to finish that business. They might not accept that they are dead.

Ghosts: Where Are They?

Ghosts can be attracted to houses and other structures or areas, to objects, and to people. They have a dense, heavy, slow vibration and are often felt rather than seen. They often feel cold, as they are draining the areas around them of vibrational warmth.

Ghosts might live in a house where they lived when they were alive. They might live in a house that they like and that for various reasons attracts them; for instance, it might be in an area in which they previously resided and resemble a home that they inhabited at that time. Ghosts might be occupying a space in which they once had a home, but that home is long gone. They might be in a location—woods, river area, lake—that was a favorite retreat when they were alive.

Ghost soldiers have been known to follow their gun, their medals of honor, or other military items. This happens more often if the death was attached to military service or if there was a particular pride in the time spent in the military. The ghost of a wealthy dowager might follow her favorite diamond brooch or ring to wherever it goes. Old furniture may attract ghosts.

Ghosts can attach themselves to people and sometimes target people with permeable boundaries or people who have mental or chemical health issues—people who are vulnerable in some way. This does not mean that the ghost can or will cause harm, and frequently, people are unaware, on a personality level, that the ghostly presence is at hand. However, if a ghost is hanging out with someone, it is because someone has, in some manner, allowed the energy to make itself manifest.

A Ghostly Presence: A Haunting

Most people can be in the presence of a ghost and be largely unaware of it. Although there are members of my family who are exceedingly conscious of ghost energy, I am not one of them.

A friend and I had gotten into the habit of visiting antique stores. Our families had owned similar items to those we found there, and we would go look at them and take little trips down memory lane. Generally we stayed in the stores only a short period of time and, although we could both feel the denser energy, we were not bothered by it.

However, we discovered a new antique store and out of curiosity visited it. We were fine when we were on the main floor, but when we decided to go downstairs and look at the furniture, within seconds we both began to get headaches, felt dizzy, and disoriented. We left immediately. As soon as we were outside of the store, we were all right; a bit tired but fine.

Ghost Sending

No ghost has a respectable or satisfactory reason for staying, and it is never a good idea to promote a continued earthly presence. It is in the ghost's best interest to give up that form of existence and to cross into the World of Spirit.

If we are aware of a ghost presence and want to encourage a crossing, we can assert ourselves and ask the ghost to leave and go to the Light. If possible, think and speak of that entity's "highest good." We do not have to do this aloud but can simply think the words; thoughts are energy, and we are dealing with energy. It is all happening on an energetic level.

Sometimes this is all that is required. If the ghost has not been here long, or if it is confused and simply lacks direction, this might be all that is needed. We do not have the power to force the ghost to the Light; however, we do, almost always, have the power to get it out of our space. Tell them to go to the Light, that they are not welcome here, and to go in peace. Do not be timid.

Several members of my family are in the law enforcement community, and one of them was asked to visit the home of an elderly, disabled woman late one night. The woman had complained that two other women were sitting at her kitchen table and were refusing to leave. When he got to the home, he saw no one and so asked the woman if they were still there. She said they were and did he not see them?

He told her he could not see them and asked her if she thought they might be ghosts. She agreed that if he could not see them, the visitors must be ghosts. He told her to tell them that they were not welcome in her home and that they should go in peace to the Light. She did, and they left.

She had no power to force them to the Light. She did use her own power to get them out of her home, however. We do not know where they went, but we do know that they no longer troubled her.

If we find a ghost's energy frightening or off-putting in any manner and do not want to deal with it personally, there are ghost senders who are happy to assist. Ghost senders are intuitive or psychic people in the community who have a particular interest in and a talent for contact with ghost energy. They are able to help identify the denser energies of ghosts and send them on their way.

I do occasional parties in a home that used to have a great deal of ghostly energy. That energy concentrated itself in the bedroom of a younger family member. The bedroom was markedly colder than the other parts of the house, and the young person refused to sleep there. I am not a ghost buster, but I know people whom I trusted to do the job. My client hired them. They identified several ghosts and sent them on their way. The bedroom is now as warm as the rest of the house.

The Sea of Faces

Any Soul can be rescued and no Soul dies; all earth-bound Souls, all ghosts, should always be encouraged to go to the Light. However, a Soul that chooses to remain on Earth may require special attention and extra effort.

Sometimes a ghost's energy vibrates at an especially low, dense level, particularly if that entity has existed in this form for a long period of time or if the ghost has lived a damaging life in the human experience here on Earth. If the vibration is very low, it might be difficult for that being to cross over into the Light. Groups of Souls who have once been ghosts themselves but who have now crossed, form teams to assist these low-vibrating entities. When they cross, they enter the lowest level of the World of Spirit to a place some call the Sea of Faces. There, they heal until they are able to raise their energetic vibration to a level high enough to allow them to continue the journey. As with all else, free will operates, and it is the ghost's choice when and how it will cross.

Ghostly Energy

There is also a phenomenon that is not a ghost at all but is ghostly energy. This generally happens when something traumatic or intensely emotionally charged has occurred in a specific location. The location imprints this event or portions of the event, which then becomes stuck in time and so the event is replayed over and over. Ghostly energy can be mistaken for a ghost.

Clearing Ghosts and Other Negative Energies

Ghosts can attach themselves to places and objects. However, anything in the material world can absorb the energies of those who have previously owned them, used them, or lived in them. This might be ghost energy, but it could also be energy from a living person or from a person who has died and crossed to the world of Spirit.

When we acquire something, if we feel that there is ghost energy or any other kind of negative energy attached to it, it is an excellent idea to clear the space or object. There is no particular right way to do this, and our intention to clear it is the most important component in our endeavor. There are, however, rituals, processes, and techniques that can help us clear an object so that the energy of the previous owner diminishes and eventually disappears.

The most important element in clearing anything is intention— words and thoughts. Think or say what it is that you are intending to do. You might say something such as: "I release (item) of all old energy; I release (item) of all negative energy. I surround (item) with light and love." Visualize higher vibrating, positive energy surrounding that which you are clearing.

When clearing an object, the first thing that should be done if it can be done is to wash it. Many items cannot be washed, however, so do not wash it if it is not indicated. Whether or not it is washed, the object can then be smudged, which is done by blowing smoke across the item in question. Smudging involves the burning of plant materials, such as sage, cedar, or sweet grass, or wood, such as palo santo. Burning your substance on an abalone shell is recommended but not necessary.

Other clearing techniques involve placing the object in the sunlight or in the moonlight. You can use sea salt to clear an object but care must be taken if we are using salt, as many items will not tolerate it (particularly certain crystals). We can draw upon the power of repetitive sounds and create a clearing ritual using bells, drums, and chants. Whatever our choice, however, intention remains the most important component of any clearing that we might do.

When clearing a house or building, first remove and discard any items that trigger depressing, pessimistic, or hurtful thoughts or feelings. Smudge the house. You can also set a bowl of sea salt in the middle of the room and allow that salt to absorb the negative energies. Be sure that your salt has no additives or preservatives and do not use it for anything else when you are finished with it; discard the salt. Be sure to state intention.

If you are clearing ghost energy from the house or building, you might consider using crystals to discourage reentry (see Chapter Nine). Selenite can be placed at the four corners of the home. Others prefer a black stone, as black is the color of protection; hematite and obsidian are useful if you prefer a black stone. Additionally, it is helpful to ask for the protection and assistance of your Guides and Angels. Many of us find comfort in "posting" Angels at the four corners of the home.

When we are finished clearing the house of negative energy, we can introduce aesthetically pleasing scents and sounds. This attracts positive energy and helps balance the chi in the new space. The longer we live in a home or own an object, the more our own energy imprints on that home or object.

Experiencing Higher and Lower Vibrations

We are, all of us, most comfortable in a vibration that is similar to our own. When contacting entities of higher vibration, we must raise our own vibration as much as is possible (see Chapter Seven). Higher vibrating entities must also reach toward our lower vibration to help us communicate.

We are more comfortable in the presence of a higher vibration than in the presence of a lower vibration. Vibration that is a great deal higher than ours, such as Angels and Guides, may alarm us in that we experience the awesomeness and mystery of it, but it does not *feel* bad.

On the other hand, lower vibrating energies often feel distressing or unpleasant. This is why we find ghosts or other negative energies so deeply troubling. Lower vibrating energy *feels* bad. Souls here on Earth who are much younger than we are in terms of reincarnational evolution can be stressful and difficult for us to be with for any length of time as well. The lower vibration of their energy can exhaust us when we spend time in it; it depresses and distresses.

Our tolerance for lower vibrating energy decreases as we get older, just as our tolerance for higher vibrating energy increases. This is as it should be. It encourages our reach for the higher vibrations.

Chapter 4: Laws of Evolution: Reincarnation and Karma

- Reincarnation
  - ❖ Free Will
  - ❖ Our Reincarnational Journey: An Analogy
- Reincarnation and the Soul
  - ❖ Soul Groups
  - ❖ Other Soul Choices in Reincarnation
    - o Soul Splitting
    - o Twin Souls
    - o Soul Mates
- Karma: Its Link to Reincarnation
- Death: The End of the Incarnation and the Journey Home
- Home: The World of Spirit and Preparation for the Next Incarnation
- What Is the Akashic Record?
- Past Lives
  - ❖ Past Lives and Children
  - ❖ Resolving Past Life Issues in the Present
- Reading the Akashic Record: Past Life Examples
  - o Victoria
  - o Katherine
  - o Alexandra
  - ❖ Why We Are Allowed to Glimpse Our Past

Reincarnation

Our Souls are eternal aspects of the Universal Mind; they are Divine energy that came from and are a part of Source Energy. As with Source Energy, they cannot be destroyed and have no end. The Universe is ever expanding, and the Universal Mind is constantly in the act of creation. We are cocreators, and reincarnation is the path our Soul takes as it moves to create with the highest of all vibrations, Source Energy, or God.

All things are evolving toward God. It is our Soul's intent that we push ourselves into higher and higher vibration as we reach for the perfection that is God. It is through the human experience that our Soul drives our growth into those higher vibrations. With each incarnation, we learn, grow, and evolve. But significant evolution is only truly found through cumulative incarnations. Reincarnation is the journey our Soul takes through cumulative incarnations.

It is through reincarnation that we are able to transmute and transform the lower vibration into the higher vibration. Within each lifetime, we are called upon to use our power and to pull the lower vibration higher. We are given countless opportunities to move away from fear, hatred, and revenge and to move into love, joy, and gratitude.

We are not able to accomplish all that our Soul wishes to accomplish within each lifetime, however. It is a long climb up the mountain and into the highest vibrations. And so we are granted additional opportunity and further possibility to embrace benevolence, generosity, and compassion.

We have approximately 550 to 600 incarnations here on Earth. When we begin the reincarnational journey, our Souls are primal, primitive, and raw; the Soul is in the earliest stage of individual existence. We travel through various stages of development as we reincarnate and evolve into the higher vibration (see Chapter Five).

As we move from incarnation to incarnation, we experience time sequentially, although on a Universal level, time may not be chronological (Albert Einstein, as well as certain quantum physicists, imagined time as happening all at once). However, for our earthly journeys, chronological time is an effective way for us to learn as we build upon past experiences from each life and as we move from lifetime to lifetime.

With each incarnation, the veils between heaven and earth are pulled; they are closed so that we can concentrate on the life at hand and can experience all that which we came here to experience. If the veils were not pulled, we would be significantly distracted and would not give the current life the attention that it needs. We would not live within the complexities of the existing journey and so would compromise our reach for the higher vibration.

And yet we often recognize that we have had a previous experience or prior knowledge of a person, place, or situation. Déjà vu is defined as a feeling that something or someone is familiar when we believe that we are actually experiencing it for the first time. We may not have confronted it yet in this life, but that something or someone has most assuredly been experienced in past incarnations. This is why we have the feeling of familiarity.

Free Will

All life is choosing. When we choose to reincarnate, prior to our births we choose all the pertinent or relevant people we wish to bring into the life. We require their consent, of course, as they too have free will. We choose the major experiences, situations, and circumstance for the upcoming life. We choose the places we will live and visit. We choose our names, birthdates, and birthplaces.

Once we are on the planet, we continue to exercise free will and can always change our story. It is not likely that we will do this with the relevant people, the major circumstances or situations, or the pertinent places. We have come here to raise our vibration, and we do this by learning through specific experiences that we ourselves have predetermined.

Even though we may encounter difficulties and challenges, on a Soul level we may decide to continue with any given event or relationship. We have chosen this particular situation at this particular time because we know that we can raise our vibration by providing ourselves with the knowledge and understanding that can be gotten here. We always have free will regarding how we choose to live within our experiences and our relationships, however. It is the power of free will in our most difficult challenges that will ultimately help us raise the vibration.

Our Reincarnational Journey: An Analogy

Our reincarnational journey can be compared to a trip, an expedition, or an excursion that we might decide to take in the current lifetime. Perhaps we have decided that we will go to Europe with three of our friends. We go to the travel agency and begin to make our arrangements. We commit ourselves to the trip and pay for it.

We mutually decide that we will fly to New York, where we will spend a few days shopping. Following our shopping trip, we will join a tour group and travel on to Europe. One of the friends will fly to New York with us; the other two are coming on later flights the following day into different airports. We make arrangements to meet them.

We have many experiences in New York, some of them planned and some unplanned. We encounter situations and circumstances with which we are unfamiliar and must develop some creative and innovative solutions. One of our friends has shown some considerable leadership skills, and we begin to rely on her for resolution to many of our problems. Another friend tires easily, and we must slow our pace to meet her needs.

We complete the New York part of our journey and fly to London with our tour group to Europe. Our group includes thirty additional people and two tour guides. The tour begins in London; we will then travel to Amsterdam and Rome. Hotel accommodations and breakfast are provided. Other arrangements include various theatrical events, sightseeing at different historical sites, and a diverse assortment of museums. We have chosen this particular tour because the scheduled activities are of interest to us, and yet we will be having a great deal of free time and can see new things and have new experiences.

We are going with our friends because they are familiar to us and give us comfort and support, and yet we are eager to meet other people on our travels. We soon learn that we are happy to have our friends' soothing presence, as several of the other people in our group are presenting some significant challenges to us and to the group as a whole. One individual complains incessantly, while another bullies the tour guides. Still another wanders away from the group, and we have almost missed important events as a result.

We all have to decide how we are going to respond to these individuals. Should we confront them? Should we ignore them? Should we defend the tour guides? Some of the others in the larger group will be our allies, some will present solutions that we find disturbing, and some will remain in the background.

We visit all of the scheduled historical sites and see all of the scheduled theatrical and musical events. During our free times, we sometimes rest, but we often explore our new environment. We are disappointed in certain experiences but are unexpectedly pleased in others; many of our experiences offer no surprises and meet our expectations. At times, we are amazed; at other times, we are bored. Most of the time, we are comfortable but do have a few disconcerting or even fearful moments.

This earthly trip is metaphorically comparable to a Soul journey trip. We know before we begin the journey what we want or need. We know that we choose certain people to accompany us on the journey, but that we also wish to meet new people. We have decided to have certain defined experiences, but we also allow for new experiences. We have spent a good deal of time making the preparations, and when we choose the body and the life, "we put our money down."

Reincarnation and the Soul

Our Souls are radiant Divine Energy. When we incarnate, our Soul moves into physical form; the Soul remains Divine Energy but has now moved into and become a part of a body. Living in the human experience is often difficult, but on a Soul level, we chose this form at this time in our spiritual evolution, as it is optimum for our learning and growth.

We return to the planet so that we may increase our understanding and awareness. We wish to comprehend that which has previously been incomprehensible. We come here to learn. Everything that we experience, encounter, discover, or realize within each lifetime is intended to ultimately raise our Soul's vibration.

We also come back to the planet so that we can resolve imbalances created in past lives; we "learn lessons." As we learn and balance, we raise our vibration. Our vibration is intertwined with the whole of the Universe and so our accomplished vibrational increase is of universal benefit. This is what is meant by cocreating with God.

Soul Groups

We incarnate in massive Soul groups, and most of the people in our current incarnation have shared lives with us before. When we decide to incarnate, we also decide which Souls we would like to share the journey with us. We must ask other Souls to accompany us on each and every reincarnational journey. They can accept or refuse, depending on their concerns regarding that time and space.

We may ask certain Souls to come with us to Earth to support us and to complement our journey. We may ask them to provide emotional or spiritual comfort; we may ask them to provide information or knowledge. These Souls can come from our family group, friend, or important other group. Any Soul from any group can play a small or large part in our incarnation.

For instance, a Soul from our family group may make a passing appearance in our life. We may think on an earthly level that this person is relatively unimportant to our current journey. We may have a brief encounter or a chance meeting with this Soul, yet this person imparts wisdom that affects the remainder of our life. In this particular incarnation, we experience this person as a fleeting presence; nonetheless, this Soul is from our family group and has agreed to cross paths with us to give us just the right message at just the right time.

Or we may have a Soul from our friend group or our important other group that is with us for most of the life. This Soul may incarnate with us as a sister, brother, or a lifelong friend and provide a lifetime of compassionate benevolence. We may have a Soul from the friend or important other group that is with us for part of the life but even so plays a significant role. He or she may be from a religious community and provide spiritual information and comfort. Perhaps this person is a teacher who encourages us to fulfill our potential or a nurse who provides physical relief and healing.

We may ask others to accompany and challenge us in a way that is intended to compel questioning and increase our vibrational growth. Again, these Souls may come from any of the Soul groups. For example, we may ask a Soul from our family Soul group to come to us as a member of a dissimilar culture and with a philosophy that is difficult for us to understand. This family-group Soul may have agreed to help us expand our tolerance, patience, and compassion.

We may ask a Soul from the friend or important other group to come into the current incarnation as a troubled sibling or parent with mental or physical challenges; we will spend a large portion of the life with that person. Or we may ask for a shorter-term challenge and request this Soul's appearance as a client, customer, or patient.

Other Soul Choices in Reincarnation

Soul Splitting

We live here on Earth and are grounded to the energy of this planet. We see ourselves as individuals with one body, one mind, and one set of emotions. We perceive these selves to be complete, singular entities. It is hard for us to imagine that we might be capable of more than this. We can conceive of our Souls taking on a body and a life, but it is difficult for us to imagine that our Soul may decide to experience two or more lives simultaneously.

Once we become older Souls, however, we often like to enhance or accelerate the reincarnational process. We begin to understand that in many ways we are much more than the sum of our parts. We become adept at doing our reincarnational journeys and so look for ways in which to increase our vibration at a more rapid rate. We Soul split.

Soul splitting is exactly that. By splitting, one Soul chooses to have more than one body, more than one personality, and more than one life experience and does so simultaneously. Remember that our Souls are pure energy; as we get older and wiser, our vibration is raised. Once the vibration is raised to a certain level, Soul splitting becomes a possibility. One Soul may be having a lifetime as Mary from San Francisco while at the same time being Boris from Moscow.

Quantum entanglement or quantum nonlocal connection is a quantum physics theory that informs us that when two or more particles are entangled, even if they are in different spaces in the Universe, they maintain a connection. If something happens to one particle, the linked particles will respond.

The entangled particles in this example would be the energy that is the Soul; the "two or more particles" are Boris and Mary. Mary has her life experiences while Boris has his, but they are linked by a shared Soul energy. When Mary does something that alters the vibrational energy, it affects Boris, just as when Boris does something to raise or lower the vibrational energy, it affects Mary.

Twin Souls

When a Soul has chosen to Soul split and the personalities are here on Earth, those personalities may have feelings of being incomplete. The Soul knows that it is complete, but the personalities may have a longing or a yearning for completion.

Because we live here on Earth, we most often think that this person is separate from ourselves. We do not understand that Twin Souls are actually one Soul, and the longing is for reunification of the Soul energy. Instead, we believe that the Twin Soul is the perfect mate or the perfect friend, and we may spend a great deal of time searching for the missing person.

When we choose to Soul split, we know on a Soul level that we will experience feelings of incompleteness. We know that we will long to return to the whole. And so an additional component of the yearning or the longing is actually a desire to return to the wholeness that is Source Energy. We came from God and will return to God, and so the longing for reunification is ultimately a longing to return to God.

Soul Mates

We often have a romanticized idea that there is a perfect Soul Mate for us—that there is a life partner who will be the one perfect complement to us. We do not, however, have a single Soul Mate but many of them. Our Soul Mates are those Souls who have repeatedly reincarnated with us and are closest to us in the family Soul group. We incarnate in massive Soul groups and have many Soul mates. One might be perfect for one lifetime, and one for another, depending on our needs.

We are multifaceted, complex entities with many needs, desires, and issues. Certain Soul energy might be the best counterpart to our Soul energy in one incarnation, while different Soul energy might best fit another incarnation. In each lifetime, we choose different areas in which to raise our vibration.

Ironically, what might be the perfect complement to us might also provide us with our greatest challenge. We are here to learn, grow, and raise the vibration. We may choose a Soul Mate who loves us enough to provide that challenge, even though the lifetime with that Soul may be arduous and demanding

That does not mean that we cannot have the love and support of a life partner; it does not even mean that we cannot have that one great love in the lifetime. But we may have chosen to forego this experience for other experiences that will raise our vibration.

Karma: Its Link to Reincarnation

Karma is a fundamental part of the growth process involved in reincarnation. Karma is about responsibility and choice, and it is through karma that we choose to learn that which we need to learn to achieve a higher vibration. Karma is not something that is imposed on us nor is it punishment for wrongdoing in past lives or this life. Karma is simply the ability to address imbalances that we have created in present and past lives so that we can attain that higher vibration.

Karma is the law of cause and effect. That which we do comes back to us. Or, as the King James New Testament, Galatians 6:7 tells us, "Be not deceived; God is not mocked: for whatsoever a man soweth, that shall he also reap." And so we cannot fool the Universe and are held accountable for our actions.

Karmic chains are created as we move through lifetime after lifetime and create imbalances. The more unwilling we are to address them, the more chaining that occurs. If we have an opportunity to address an imbalanced situation, and we choose to forego the opportunity, we then create another link in the chain, so to speak. We break the chain by addressing the imbalance. If we have added link after link over many lives, it may take some time and effort to break the chain.

We must balance our karma if we are to accomplish higher vibrations. If we don't balance it now, we will always be given another chance. It won't go away and must eventually be corrected.

Love will break a karmic chain. When we act out of love, compassion, and in the present moment, we can bring a situation into balance more quickly. If we act out of vengeance or retribution, we create additional imbalance. Revenge is anti-healing always and in all directions.

We accept the karma of anything to which we belong—any organization, agency, business, our families, our friendship groups, and our country. Karma is created by the beliefs and actions within any of these systems, and as long as we maintain a commitment to the system, we share the karma. If karmic imbalances are being created, and we are embracing the actions that cause the imbalances, we share the karma. The accumulation of karma dies when the commitment to the system dies.

Our karmic imbalances may be personal and about how we care for ourselves. It is just as important for us to love, honor, and respect ourselves as it is to love, honor, and respect others. Failing to take personal responsibility for ourselves when it is within our ability to do so will create an imbalance.

We may have relational imbalances that have been created as we interact with others. How are we behaving toward others in our life and in our environment? What conduct and behavior are we tolerating from others?

How tolerant are we being in terms of the lives and philosophies of those around us? What is our relationship to our planet? Disrespect for anything created by Source Energy will produce an imbalance and will generate karma that must be addressed—if not now, later.

We are not the victims of our karma. When we decide to come into life and address and rectify the imbalances that we have created, we are doing so for our own Soul's growth. When we balance karma, we create "good" karma; good karma is simply the dissolution of negative karma by bringing balance and harmony into a situation. When we balance karma and create good karma, we raise the vibration and have the benefit of those energies.

The karma and imbalances in another person's life are not our business, and we can never know the nature of another person's issues or their karma. It is easy to judge when we do not know the cause, but we must be careful indeed when we bring our opinions and judgments into the life of another. Doing so may add another link in our own karmic chain.

Death: The End of the Incarnation and the Journey Home

Just as we choose our lives, we also choose our deaths. We have between three and five exit points during each lifetime; these exit points are times during which we could and might make the choice to leave the current life and to die. As a general rule, we choose to stay until the "final curtain." But if the life has been arduous and the personality is weary, the Soul may decide to take it Home.

Just as we never know another's life journey, we also don't know another's exit points. Sometimes people choose to die at a young age, and then the tendency is to lament that person's abbreviated lifetime. But it may be that the lessons are learned, the work is accomplished, and the journey is done. In the context of 550 to 600 lifetimes, one short lifetime is one short lifetime. Within each lifetime, however, it is difficult, even impossible, to understand this or to take something less than a grievous and despairing attitude.

Or someone who is very old and sick may linger on, and we lament that as well. We believe that it might be in that elderly person's best interest—and in the best interest of those around that person—if this individual would give up the journey and go Home. But again, this elder may be continuing with the final lessons.

It may also be that he or she is assisting others with their lessons. For example, the person may be aiding another in learning to put personal needs aside for a time and comfort the dying. He or she may be helping others learn patience. Perhaps this individual is teaching someone that death is a journey, just as life is, and that there is no reason to be afraid. We do not know, but the elder will go at just the right time.

When we die, our Souls leave our bodies through the Stellar Gateway, the eighth chakra that is located just above our earthly bodies. Most Souls cross to the Light; it is a rarity, even in the very troubled personalities, for the Soul to linger on as a Ghost. Souls who have crossed can and do come back to visit us.

Home: The World of Spirit and Preparation for the Next Incarnation

After our death, we return to the World of Spirit. The historical belief is that we spend approximately fifty years here. Some Souls may spend more time, some less, depending on issues and needs. Now, however, many in the New Age communities believe that numerous Souls are more rapidly reincarnating, and spending much less than fifty years in the Spirit World. This is due, perhaps, to the changing planetary energies.

When we are between incarnations and are in the World of Spirit, we review our lives. With the help of our Guides, we examine the life that we have just left. We study the akashic record and the lives of our past to see what issues continue to need to be addressed—what karma remains imbalanced.

We look at the areas in which we have grown and raised our vibration. We look at our karmic issues and what balances we have achieved. We look at the karmic issues that we have failed to balance and areas where we may have accumulated additional karma. We determine what challenges remain to be met.

We examine relationships, families, and groups in which we have participated. We scrutinize the work that we performed—the work where we were compensated in equal measure, the work that we did out of generosity and compassion, and the work where, perhaps, we exhibited some laziness. We study our worldview, both what we believe we should have lived and what we actually lived. We examine everything.

When we are readying ourselves to incarnate again, with the help of our Guides, we choose all that we will be bringing with us back to Earth. We choose our next life experience. We choose individual forms—our personal appearance. We choose specific situations, particular opportunities, and special challenges. We choose that which will detract us from our life lessons

81

and that which will support us. We choose our Spiritual Guardians. We choose our time and place of birth and what we will call ourselves. With the consent of the other Souls, we choose our people, all of them. And then, in our time and place, we reincarnate.

What Is the Akashic Record?

With each incarnation, the veils between the World of Spirit and Earth are pulled; they are closed so that we can concentrate on the life at hand and can encounter all that which we came here to experience. If the veils were not pulled, we would be greatly distracted and would not give the current life the attention that it should have. We would not live within the complexities of the existing journey and so would compromise our reach for the higher vibration. To remember all of our past lives would be overwhelming and confusing.

It is all recorded, however, in the big book of past lives called the akashic record. Obviously, this isn't a book in the way that we think of books, but we must put it into terms that we can understand.

Akasha is a Sanskrit word meaning "ether"; akasha is Universal energy that is a part of and is interwoven into the fabric of all things. The akashic record then is an energetic transcription. It is a Universal library or filing system that is written into and recorded in the Cosmic Mind.

The akashic record chronicles all events and responses to those events. It is the energetic record of all beliefs, thoughts, feelings, and occurrences that have ever happened or will happen. When retrieving information from the past, information is generally clear and comprehensible. When asking about the future, information is given in probabilities.

The akashic record can be accessed through meditation, channeling, and prayer. It is a minimal access, however, and even the most accomplished psychics cannot go into the record in great depth. As humans, we are not designed for this; we are here, as stated earlier, to address the current life and learn the current lessons.

This is not a storybook that we can simply open and read. Past life information is given to us only as it is relevant to the current life. There are a number of ways that we can get past life information, but it is helpful to have another person involved, as it is difficult to be objective when dealing with our own issues. There are many practitioners now who are trained in hypnotherapy and are able to facilitate past life regressions. There are also readers who are capable of accessing this information. Again—be sure that you get references and know your practitioner's training and experience.

Past Lives

We have lived many lives and have had many experiences. Some of our lives have been more comfortable than others. In certain lives, we suffered terrible trauma, and in other lives, we participated in causing others trauma. We have behaved honorably; at times, it was a passing kindness, and now and again, we made notable sacrifices to serve the common good. We behaved dishonorably; often it was a simple slight, but from time to time, we contributed to great harm to others.

Past Lives and Children

In the early years of each incarnation, when we are babies and little children, we are often able to remember past life experiences. Generally, our access to this information begins to fade when we are between ages six and eight. Pay attention to what children say. What we often think of as stories created out of a vivid imagination may well be a narrative of a past life.

One of my family members asked her mother and me if we remembered that time when I was her grandma and she and I were the only ones in the family. She was thinking about our dog, Murray, who had all those puppies. We did not remember that time or Murray, much to her frustration. But even though we do not remember, we can ask them to tell us what they remember about it.

Notice the tiny baby who is sound asleep and begins to smile or the infant who startles suddenly and begins to wail. These little ones are still close to Home and have heightened access to past life information. (When infants are distressed, I generally tell them that they are just fine, that they are here now with us, and we are so glad to have them.)

Eventually, most children begin to forget. It is not necessarily because the situation is resolved but rather that they are getting on with the tasks of this life. However, reoccurring dreams, unexplained fears, phobias, likes, and dislikes should be taken seriously; they should not be negated as these issues might well be Soul memories from a past life.

For instance, a little girl in my extended family has been exceedingly fearful of loud noises. During a weekend retreat, her mother, her aunt, and I were discussing the situation. Her aunt asked if this issue might have its roots in a past life. I asked our Spiritual Guardians if they had information for us. They did, and so we became aware that she had a past life in London for the duration of World War II. During the bombings, she had sometimes been able to shelter in the underground; at other times, however, she had been caught in the city and remained above ground when the air raids shrieked and the bombs fell. Any loud noise in the current life (here and now) would cause her severe distress, and she would become fearful and anxious. For the first four years in the present incarnation, this situation was difficult for her and for those who were close to her. However, as time went on, this "memory" receded, and she grew more accustomed to today's loud noises.

Resolving Past Life Issues in the Present

Additionally, we bring significant issues into the current lifetime from past life experiences. We do this so that we can understand and heal them and begin to bring ourselves into balance and equilibrium. We may replay certain themes because in past lives we have been wounded or traumatized or caused harm to others.

For example, all of us in many lives have been without enough food; in certain lives, we may have died of starvation. In the life of the here and now, we may have chosen to develop an eating disorder. We may eat too much or too little in an attempt to understand the issue and begin to bring balance and healing to the situation.

Furthermore, we have all experienced war, and physical and sexual violence. Very young Souls (see Chapter Five), in an effort to organize and understand the experience, may replay the trauma in future lives by engaging in violent behaviors themselves. Older Souls are more likely to seek understanding by working in rape crisis centers or victim support organizations. They may participate in organizations such as Doctors Without Borders or the Children's Defense Fund.

Souls, particularly Souls who have had many incarnations, may also choose to experience violence again but in a setting where help is available. For instance, that Soul may experience date rape but in a circumstance where therapy, good friends, and supportive family are available.

Reading the Akashic Record: Past Life Examples

I once did a reading for a man who had a past life that involved being a Welch miner trapped in the mine. We began to talk about his current life experiences, and he told me that he had recurring nightmares about being trapped in the dark and the terror that went with those dreams. We were able to discover this information because it was useful for him to know that this was trauma from a past life, and that he was healing this trauma, bit by bit. Interestingly, he had chosen a current life experience in the wide-open spaces; he owned a boat and was a salmon fishing guide on one of the Great Lakes.

Those of us who have had readings know that our Guides and Angels give us information in a way that we can understand. They are not averse to stretching our imagination, however. My Spiritual Helpers sometimes use language that is familiar to me but is archaic and not in my usual speaking or writing vocabulary. Sometimes the cadence of the language is unusual. My Guides frequently use language such as, "At this time in your life, you are wanting …" instead of "Right now, you want …"

I try to stay as true to the message as I am able to do, so sometimes the presentation of the information sounds odd or stilted. At times, it is my own struggle to move back and forth between the right and left brain; the information is often coming quicker than I am able to speak or write. The following examples are "unedited" and are given to you as they were given to me. I prepare Metaphysical Blueprint Charts that include numerology, astrology, and cardology, and the last part of the Chart includes a Past Life Reading. The past life examples are from three of those Charts.

➢ *Victoria:* The woman in the following example is a woman who experienced a difficult childhood with a certain amount of emotional and verbal abuse. This abuse was frequently not directed at her, but she was witness to it. In the current life, she is healing on a Soul level bits and pieces of trauma that she suffered from violence in the past. She is keeping some amount of violence as a theme in her life but not an overwhelming amount. Her goal on a Soul level is to heal. With the help of a therapist now, she is taking those childhood experiences, examining them, and is in the process of healing them.

In her current experience, she herself is a therapist and a great talker. However, her concern was that, although she was able to help people get through and beyond their own issues, she herself often felt immobilized. She could see what she perhaps might want to do, but to bring herself to do it was very difficult.

She also tended to put herself in employment situations where she dealt with the poor and the issues that arose from their poverty. She has family members who, because of health issues, were living in very poor circumstances; she often felt that she needed to assist them financially, physically, and emotionally. Here is her past life reading:

The past life that your Spiritual Guardians are showing for you takes place in the French Revolution. You are a little girl, and you live in a bourgeois, or middle class, household. Your parents are very "forward" thinking and hold in high regard the principles of liberty for all persons. As your own family has plenty to eat, they are less concerned for the poor but hold some concern for the poor, nonetheless. For them it has more to do with inclusion for all persons in the workings of society; it has to do with enfranchisement into the culture. They do understand on some level the hunger and poverty of the poor, but they want them to be able to be included into the political structure as a solution to the problem, so there is only a rudimentary understanding of what poverty means to the impoverished.

There are you and one or two other children living with your parents. Your parents are involved in many secret meetings with other persons who hold the ideals of "liberty, brotherhood, and equality." And they are pursuing this on an intellectual level—they want to move the system so that the system responds, so there are a great many discussions. There is much meeting and talking.

Eventually, however, they are brought down into the world of action, and action out of their control. They get swept up in one of the many protests—mobs, hungry mobs—who are protesting their situation. And your Guides and Angels are asking that you remember that the concerns of the poor were different from the concerns of the middle class. The middle class wanted change, enfranchisement, equality, and liberty; the poor wanted food and shelter. But both groups wanted change, and many of the poor saw that the ideals of the middle class would help them get what they wanted, too. And so your parents went from intellectual discussion into action. They were literally swept up by the mob and carried along. And, of course, the existing nobility was having none of it, so the French armies fired on the mob, and your parents were killed.

You are working through many issues from this French lifetime in the current lifetime. For one, you are integrating more the difficulties of being poor, and you are exposing yourself to very personal situations in the life of the here and now. You are giving yourself information about how difficult it is to be poor.

Additionally, you are examining the difference between words and action—how effective are words and what happens when you carry them into action. Words are noble and high sounding, and they help us frame and communicate the issue, but words in and of themselves do not fix the problem. Action is required. And when action is "let loose," we are not always in control of what happens; others are involved, and we cannot control how others behave. And part of your paralysis in terms of taking action in the life of the here and now is your observation in the French life of your parents getting murdered by the French army. And so your Spiritual Guardians are asking that you remind yourself that you are living in the here and now and are no longer the little French girl with the murdered parents. Your emotional response often comes out of this life, so it is extreme for the situation.

And a third issue is your desire to assist others. Part of this desire stems simply from the disenfranchisement that you witness—what happens to people who are poor. But also you want to help others in this current lifetime to be more personally powerful—to have personal liberty and equality and to be able to be brothers in the sense that we are all of equal worth. And so your French parents' ideals remain with you on a Soul level. You are carrying on the inheritance or the mandate, so to speak.

> *Katherine*: The woman in the following example is a very pretty young woman who is a scientist and a teacher, with advanced degrees in her field. In the current life, she is working hard. She is married to a man in the "helping professions" who has unpredictable hours, she has a full-time job outside of the home, and she has young children. She grew up in the city but spent a part of her life living in small communities as her husband advanced his career. She is a soft-spoken, reserved person.

One of her concerns in the life of the here and now is her lack of ability to speak up for herself. Often this is not a problem, but sometimes she does not express herself in a timely manner (or at all), so what should have been a minor situation becomes a big problem.

An additional concern is that she often allows other people's opinions of her and her actions matter too much. She believes that she sometimes defines situations as very confining or limiting, when in fact they are more minor obstacles than she at first believed.

In the life of the here and now, she has chosen to "get down and get dirty," as they say. She has decided to address issues from past lives and to raise her vibration. Here is her past life reading:

The life that your Spiritual Guardians are showing for you takes place in the United States in California in the 1910s and early 1920s. You were female, very pretty, petite, delicate, and graceful. And you were this from early childhood. Particularly your Guides and your Angels show your hands and your feet and are saying that "even your gestures were poetry." You grew up in a small town—kind of the stereotypical small town of that time. It is likely that this town was in California or close to California. You were a movie actor during the time when silent pictures were being made, and it is possible that you also made movies when the films became "talkies." However, your renown or distinction or recognition in the movie industry took place during the silent film era.

Because you were so attractive, it was difficult for others around you to see you as really "one of us"—you seemed more like something to own, and those around you had a difficult time seeing you as fully "human," so to speak. As a result, your intellectual, emotional, and psychological development was atypical, and you had an indistinct sense of self. You were an intelligent woman but did not always present yourself as such. Others appeared to run your life for you, and you allowed this for the most part; frequently you did not own your power. However, this is (as stated) for the most part and when you desired something that was not being freely given, you knew that the withholding of yourself would likely get the result that you wanted, and you would get what you wanted.

They are showing this life for several reasons. It is significant that your Spiritual Guardians show a life in which you were in silent movies and played a major role in the movie culture of that time, and that when movies became "talkies," you played a less significant role. In the life of the here and now, you are to talk; you are to express yourself, your ideas, your thoughts, and your feelings in words. In the silent movies, you played the part of the overly emotional female, and your gestures were exaggerated, possibly as they needed to be, to get your point across. In the here and now, however, there is no need of dramatic gesture (although you may occasionally be tempted), and you are to speak your truth, as it is important for you to express yourself verbally. Ask for what you want, say what you think, let others know when they tread on your toes.

The other part to the expression of yourself is within the theme of withholding yourself to get what you want. In the here and now, you are to define what it is that you desire and then go about getting it in a straightforward manner, using your verbal skills—frank, forthright, and direct.

In many respects, things came easy for you in the life of the 1920s because people wanted to please you; they saw you as an "exquisite thing" (as your Guides and Angels say), and herein lies another issue. When things do not come easy in the life of the here and now, you tend to see it as a problem bigger than it is. You may see hardship and limitation in situations that are not necessarily difficult or limiting but just need your full attention and some hard work. Additionally, you will not always get what you want, although you yearn for that and "remember" back to this past life when you generally did get what you wanted. The other part of this is that others saw you as "thing." In the life of the here and now, your desire is to be "fully realized." You want to be who you are; you want independence and individuation. This is reflected in your Soul Urge Number One and also by your Rising Sign of Aries. Both of these energies help you to "become" in this desire to be "fully realized."

> *Alexandra:* The woman in the following example is a woman who has also worked very hard in her life. She had a child at a young age and so, although a very bright woman, did not purse the education that she had intended to pursue but rather pursued the education that she needed so that she could support herself. She dedicated herself to the raising of her child, doing an exemplary job.

She has frequently worked two jobs to support herself and her child. One of her jobs has been as a dispatcher for police, fire, and emergency personnel. Although she presents herself with a tough crust, she is, in fact, sensitive and concerned for others to the point that advantage can be taken.

In the life of the here and now, she has a great curiosity for things alternative. She has an enormous respect for her body, has an excellent diet, consumes food and alcohol in small to moderate quantities, and exercises not only on a regular basis but in a variety of formats. Because she is interested in her spiritual life, she wanted a reading. Here is her past life reading:

What your Spiritual Guardians are showing us now is a young man, and he is golfing. He is wearing argyle sox, wool half pants, and shoes that are brown and white. He is golfing on a magnificent golf course—something that looks like a castle is in the background. This young man is you, and this is Scotland; it is in the time of World War I. You come from a very wealthy family, and you, of course, do not go into the War. What your Guides and Angels are saying is that you golfed your way through the War, and not, they are saying, that it would have been right or good for you to go into war, but many sacrificed, and you did not. It isn't that you lead a debauched life, but you drove the little roadster-type car and drank the expensive whiskey and went to rather lavish and wasteful parties. You had a good life, as many would define it, and you learned very little. And so in this life of the here and now, you have decided to address this. It is almost like you are making up for lost opportunity in terms of Spiritual learning in the present life.

On the estate where your family lived, there was an old "cottager" (what this person is calling himself), who you were close to as a boy. Oh, Shamus you can call him, he says. And this person has agreed with you, in this life of the present, to be your Guide—one of your Guides. He was an Old Soul (see Chapter Five) already in the Scotland life, and he was, in many, many ways, your guidepost, comfort, and solace when you were a boy. As you grew older, you forgot about and neglected him, but he is not minding about that. He says that he was there for you at the time that you needed and now he is there for you as your Guide. You have lived many lives with this Shamus.

Shamus is saying that you ended your life in Scotland by drinking Scotch all night long and then driving your little car. You died behind the wheel of your little roadster, just as Steely Dan so eloquently sang in "Deacon Blues," and you are still having some trauma about this abrupt ending of the life. Although you had decided this was how and when you were going, still it was a trauma. So there are some issues and working through them in the life of the here and now. You are involved in trauma, but you have put it at a distance by putting yourself in a position to assist by dispatching help to the place in which it is needed.

Why We Are Allowed to Glimpse Our Past

These examples are relatively simple in that they present imbalances that have evolved to a point where they are reasonably easy to understand; with some effort, the situations, circumstances, or relationships can be made whole. Often, however, difficult or complicated issues that we are experiencing in the here and now are rooted in multiple past life hardships and traumas. Having past life history can assist us in putting our current troubles in a continuous framework; the issue came from somewhere and is going somewhere else. We can put it in context in terms of our past lives.

Eventually, after many, many lifetimes, we are "done" and are ready to move into experiences that are not of the earth. Before our vibration is increased to this level, however, we will have been so many things and have lived in so many places here on Earth. We will have been African, European, Asian, and Indian. We will have been male and female; we will have been straight and gay. We will have been Pagan, Buddhist, Christian, Muslim, Jewish, and a host of other spiritual expressions. We will have lived in democracies and dictatorships.

We will have had innumerable religious and political expressions and experiences. We will have faced poverty and wealth, oppression and freedom. Our horizons will have been inestimably expanded.

Chapter 5: Soul Stages and Ages

- Souls
  - ❖ Soul Growth: An Increase in Vibration
  - ❖ Beginning and Living the Journey
- Paradigms and Shifts
  - ❖ Locus of Control
  - ❖ Roles
  - ❖ Rules
  - ❖ Norms
  - ❖ Narcissism and Philanthropy
  - ❖ The Common Good
  - ❖ Reciprocity in Relationships
  - ❖ Moral Judgment
  - ❖ Concrete and Abstract Thinking
  - ❖ Executive or Administrative Ability
  - ❖ Relationship to Source Energy
- Soul Stages
  - ❖ Baby Soul Stage (with Paradigms)
  - ❖ Child Soul Stage (with Paradigms)
  - ❖ Adolescent Soul Stage (with Paradigms)
    - o Example: Adolescent Souls at Work
  - ❖ Mature Soul Stage (with Paradigms)
  - ❖ Old Soul Stage (with Paradigms)
  - ❖ Transcendental Souls
  - ❖ Infinite Souls
- Other Factors That Influence Soul Age Expression
  - ❖ Family of Origin in the Current Life
  - ❖ Birth Order
    - o Only Children
    - o First Children
    - o Second Children
    - o Third Children
    - o Fourth Children
  - ❖ Gender
    - o Male
    - o Female
  - ❖ Intelligence
  - ❖ Past Life Issues and Karma
- Conclusion

Souls

Our Soul is an eternal aspect of Source Energy or God; it lives within each of us. It can never perish nor can it be corrupted. The Soul is pure, radiant energy, and although our Souls are a part of us, they are not in physical form. Our Souls are Divine Energy that came from God; as with God, they cannot be destroyed and have no end. God is always in the act of creation, and we are cocreators with God through our Souls. God has no end and is not finished with the creation, so Source Energy is constantly seeking out new experiences and new growth.

Soul Growth: An Increase in Vibration

Soul development or Soul growth occurs as a result of reincarnation. With each incarnation, we bring people, experiences, and situations into the life, and we learn from them. As we learn, we grow and develop, and as we grow and develop, we increase our vibration and acquire wisdom. Wisdom is a process not a product.

Reincarnation is a progression that leads to vibrational expansion. With each incarnation, we discover ourselves more fully and understand ourselves more wholly. We begin to comprehend our interconnection and interrelation to all life. As we reach higher vibration, we start to appreciate the importance of giving and receiving love, of experiencing joy each day of our lives, and of expressing gratitude for all of our blessings. We become increasingly conscious of Source Energy, of the Universal or Cosmic Mind, of God and begin to realize that we can and must have trust in "All That Is."

Before we are finished with our many journeys here on Earth, we will have spent numerous lifetimes in each stage of Soul development. For ease and clarity, these stages will be presented as follows: Baby, Child, Adolescent, Mature, Old, Transcendental, and Infinite. Soul development stages are never entirely concise or exact. When precisely do we move from adolescence to maturity, and at what point do we really become old? There is no magic number or series of events that mark a clear boundary for movement from one stage to another.

Nonetheless, there are some things that are common to each stage. There are certain behaviors and skills that children have that babies have not yet developed. Children are capable of learning concepts, such as colors and numbers, which are out of the intellectual grasp of babies. Conversely, babies have certain behaviors that they outgrow as they learn and develop. For instance, as babies grow into maturity, they eventually stop putting everything into their mouths and learn to use the potty. And, of course, mature people have certain skills that children cannot have, simply because it is not developmentally possible.

Many lifetimes are spent in each Soul stage. Baby Souls do not advance to a Child Soul status until they have completed many incarnations as Baby Souls. Concepts and skills must be acquired before they are ready to move forward; it is through this acquisition that the vibration is increased. The reincarnational process is constant, consistent, and coherent and requires numerous lifetimes in each Soul stage. It takes us approximately 550 to 600 incarnations to complete the entire process from our beginning as Baby Souls through to the end of the Old Soul stage.

So if you are a Mature Soul and are in a relationship with a Baby Soul—that is exactly what you are: a Mature Soul in a relationship with a Baby Soul. No matter what you say, no matter what you do, that Baby Soul will remain a Baby Soul for the remainder of this lifetime and in more lifetimes to come.

We can never truly know the age of another Soul. We can frequently make reasonably accurate assessments, but we do not know the entirety of another's journey. We do not know that person's reincarnational history or what they are here to learn now. That is the business of each individual Soul. It is difficult enough for us to understand one another in the human life of the here and now; adding the past life component makes this understanding even more difficult. It is essential that we temper the judgments that we make about each other, in all directions and across all time and space, as we possess incomplete information.

Beginning and Living the Journey

When our Souls separate from Source Energy, they move from the all-embracing wholeness of being enveloped in the One. They move from the Unconditional Love that is God. They become distinct. Initially, our Soul energy is primal and undeveloped. The goal for each and every Soul is to progress through its reincarnational journeys as it moves to reunite with God. With each incarnation, the Soul chooses relationships, localities, work, play, situations, and issues; it is through each all-encompassing, all-inclusive life experience that the Soul develops. It is important to live in the present moment, in the here and now, because this is how we acquire wisdom and growth. This is how we increase our vibration and reach for God.

As we travel through our lives, we have adverse experiences and meet challenging or demanding people. It is often difficult to understand how this relates to our reach for higher vibration. However, each lifetime, each person in every relationship (no matter how significant or insignificant), and each experience we have is about gaining information, understanding, and ultimately wisdom. All of our experiences support our move toward higher vibration; it is by way of this vibrational increase that we cocreate with God.

The Infinite Soul, Jesus, came to Earth to teach Love; the Infinite Soul, Buddha, came to Earth to teach Oneness. As we move into higher vibration, we begin to gain an increasing understanding of the concepts of Love and Oneness. Soul development has nothing to do with intellectual aptitude. Instead, it concerns itself with an increase in our capacity to understand higher Spiritual principles relating to Universal Oneness, Love, and the Common Good. One can be a Baby Soul and be clever and intellectually gifted. One can be an Old Soul and have compromised intelligence.

Paradigms and Shifts

We all have values and beliefs, experiences and encounters that affect how we perceive reality. The significance or importance that we place upon a circumstance, situation, or event varies from person to person. There is a wide range of individual difference in the levels of confidence that we have in the people and groups around us. Some have strong convictions and principles and act on them quickly; others have few or weak opinions and seldom take a position or stance.

We all define reality differently. A paradigm is a philosophical framework that defines a reality. It is how we think, what we believe, and what we value. It is the habitual or usual manner in which we respond to our environment as a result of what we accept to be true and what we think is of value.

A paradigm shift is a change or a modification in the paradigm. For instance, we define our society as "safe" and then become aware that there is a group in our midst of which we have been previously unaware. We meet several members; they seem to have unusual beliefs but appear to be nice people. We do not give them much thought, believing they are odd but harmless. However, some time later, they bomb the local courthouse. Now we are giving them a great deal of thought. We change our belief and perceive them to be violent people with dangerous convictions and no longer define our society as "safe." Our reality has been changed; we have had a paradigm shift.

Or we have previously felt ourselves to be superior to a certain ethnic group but have not bothered to inform ourselves about their habits or customs. Occasionally, we have been heard to make disparaging comments about them. Our daughter marries a member of this group, however, and blesses us with a granddaughter. We fall in love with this little girl, and so, for her sake, we learn all that we can about "her" culture. Now we are outraged when we hear negative remarks and express concern regarding the narrow thinking that cannot accept diversity. We have had a paradigm shift.

93

As we move from Soul stage to Soul stage, our paradigms shift. This chapter discusses several areas in which these shifts occur:

➢ *Locus of Control* refers to the extent to which we believe that we can control the events that affect us. If we have a low internal locus, we believe that events are dominated or dictated primarily by something outside of our control; other people, the environment, or God, for instance, are to be held accountable for our experiences. If we have a high internal locus, we believe that the events of our lives are primarily a result of our own actions and behaviors.

➢ *Roles* refer to our function; it is the part we play in our relationships and in our own lives. It is the standard or typical expectations regarding behavior and conduct, rights and privileges, and obligations that are associated with those functions.

➢ *Rules* are the principles that guide or govern conduct and behavior within societies.

➢ *Norms* are the rules that define appropriate and inappropriate behaviors, attitudes, beliefs, and values within groups, cultures, and societies.

➢ *Narcissism and Philanthropy* are on opposite ends of a continuum regarding self-interest as opposed to an awareness of others. If we are narcissistic people, we are inwardly directed and disproportionately concerned with our self; we are egotistical and selfish. We have limited understanding of or consideration for the consequences that our actions may have on others. If we are philanthropic, we are outwardly directed; we are concerned for the people around us and for humanity as a whole. We have empathy for others, understand the concept of the Common Good, and believe that it has relevance in our lives.

➢ *The Common Good* refers not just to what is in the best interest of the largest portion of the population but what is in the best interest of each member of society. It understands that each person is, indeed, a child of God.

➢ *Reciprocity in Relationships* refers to giving and receiving in equal measure; it is responding to and exchanging in-kind behaviors, actions, and emotions.

➢ *Moral Judgment* refers to an understanding of the consequences that our behaviors and actions may have on others.

➢ *Concrete and Abstract Thinking* are on opposite ends of a continuum that describes mental processing or reasoning. Concrete thinking is surface thinking; facts are considered truths. There is a generalized idea of concepts and a belief in what is seen or otherwise perceived with the senses. Abstract thinking involves more complex mental processes and is deeper thinking. Abstract thinking involves ideas; the concepts of figurative communication, as well as symbols, or metaphors, are understood. Multiple meanings within ideas and expressions are acknowledged. How we think greatly contributes to what we think; it helps us define our reality.

➤ *Executive or Administrative Ability* refers to our capacity to make a plan and achieve a goal. Successful planning requires an ability:

- to give and sustain attention to detail
- to inhibit our impulses
- to be self-initiating in our activities
- to control our emotions
- to organize ourselves
- to manage our time.

➤ *Relationship to Source Energy* refers to how we define Divine Energy, what we perceive it to be, what we choose to call it, and how we experience it.

Soul Stages

Baby Soul Stage

Baby Souls are primal and undeveloped, inexperienced and raw. They are just beginning their reincarnational journeys and so need sustenance, safety, patience, and guidance. They will remain in the Baby Soul stage for many lifetimes. It is difficult to be in a relationship with them, but it is important to remember that we all started here.

Narcissism and Philanthropy: Baby Souls are unreservedly self-concerned and operate out of pure egoism; they are "me" and see the rest of the people in the world as "not me." Baby Souls are narcissistic. They see themselves as the center not only in their own lives but in the lives of others as well. They have unreasonable expectations of favorable treatment and expect others to comply with their wishes and demands. They are not able to identify with the emotions of others and so lack consideration for those around them. Empathy and compassion are concepts they do not yet have the capacity to grasp. As a result, on an interpersonal basis, they are exploitive and frequently dictatorial.

Because Baby Souls are so utterly self-involved, they see their own and other people's actions and behaviors only in terms of the consequences those actions and behaviors have on them. As a result, Baby Souls can engage in very hurtful and damaging activities, and if they are not adversely affected, they will see no reason to stop. They are unable to see the effect that their actions have on those around them. Baby Souls have not acquired the conceptual skills necessary for thinking in philanthropic or humanitarian terms and are unable to identify with other's emotions.

Baby Souls are not aware of themselves in the context of other human beings. Those around them, even those they love, are psychologically invisible to them. Baby Souls do love, but it is so tied to dependency and need that is difficult to differentiate the love from the need.

Locus of Control: Baby Souls have a low internal locus of control. They do not believe that they have control over events around them, but rather something or someone else controls situations, occurrences, and experiences. As a result, they lack accountability and blame their negative circumstances, behaviors, and actions on something outside of themselves.

Because Baby Souls do not understand that they are the cause of their own experience and believe that others are to blame, they have difficulty learning from their mistakes. They often struggle with the complexities of society; as a result, they may find themselves institutionalized in hospitals, treatment centers, or prisons.

Relationships and Reciprocity: Relationships infer shared interests and efforts. The Baby Soul's focus is so egocentric that shared interests and efforts have limited possibility and restricted expression. Baby Souls have inadequate or deficient ability to have reciprocity in relationships. They are not able to take and give in the equal measure that is so crucial to a healthy relationship; instead, they take and the other person gives. Baby Soul's who are in relationship with each other are living side by side in a parallel, self-focused existence rather than in a true relationship.

Baby Souls measure the relative incorrectness of their behaviors and actions based on the consequences (or punishments) that they receive. If there is a harsh consequence, the behavior is perceived to have been bad. If there is little or no consequence, it must have been all right. For example, if a Baby Soul steals a candy bar from a store and the consequence is disproportionate to the act—the storeowner beats the thief so badly that hospitalization is required—the Baby Soul understands his action to have been terrible. But if he steals the candy bar, stabs the storeowner, and nothing happens to the Baby Soul, the act is understood to have been acceptable.

Guilt is a concept that is not acquired until later Soul development. Baby Souls are not driven or affected by guilt; therefore, appealing to the feelings that are associated with guilt and shame will fall on deaf ears. It will be many more lifetimes before the concept of reciprocity in relationships will be recognized. We must be emotionally aware of other people before reciprocity can occur.

Moral Judgment: Baby Souls have a very limited understanding of the consequences that their behaviors have on other people. They do not believe that they influence events around them and live a very self-absorbed existence. As a result, they do not see the correlation between their actions and other people's outcomes.

The Common Good: This concept is beyond the grasp of the Baby Soul.

Rules: Baby Souls have a difficult time with rules. If the rule supports or is in harmony with their needs, it will be followed. However, if a rule does not serve their best interest, it is seen as irrelevant or extraneous and is ignored or violated. Baby Souls have a low internal locus of control; they see others and not themselves as responsible for what happens to them in their world. This is particularly true when their behaviors are socially inappropriate, offensive, or illegal, and they are being asked to account for themselves. Baby Souls blame; they do not take responsibility.

Norms: Because Baby Souls are self-focused, beliefs and values lean toward that which will serve and support their desires. Whether or not the action is appropriate or inappropriate as defined by the larger culture is often irrelevant. In their more extreme expressions, Baby Souls refuse to comply with culturally accepted norms and will engage in socially pathological behaviors. They exhibit reckless disregard for others' well-being, have no remorse for their behaviors, and are indifferent to the harm they may be causing. They may deceive others, act impulsively, aggressively, or violently, and rationalize their actions. When Baby Souls express themselves in an exaggerated manner such as this, they move from narcissistic to sociopathic.

Roles: Baby Souls are not overly concerned with cultural norms. Roles are closely tied to normative expectations. Baby Souls tend to cling more to the rights and privileges inherent in their roles and less to the proper conduct and obligations. As employees, parents, spouses, or friends, they are focused on their rights even when they are failing to fulfill their obligations.

Concrete and Abstract Thinking: Baby Souls think very concretely and lack the ability to engage in abstract reasoning. Even though they may have high intelligence, they lack the ability to engage in complex mental processing. Facts are truth; truth is based upon that which is perceived by the senses, particularly what is seen and heard. Concepts are generalized and have a single meaning.

Baby Souls are rigid, concrete thinkers. Accordingly, it is vital to follow statements of consequences for behavior with actual consequences for that behavior. Baby Souls understand action, as words are frequently meaningless to them. This is not because they are being contrary or malicious. They do not understand the concepts that are being articulated, and so if action does not follow verbalization, communication is pointless.

Executive or Administrative Ability: Baby Souls have compromised abilities in this area. They lack impulse control and have difficulty managing their emotions. Their talent for sustaining attention to detail is marginal. Their skills regarding time management, organization, and self-initiation are underdeveloped. Baby Souls have difficulty making and following a plan and tend to live day to day.

As a result, Baby Souls are often unreliable in their endeavors and their relationships. Baby Souls define activities and relationships as a means to an end. When the relationships and activities are no longer serving the

97

interest of the Baby Soul, those activities and relationships are discarded or deserted. There is little thought given to that which has been abandoned.

Relationship to Source Energy: Baby Souls generally pay little heed to God. When they do express an interest, their concept of God is literal and rigid. They may use God as a means to exploit or manipulate people in their environment.

Child Soul Stage

Child Souls define the world around them as "me" and "others who are like me," so they are beginning to expand their experience to include relationships. They can find solace and security within the group of "others who are like me," and this safety gives them the foundation to begin having reciprocal emotional connections. They do not generalize their growth into higher vibration to the general population; rather, they confine this expansion to those they define as their group. Their focus remains largely self-centered, and they see value in people primarily as those people relate to the Child Soul.

Locus of Control: Child Souls have a low internal locus of control and believe that someone or something outside of themselves dictates what happens in their world. They are committed to vertical power structures. Child Souls believe that authority figures know what is best, and they trust them to correctly establish and properly enforce the rules.

Rules: Child Souls are rule-bound. Once the "real" rules are determined by the appropriate authority figure, Child Souls will steadfastly adhere to them. There is little to no questioning of the rules or persons in power. The emotional and physical well-being of the Child Soul is dependent on a valid power hierarchy and on the "authentic" rules. Power hierarchies are a hallmark of Child Soul development, and Child Souls see almost everything around them in terms of who has the most influence and control. The concept of worth is attached to the power structure, and the higher the status, the more worth one has.

Norms: Appropriate and inappropriate behaviors are defined by the authority figures within the group. Beliefs, values, and attitudes are similarly identified and described by those who have power in and control of the group. Strict attention is given to normative expectations within the group but this does not generalize to the larger society.

Roles: Within the context of their group, Child Souls are able to function very well within their roles. They are able to be personally accountable as well as responsible in their relationships. Their behavior and conduct conforms to the group norm. They understand their obligations and are prepared to enjoy their rights and privileges.

Reciprocity in Relationships: Child Souls have self-interested concern for members in their group of "those who are like me" and a limited interest in the well-being of others in the general population. Interest even in the members of their group remains self-involved, however, as they are as interested in what benefits them as they are in the welfare of others close to them.

Child Souls have an immature understanding of reciprocity in relationships; they struggle with the concept of in-kind or similar exchanges regarding behaviors and actions. Child Souls often have a disproportionate sense of the kinds of responses certain behaviors and actions elicit. They may not recognize that a particular action may lead to a definite reaction or that a certain behavior may lead directly to a specific consequence. Inaccuracies in their perceptions are often frustrating to them and to others around them.

Child Souls have significant issues with control and believe that those around them must be monitored, regulated, and in some instances, dominated. This includes people in the larger society but also people in their group. Child Souls are most comfortable with a vertical power structure. They know their place in that structure but will attempt to gain more expanded authority or make a vertical move in the power structure if it is possible.

Narcissism and Philanthropy: Child Souls remain self-absorbed and self-centered. They have not yet gained the ability to be empathetic, compassionate, or generous. They are able to respect and even to revere specific members of their group; however, members of the general population remain people who should be ignored or controlled.

The Common Good: Although the Child Soul has a self-interested concern in the members of the group, the concept that all members of society are individually relevant is beyond their grasp.

Moral Judgment: Child Souls see their own belief system as true and correct. Accordingly, they see themselves as the guardians and protectors of culture and society. They follow the rules and are comfortable forcing others to follow them as well. If the society and culture in which they are living permits it, they will fight and kill for the beliefs that they espouse. They have a biased, one-sided understanding of the consequences that their behaviors and actions have on others.

Child Souls are comfortable with earthly authority and are attached to their vertical power structures. Laws, rules, rituals, and tradition have an almost legalistic fascination for them. Child Souls want structure and prefer security within that structure. They are resolute and unwavering in their attachment to their traditions and rules. Child Souls do not like to be confronted or challenged about their belief systems, and when they are, they may become confused and hostile.

Concrete and Abstract Thinking: Child Souls are concrete formulaic thinkers and use sets of words that express concepts definitively and authoritatively. As a result, they are very open to religious, political, or social dogma. Child Souls are the "fundamentalists" in all societies. As previously stated, they are authoritative in their expression, believe that there is "one true" belief system, and are willing to fight to defend and disseminate their worldview. Philosophies, values, and beliefs for which they are willing to wage war can be religious, political, economic, or social. Creative thinking, discussion, and exchange of ideas are not within the conceptual range of the Child Soul.

Child Souls are concrete dichotomous thinkers as well. Situations are either black or white. People are either good or bad. Sometimes, they are saintly, and sometimes they are evil. Child Souls are unable to recognize the mix of positive and negative that lives in all of us; in this regard, they are vulnerable to cults and their leaders. If the leader or authority figure in a cult (or indeed in any religious, political, economic, or social structure) is initially perceived and defined as "good," and that leader's message is "true," the attachment to the leader is made. Once the attachment is made, the Child Soul will trust that the leader will continue to represent the truth even when there is contrary evidence.

Child Souls are attuned to form and not to content. They see how things look, as opposed to how things actually are. This includes people, situations, events, places, and times. If the person, circumstance, event, time, or place is concretely presented as good, and that presentation is embraced, it is good. Any attempt to dissuade using intangible theory will be ineffective. Imaginative investigation or research involving abstract ideas is not within the conceptual reach of the Child Soul. If more complex, abstract information is provided that refutes the concrete presentation, the abstract will be ignored or rejected.

Executive or Administrative Ability: Child Souls are beginning to develop skills in organizing and managing their time, initiating activity, and paying attention to detail. They continue to prefer the direction of a leader, but within certain parameters, they demonstrate independence. Impulse control and managing emotions remain immature.

As a result, Child Souls have the ability to make plans and achieve goals; indeed, plans and goals are often important to the Child Soul. Plans and goals, however, are interdependent with rules and power structures.

Relationship to Source Energy: Child Souls are concrete thinkers with a significant attachment to vertical power structures; when they look at God, they tend to see him as the Supreme Boss. Child Souls attach themselves to a "true" belief and are willing to dominate, often even destroy, to preserve and present their truth. Their concept of God is reflected in this worldview; hence, God has a revengeful and punishing part of his being and is willing to obliterate his creation if there is not strict adherence to his rules.

Adolescent Souls have mastered the world in many ways and are now interested in how powerful they can become. They have a well-developed sense of personal entitlement, and competition permeates the very air around them. An Adolescent Soul sees the world as "me" and "you." They always have an eye on the prize and intend to emerge from their competitions victorious and triumphant. They want dominance, authority, recognition, status, and wealth and see no reason why they should not have it. Adolescent Souls believe that the end justifies the means; they have no issue with using negative means to get to what they consider to be a positive end.

Locus of Control: Adolescent Souls are moving into a higher manifestation of internal locus of control and often believe that they are in charge of their world. This is particularly so when they are winning the competition. Their move into a higher expression of internal locus is in progress, however, and remains incomplete. When success is illusive, the Adolescent Soul will revert to a lower internal locus and blame something outside—other people, the environment, or changing circumstance.

Reciprocity in Relationships: Adolescent Souls do not necessarily pursue what they want but rather what will make them successful. Additionally, form (how it looks) is often more important than content (what it is). These influences often dictate the types of relationships the Adolescent Soul will pursue. For example, they may choose to marry the beautiful person rather than the beloved person, simply because the beautiful person has more currency in society.

Adolescent Souls are moving into a larger understanding of reciprocity, and in-kind exchanges are frequently a part of their relationships. For example, there may be an agreement to marry, remain affectionate toward each other, and raise children, and each person in the couple will work toward achieving that end. There may be other similar but distinctly different in-kind exchanges in relationships. For instance, in a marital relationship, it may be one person's "job" to make a great deal of money and the other person is to remain attractive and host social events. Or if the children do well in public school, decide to go to college at a prestigious institution, and continue to attend the Episcopal church, the parents will pay for their education. There is a serious understanding of the axiom, "I'll scratch your back if you scratch mine."

Concrete and Abstract Thinking: Adolescent Souls are beginning to be very skilled at abstract thinking. When addressing the physical and material world, they are deep, creative thinkers, capable of complex mental processing. They generate and contemplate ideas; they are often inspired thinkers and are able to discern multiple meanings and multiple purposes in their designs, proposals, and imaginings. Socially and emotionally, however, Adolescent Souls remain conventional thinkers and see the world in stereotypes.

Executive or Administrative Ability: Adolescent Souls are conventional thinkers; they are conservative and traditional. They have very well developed executive and administrative abilities, however, and are able to organize themselves and their worlds. They can make a plan or a goal and follow it through to its completion. Adolescent Souls are able to sustain their attention and manage their time. If they stand to gain something they want, they have tremendous impulse control and can manage their emotions. Adolescent Souls can be wonderful self-initiators.

Rules: Adolescent Souls have fixed ideas about social and political roles, functions, organizations, and events. Adolescent Souls have defined their place in the culture and wish to, in the very least, maintain it. Accordingly, they believe that rules and authority exist in large part to maintain societal stereotypes and so are willing to support law and authority if it continues to assist them in preserving their place in society. They do not want to see the status quo disrupted.

Roles: Adolescent Souls are interested in status, power, and wealth. As a result, they appreciate the inherent value of living up to society's expectations and are prepared to fulfill societal roles. They have competency in self-regulation and can make a plan and execute it. They make an effort to understand motivation for their actions, and if a desired result is not achieved, they are willing to look at alternatives.

Norms: Adolescent Souls rigidly define socioeconomic status and embrace cultural norms as they apply to the various socioeconomic strata. They are very aware of appropriate and inappropriate behaviors, beliefs, and values in all levels of society. Because they are extraordinarily interested in increasing social status, wealth, and power, they pay special attention to rules, roles, and norms that support a move upward. They are conventional thinkers, though, and like things to remain the same, especially as it applies to others. They count on roles and rules remaining consistent and predictable in the dominant culture. Status quo does not necessarily apply to them, however, if they are able to make a vertical upward move. They are often intensely focused on making that move, and this can drive much of what they do.

Narcissism and Philanthropy: Adolescent Souls are beginning to at least explore the higher concepts of charity, generosity, and compassion. Indeed, it is the Adolescent Soul who often *acts* as the philanthropist in society. This is due in part to the need for status, wealth, and power, but it is also due to a burgeoning and genuine interest in society and culture.

The Common Good: Nevertheless, Adolescent Souls do not yet understand or embrace the concept of the Common Good; they remain largely self-interested.

Adolescent Souls are the power elite in all societies. They are the captains of industry, the empire builders, the wolves on Wall Street, and the robber barons. They see the business opportunity inherent in the invention. They are the people who "modernize" the culture and make technology available to us all. They are responsible for the creation of corporations, industries, and businesses. They generate jobs for millions.

Yet, they are responsible for the exploitation of their human resources, often exhibiting little concern for the health, social welfare, or education of their workers. It is the Adolescent Soul who is willing to poison the migrant worker with pesticides or to move industry to developing nations where men, women, and children will work long hours in sweatshop situations and with little pay. It is the Adolescent Soul who is willing to topple the world economy for personal gain.

Additionally, they are responsible for the exploitation and devastation of our natural resources, which does not, of course, support the concept of Common Good. Again, it is the Adolescent Soul who, for personal gain, is comfortable destroying the rain forest, pouring oil into our oceans, or setting the Cuyahoga River on fire.

Of course, many Adolescent Souls do not rise to the top as they would like to do. Nonetheless, they retain their sense of entitlement and may become envious, bitter, and depressed people if success is not forthcoming.

Moral Judgment: Adolescent Souls do not fully understand the consequences that their behaviors and actions have on others or on the larger society. They also embrace the concept that the end justifies the means; as a result, they are frequently willing to allow people and places outside of themselves to pay a price. Adolescent Souls may realize that their behaviors and actions are damaging but seldom understand the magnitude of the issue. They may use their new abstract thinking skills to rationalize their behaviors.

Relationship to Source Energy: Because of their attachment to wealth, power, and status, Adolescent Souls are frequently more interested in the proper way to relate to God than in actually relating to God. Adolescent Souls are heavily identified with their bodies and very often are not sure their consciousness survives their physical death. This fuels the relentless pursuit of power, status, and wealth. They may be terrified of dying and take extreme measures to cheat death. For example, cryogenic freezing assumes we only have one life, and so upon death, the very rich have the option of having themselves frozen until such time as a cure for their ailment or a way to extend the current lifetime can be found. Old age as the precursor to death may also be frightening, and Adolescent Souls may go to great lengths and spend large amounts of money to look younger than they in fact are.

Adolescent Souls at Work

The following is an illustration of Adolescent Souls at work. The people and the process described are complex, and it is not entirely known who among them was an Adolescent Soul and who was not. The behavior is Adolescent Soul behavior, however, and so I use this as an example:

In the late eighteenth century, during the time of Napoleon Bonaparte, a reliable method for canning food was invented. In the early nineteenth century, several Englishmen (Adolescent Souls) saw the business opportunity inherent in this invention and built the first commercial canning factory. At this time, another Englishman (Adolescent Soul) brought this process to the United States and established the first canning factory here.

Canned food significantly improved people's lives. It was convenient, traveled well, and made foods available in places and at times where they would previously be unavailable.

By the early twentieth century, there was a significant shrimp and oyster canning industry in Mississippi and Alabama, and Adolescent Souls throughout the Gulf Coast area owned canning factories. In order to make a suitably high profit, however, cheap labor was desired. And so the canning factory owners sent "bosses" north to enlist thousands of Polish and Bohemian immigrants; men, women, and children as young as five years old picked shrimp and shucked oysters. Again, Adolescent Souls have stereotyped and fixed ideas about social roles. To them, it is perfectly all right to exploit immigrants and their children. Immigrants are, almost without fail, categorized as second-class citizens in society.

Children worked in oyster shucking factories from 3:00 a.m. until 8:00 a.m., when they were then allowed to go to school for several hours. At 1:00 p.m., they went back to oyster shucking for an additional four hours. Shrimp pickers had similar long hours. Due to the high acid content of the shrimp, swollen and bleeding fingers were common among those children who picked shrimp.

Working conditions were poor, illiteracy was high, and wages were bad, and there was little concern for the health, social welfare, or education of the workers. (For additional information, Lewis Hine has given us an excellent photographic record of child labor in the New South at the turn of the twentieth century.) American corporations participate in similar situations in third world countries and even in this country now.

Mature Soul Stage

Mature Souls want a life that is personally satisfying, and they will pursue their interests without regard to wealth, power, or status. Mature Souls see the world as virtually an undifferentiated mass of "me's." Accordingly, much of the work that will be done in this Soul stage involves individuation and self-definition. Mature Souls may engage in "Soul searching" in a private, emotionally aloof, or remote manner. However, they frequently discover and define themselves within the context of relationships.

Furthermore, Mature Souls are now ready to embark upon a journey that will ultimately lead to expanded spiritual awareness. This stage of Soul development is the stage of utmost stress to the human personality. On a subconscious level, Mature Souls now actively desire vibrational evolution; however, in the early stages, they are often ill equipped to cope with the attendant availability of psychic energy. The Mature Soul is opening the mind to self-improvement, the heart to relationships, and the spirit to psychic interaction.

Reciprocity in Relationships: Mature Souls understand the concept of in-kind exchanges and responses. They are aware of and want to enter into relationships where give and take is in equal measure. Mature Souls, however, repeatedly have difficulty being true to themselves while in relationships; the boundaries that separate one individual from another frequently break down. As a result, Mature Souls may not be able to properly distinguish where they end and where the other person begins. They may not know who is feeling or thinking what; they may over-involve themselves in the emotional, mental, and physical issues of the other while neglecting their own affairs. They are vulnerable to codependency and may enter into relationships that are one-sided and emotionally abusive or destructive.

Relationship to Source Energy: It is not until the Mature Soul stage that people are able to access a considerable level of psychic energy. In the earlier Soul stages, individuals may have had access to a certain amount of psychic input, but it was not fully understood. Instead, attention was given to learning about the material self and the physical world. Now, at the Mature Soul stage, psychic interaction and communication are coming into the conscious awareness. The Mature Soul desires it but is overwhelmed by it as well.

Psychic communication comes from a non-sensory source that is not explainable by current scientific theory. It is an awareness of the still, small voice that exists in all of us. It is the capacity to know something without knowing how it is known. It is diverting the conscious mind and focusing the subconscious mind as we begin to seek out information that is beyond the range of typical, natural, or standard perception. It can be through intuitive knowing, psychic seeing, or psychic hearing that uses the subconscious capability rather than the physical eye or ear. It is learning to accept the information that we are given and then learning how to interpret it. Psychic interaction is interaction with Universal Source Energy.

Occasionally, this infusion of psychic input can result in mental health issues, such as anxiety disorders, panic disorders, phobias, obsessions/compulsions, and post-traumatic stress. Often, the vibrational energy that attends the psychic input is so high that the Mature Soul lives in a persistent state of what is perceived to be anxiety. Or the Mature Soul may be having subconscious memory of past life encounters and be experiencing symptoms of post-traumatic stress disorder, panic attacks, or phobias that seem unrelated to the current life. In an attempt to organize this psychic energy, Mature Souls may engage in obsessive/compulsive behaviors.

When Mature Souls begin to experience psychic input, they may believe that they are crazy and so refuse to give it attention, explore it, or discuss it with others. Anyone at any Soul level can have mental health issues, and mental health issues are not always the result of psychic input. However, more than at any other Soul level, a person in the Mature Soul stage is vulnerable.

Mature Souls may also have issues with drug and alcohol abuse or addiction. When psychic input becomes confusing to the Mature Soul, there may be a desire to retreat and escape, and so drugs and alcohol are used to avoid the experience. However, the Mature Soul may desire to enhance the psychic experience and so may use drugs in an attempt to open the mind more and more. In this instance, hallucinogenic substances are a common choice. Drugs and alcohol are a shortcut to psychic experience and cannot be trusted to give accurate information; pretty information perhaps or frightening information at times but not necessarily accurate.

Of course, all Mature Souls do not have mental or chemical health issues, at least in most of the lifetimes at this level. Mature Souls actively desire on a Soul level raised spiritual vibration and so they invite psychic input and communication. As they raise the vibration and move toward the Old Soul stage, they are better able to understand and organize psychic energy.

Locus of Control: Mature Souls generally have a high internal locus of control. They understand on a fundamental level that they are responsible for their lives and their choices. Achieving self-determination is important. Mature Souls have their own priorities and want to be left alone to pursue them. Mature Souls do not have a great deal of concern for the opinions of others but believe that people are to be respected, and that no single viewpoint or choice is absolute or correct. They believe that people should be allowed the freedom to do what is best for them.

The Common Good: The concept of Common Good can now be understood in a much more complex manner. All of humanity is not yet embraced in their understanding of the concept, but the number of people included is vastly increased. Law is seen as a social contract that must serve the greatest good for the greatest number of people—not all people but the majority. If the law is not serving the people, the law can and must be changed. Mature Souls are also beginning to have a solid understand that the end does not justify the means, and that the end and the means are the same thing. How one gets to the outcome is as important as the outcome itself.

Narcissism and Philanthropy: Mature Souls are able to bring respect, empathy, generosity, and compassion into their relationships. Indeed, they are sometimes more aware of the circumstances of others than they are attentive to their own situations.

Moral Judgment: When they are mentally and emotionally healthy, Matures Souls are able to understand the consequences that their actions, behaviors, words, and emotions have on other people.

Rules: Mature Souls recognize and understand the principles that guide conduct and behavior within their society. In their search for personal fulfillment and definition, they may not always follow them, but they understand them.

Norms: As with rules, Mature Souls recognize and comprehend the social norms. They can distinguish appropriate from inappropriate behaviors. They are familiar with the dominant beliefs, values, and attitudes of their culture and society. It is not unusual for Mature Souls to act outside of the normative standards, however, as they search for identity and meaning.

Roles: Mature Souls generally realize what is expected of them in terms of their behavior and conduct in various roles. They acknowledge their rights and privileges and accept their obligations. Achieving self-definition is critical to Mature Souls, however, and so they may define their roles in their own way and may not perform as others around them desire. They have their own concerns and are not overly troubled by outside opinions.

Concrete and Abstract Thinking: Mature Souls are now adept at abstract thinking. They are flexible thinkers who are able to observe, plan, and make logical conclusions about the outcomes of their plans. They are able to see what might be as opposed to what is. Mature Souls like ideas and are capable of engaging in complex mental processing. They can see multiple meanings in beliefs, opinions, and concepts and are comfortable with metaphor and symbols.

Executive or Administrative Ability: When they are emotionally and mentally healthy, Mature Souls are able to initiate activity and sustain attention. They are able to organize themselves and manage time. Mature Souls understand the need for managing their emotions and inhibiting their impulses.

Old Soul Stage

Old Souls are beginning to understand that they are part of an integrated whole, and when they look at others, they see themselves, at least in part. They are beginning to grasp the interrelatedness and interconnectedness of all humanity. They are perceptive about individuals and have insight into the inner workings of civilization. As a general rule, they are able to see beyond mere presentation and have at least a rudimentary grasp of the complexity in people, in society and culture, and in times and places.

Narcissism and Philanthropy: Old Souls have now moved from an egocentric perspective into a point of view that includes a concern for humanity. Although they remain constructively self-interested, Old Souls are able to bring respect, compassion, generosity, and gratefulness into their interactions with others.

Old Souls generally have a refined sense of justice and equality. This may be expressed out of an emotional perspective. Old Souls may have feelings of empathy and compassion and so believe that they must show consideration for individuals and for humanity as a whole. It can be expressed from an intellectual perspective; Old Souls may have thoughts about the value of each life and embrace the concepts of egalitarianism and liberty for all people. Whether or not it is driven by emotion or intellect is irrelevant. What is relevant is that the awareness and appreciation of the "Common Good" is now within the reach of the Old Soul.

The Common Good: Old Souls now have an essential comprehension of the Common Good. They understand that principles and behaviors must be grounded in impartiality and fairness, and that people should be treated with dignity and respect. This does not mean that Old Souls believe that those who violate others or disregard the laws of civilization should suffer no consequence. Instead, it means that when consequence is indicated and must be dispensed, it should be done with concern for the individuals involved. Furthermore, the "punishment" should fit the "crime" and consequence should not be cruel or unduly harsh. Additionally, consequence should be administered impartially, without regard to social status or wealth. The rich and famous should endure the same consequence as the poor and disenfranchised.

Locus of Control: Old Souls have a high internal locus of control and understand that they have considerable power over the events of their lives. Instead of using the word "manifesting," they may uses phrases such as "self-fulfilling prophecy" or "you reap what you sow." There is in any event a significant awareness that the choices they make affect their outcomes.

Rules: Old Souls are aware of and understand the rules. If the rules do not make sense, harm someone or something, or do not serve a higher good, the rules may be ignored. Old Souls can be a law unto themselves. They do not like to be restricted and want the autonomy that will allow them to do what they want to do. As a result, they gravitate toward relationships, employment, philosophies, and creative endeavors that will allow them freedom of expression. Old Souls are generally aware of and resent petty or unnecessary demands.

Norms: Old Souls understand the rules that define appropriate or inappropriate behaviors; they recognize the dominant cultural beliefs, attitudes, and values. However, they are often very aware of alternate realities and may seek out the esoteric, unusual, and unorthodox. Old Souls are not afraid of imaginative or creative thinking and are generally comfortable exploring concepts and ideas that are beyond the parameters of conventional truth. Indeed, Old Souls are frequently attracted to the alternative and holistic. They may be eccentric, but they are generally discreet and know how to pass in society.

Roles: Old Souls understand for the most part the roles that they play in their own lives and in the lives of others. They realize that their behavior and actions affect those around them and acknowledge their obligations. Old Souls recognize that they have certain rights and privileges, both personally and within the context of their relationships. They accept the responsibility that is attendant upon exercising those rights and privileges.

Reciprocity in Relationships: Old Souls understand the concept of in-kind exchanges and responses. They are aware of and want to enter into relationships where give and take is in equal measure. There is a dawning awareness that every relationship is sacred and that honorable behavior must be a part of each interaction.

Moral Judgment: Old Souls understand the consequences that their actions and behaviors have on others. They recognize that the ends and the means are the same thing, and that the journey to the outcome is as crucial as the outcome itself. Indeed, the journey is of greater importance than is the end result.

Concrete and Abstract Thinking: Old Souls have the capacity to be deep thinkers with complex mental processes. They tend to be very comfortable with multiple meanings, and their communication is often as figurative as it is literal. Old Souls understand and liberally employ metaphors and symbols when expressing ideas.

Executive or Administrative Ability: If they are interested and find it pertinent to their life experience, Old Souls can exhibit wonderful skills in this area. They can manage time, give and sustain attention, and self-initiate; they can manage emotion and control impulse. If they do not find the endeavor important, however, Old Souls have a difficult time applying themselves to the project.

Relationship to Source Energy: Old Souls are comfortable with intuition and psychic input and often use it without being consciously aware that it is being used. They are frequently interested in Source Energy and may want to explore concepts and ideas related to it. On a personality level, they may also be utterly uninterested. On a Soul level, however, they have a growing awareness of and an appreciation for the interconnectedness and interrelatedness of all Universal energies.

Transcendental Souls do not need to incarnate on the planet for themselves but rather will do so to advance the Common Good. They have accomplished most of the lessons that Earth offers and so are on to other achievements and experiences in higher planes of existence and awareness. When the Transcendental Souls come to Earth, they come to teach. They are often "invisible"; they do not need or want recognition.

Wherever there are great leaps in humanitarian thinking, a Transcendental Soul is involved. Mohandas Gandhi may have been a Transcendental Soul. Transcendental Souls were very likely involved in such things as the writing of the Magna Carta, the Geneva Convention, and of our Declaration of Independence. Generally, however, they are not as visible as was the Mahatma and are most often unknown to us.

Whenever the collective consciousness is raised regarding universal humanitarianism, Transcendental Souls are involved. Following the Holocaust of World War II, we saw a significant increase in the discussions involving human rights and freedoms. Beyond doubt, Transcendental Souls came to Earth, lived ordinary lives, and died extraordinary deaths so that we could advance our awareness of humanitarian concerns.

Infinite Souls

Infinite Souls represent God or Source Energy and rarely come to Earth. Their presence is felt, and their coming is prophesized before their arrival. They elevate awareness and teach concepts that, in the beginning, are minimally understood. Their presence on Earth significantly contributes to vibrational increase. They are remembered for thousands of years. Their teachings come directly from Universal Source Energy, so their presence on Earth forever alters the planetary vibration. Jesus and Buddha are Infinite Souls. Jesus taught Love; Buddha taught Oneness.

Other Factors That Influence Soul Age Expression

When we choose to incarnate, we choose our families and where we will be placed within those families. When we choose our families, part of what we are choosing is our ethnic background as well as our cultural environment. We are choosing our social standing as well as our economic circumstances.

We choose our gender. We choose our level of intelligence, health, and abilities or disabilities. And, of course, we choose what karmic or past life issues we want to address.

Every choice matters and will influence the way in which Soul Age is expressed. A Child Soul will embrace gender, intelligence, birth order, or ethnicity in a different manner than will a Mature Soul, a Baby Soul, an Old Soul, or an Adolescent Soul. The attachment and expression will be different. We make choices within these areas because on a Soul level we have decided that this particular environment, gender, ordinal position, or racial background will help drive our growth into higher vibration.

Family of Origin in the Current Life

Ethnic and racial background, social status, economic standing, and religious preference and attachment are all chosen when a Soul decides to incarnate. These choices are made to assist with the drive toward higher vibration and will affect the manner in which Soul Age is expressed.

Ethnic background has a profound influence in our lives. In each life, we choose an ethnic group to which we will belong. Ethnic groups are often stereotyped, both in the world and in individual communities. Stereotypes affect the way others see us, but they also affect how we see ourselves.

A stereotype is an oversimplified, formulaic description or belief about a group of people. Most often, stereotypes focus on a perceived negative quality; they are generally intended to offend or to diminish. For instance, Jews are greedy, Blacks are lazy, Whites are exploitive, Arabs are angry, and Asians are cunning. Stereotypes affect the manner in which we relate to each other.

Even when we know them to be untrue, stereotypes can affect our performance in our lives. Recent studies indicate that when asked to perform in some manner, if you mention a stereotype, either negative or positive, it will affect the outcome. For example, when Asian women are involved in using higher mathematic formulas, if you remind them that they are women, they will not do as well as they will if you remind them that they are Asian.

Our social status and economic standing are vital influences in our growth as well. If our family has high social status, we will carry ourselves into the world in a much different manner than if our family has low social status. Having less than enough material resource poses similar issues.

Religious upbringing cannot be underestimated whether we remain loyal to that religion or not. Religious education takes place when we are young and impressionable. What we are taught about God and about human nature at this time may have a lasting influence.

Ethnicity is not an indicator of Soul Age; we can be from any ethnic or racial background and any Soul Age. Socioeconomic class is not an indicator of Soul Age. We can be rich or poor, upper, middle, or lower class in any of the Soul stages. Nor does involvement in any of the religions indicate Soul Age. Again, we can be at any stage of Soul development and be involved in any religion.

Our behavior within the context of our socioeconomic class, religion, or ethnic background is the most reliable indicator of Soul stage development. Souls will approach the blessings and challenges of their life choices differently, depending on how many incarnations they have experienced and how much vibration has been attained.

Birth Order

Ordinal positioning, or where a child is placed in the family in terms of birth, is often significant. Children tend to have different characteristics depending on birth order. Not all children will express all characteristics of their birth order positions, but the ordinal position in the family is generally informative and important. Ordinal position will affect the manner in which Soul Age is expressed.

➤ *Only children* are often uncomfortable being the center of attention. They may know how to be in the limelight, but that does not mean that they like it or that they embrace it. Indeed, a source of frustration for them is unrequested intrusion into their time and space. Only children are adept at understanding the emotional climate around them. When their emotional radar indicates that others are having difficulties, the only child may believe that they should fix the problem. Only children like stability in the environment. They are good at conceptual organizing. Others may not see them as organized or systematized, however, and may in fact believe them to be quite disorganized. However, the only child has the order of things, if only in the head; they know how to find what, where, and when.

➤ *First children* are often comfortable being the focus of others' attention or at least they *expect* to be in the focus of that attention. They may believe that they are the focus even when they are not. First children are aware of rules and authority; if a rule is found to be credible or trustworthy, it is embraced. If it is not, they may make up their own rules. First children see themselves as independent and needing less from relationships than other people need. They expect to be respected. They like information and tend to be competent leaders and good communicators. They are apt to be good with detail and like to get things accomplished. First children are uncomfortable with guilt and can be conciliatory and placating should they find themselves in a situation that inspires guilt. First children do not like to offend other people and, again, may mollify or appease others when they think offense may be taken.

➢ *Second Children* are skilled in finding the hidden information or rules and like to bring that information out into the open. They tend to be very sensitive to the emotional and mental health of those around them. Second children have a great deal of difficulty if caregivers are incompetent, ineffectual, or dysfunctional. They like a stable emotional environment and like to know their place. If their place is confused or unknown, or if they lose their place, they can become anxious and fearful. They are good listeners and like to do things right. Second children are gifted at blending logical, rational information with intuitive insight.

They are self-disciplined, logical, and determined; when others behave in a manner the second child finds to be illogical, undisciplined, or indolent, the second child will offer correction (if at all possible). The second child does not like to be criticized, but he or she finds it relatively easy to offer constructive criticism to others.

➢ *Third Children* may appear to be uninvolved in situations and relationships around them, but they are intimately and intricately aware of the dynamics. They form relationships cautiously, but once committed, it is hard for them to disconnect. Third children do not like to be treated in a manner perceived to diminish their dignity. They are self-protective; nonetheless, they are sensitive to the needs and wants of others around them. They can identify issues without taking sides. Third children move into and out of relationships depending on need and sometimes prefer ambiguity; they can be caring one minute, and detached the next. Third children can be physically present but emotionally withdrawn. They need emotional balance and harmony; if they feel trapped in an unstable situation, they will do what they need to do to gain some distance. They do not like to feel or to be vulnerable. Third children often have a diminished sense of their personal boundaries and will do what it takes to shield and defend themselves from the emotional and physical vagaries of others.

➢ *Fourth Children* are demonstrative and dramatic; they have good social skills and are able to put others at ease. Because of their apparent effortlessness in relating to people, those around them may believe that they have more importance to the fourth child than they in fact do. Fourth children will withdraw if they are emotionally overloaded; they may terminate relationships if they cannot see the progress or improvement that they have defined as necessary for their survival. Fourth children are able to look at the group as a whole as well as the individuals within the group. They may find and attempt to fix issues or situations without consultation or permission from others. Fourth children are analytical thinkers and work hard to understand their environment and the behavior of the people within it. They are not always proficient at trusting their own assessments, however. Their solution to most problems is to work harder, try harder, and control what it is within their power to control.

113

Males and females have more similarities than they do differences. They do, however, have some significant differences that influence the manner in which they relate to their environment. Men and women tend to have certain distinguishing traits and distinctive areas of strength. This does not mean that men cannot show strong tendencies concerning the characteristics that are defined as female or that women cannot express robust male attributes. However, men generally have certain aptitudes, while women have others. Gender influences the manner in which Soul Age will be expressed.

➤ *Male*
  o The brain in men is better developed in the right hemisphere. As a result, men have better skills in the following areas:
    • Visual-spatial
    • Mechanical
    • Navigating a route
  o In conversation men tend to:
    • Use conversation to gain status
    • Make more commands
    • Interrupt more often
    • Share or impart information
    • Compartmentalize communication and get right to the issue
  o Visually: men can detect movement better than women can
  o Men are seen as more aggressive and competitive

➤ *Female*
  o The brain in women is better developed in the left hemisphere. As a result, women have better skills in the following areas:
    • Social skills and certain verbal skills
    • Fine motor tasks
    • Accuracy in locating objects
  o In conversation women tend to:
    • Use conversation to establish intimacy
    • Ask more questions and make more requests
    • Use a higher quality of language and grammar with more detail
    • Be polite
    • Integrate communication, getting additional information and more emotion into the issue at hand

114

o   Visually: women can detect color and fine sensory movement better than men can

o   Women are seen as more empathetic and better at multitasking

Intelligence

Any level of Soul development can have any level of intelligence. Intelligence is measured in a variety of ways and with a wide range of tests. A number is assigned to the measurement result; this number indicates the Intelligence Quotient, or IQ. For the sake of simplicity, the standardized numbers will be used to demonstrate levels of intelligence: The range between 90 and 109 is considered to be normal or average intelligence.

Higher Intelligence
Superior = 110 to 119
Very Superior = 120 to 140
Genius = over 140

Lower Intelligence
Dull Normal = 80 to 89
Borderline Deficiency = 70 to 79
Mental Retardation = under 70

A Baby Soul can come into an incarnation with an IQ of 140 and an Old Soul can come into an incarnation with an IQ of 80. Soul development has nothing to do with intelligence, and we do not become more and more intelligent as we become older and older Souls. An Old Soul with an IQ of 140 will behave very differently than a Baby Soul with a similar IQ. An Old Soul with an IQ of 80 is learning different lessons and following a different path than is the Child Soul with an IQ of 80.

For instance, a younger Soul may incarnate with a higher IQ so that information can be more quickly collected and assimilated. An older Soul may come into incarnation with a lower IQ to experience the care and learn the lessons associated with dependency or to help others learn those lessons. Intelligence is chosen to complement the journey and the lessons needed to drive the vibration higher. Intelligence is not an indicator of Soul Age.

Past Life Issues and Karma

The significance of what we choose to bring into our current lives in terms of past life issues and karma cannot be underestimated. Perhaps when we were Baby Souls, we created karma with another Soul; in subsequent lives, we reincarnate with this person as we balance karma with that individual. For example, as a Baby Soul, we might have a child and abandon that child to a life lived in the streets. In future lives, balance with this Soul must be restored, and the Soul acting as parent must address the karma that has been created. In a sense, an amend must be made. As a Child Soul, we might stay with the child, but we would raise that child very rigidly and without regard to individuality. As an Adolescent Soul, we might not abandon the child (what would the neighbors think). We would supply that child with a wealth of material goods and send the child to a prestigious college but would never really develop a deep relationship with the child. As a Mature Soul, we might develop a very deep relationship with the child but not really know where we stop and the child starts. We would hang onto that child and the relationship so strongly that the child would feel suffocated. As an Old Soul, we would not abandon the child but would try to involve the child in activities interesting to the child (even though not interesting to us) and would love the child to the best of our ability.

Conclusion

We are not simple creatures. If we are born in 1966 into a Northern European hippy family living in the United States, we are going to have a very different experience than if we are born at the same time and place but into a Hindu Indian family. Complicate this with Soul Age, IQ, gender, and birth order, and we can begin to see ourselves as the complicated and multifaceted people that we are. And we can begin to see others in a similar manner as well.

Again, we can never truly know the age of another Soul. We might be able to make reasonably accurate guesses, but it is essential that we temper our judgments, as we possess limited information about each other. Although we may have access to all kinds of information about ourselves, we often fail to unearth or discover this information and may instead lead unexamined lives.

I was a practicing social worker for forty years, and during my time in the profession, there was a great deal of talk about being "nonjudgmental." Human beings are judgmental beings, and a nonjudgmental approach is neither possible nor indicated.

Of course we make judgments, and we often should. To verbally, psychologically, physically, or sexually abuse other people is grossly inappropriate. Nor is it appropriate to impose our beliefs on others through manipulation or violence of any kind. We make judgments about behaviors and impose consequences.

If people are thought to be a danger to society, they are removed; this is a part of the process of the Soul's learning. It is important, however, *how* we do this. All Souls come from God Energy, and no matter how reprehensible the behavior, it remains essential that we treat others with dignity and respect. This is particularly so if we are imposing consequences. Civilization and law must be the place where we stand against savagery.

Chapter 6: Attraction, Abundance, and Manifesting

➤ **Part One: Introduction**

- Introduction to the Laws of Manifestation: Attraction and Abundance
  - ❖ Law of Attraction
  - ❖ Law of Abundance
  - ❖ What Is Manifestation: Beginning to Use the Laws
- Thoughts
  - ❖ Thoughts: An Experiment
  - ❖ The Energetic Possibilities of Thought
  - ❖ Changing Our Thoughts, Changing Our Reality
  - ❖ Other People's Realities
  - ❖ Distracting Ourselves from Negative Thoughts
  - ❖ Moving toward Positive Thoughts
- Emotions
  - ❖ The Informative Power of Emotion
  - ❖ Allowing Emotion
  - ❖ Moving Toward Positive Emotions
  - ❖ Remembering Positive Emotions
  - ❖ Emotions: A Partial List
- Thoughts and Emotions: A Partnership
  - ❖ The Interaction between Thought and Emotion
  - ❖ The Alignment of Thought and Emotion (with Example)
  - ❖ Manifestation: Our Thoughts and Feelings
- The Role of Our Behaviors and Actions: Their Part in Our Drama
  - ❖ Empowering Our Manifesting by Changing Our Behaviors
  - ❖ Sabotaging Ourselves: Negative Thoughts and Emotions Stimulate Negative Behaviors
  - ❖ Regrettable Behaviors
- Crafting Our Request
- The Vulnerable: Babies and Children

➤ **Part Two: Context**

- Context: Our Reincarnational History
  - ❖ Reincarnational Issues: "I Cannot Believe I Would Have Chosen This"
  - ❖ Manifesting within Karmic Imbalances
- Context: Living with Other People's Realities

Part One: Introduction

We create our own reality; with the assistance of our Spiritual Helpers, we construct our lives. As we reincarnate, we heal and balance that which needs resolution and create new situations and circumstances. No lifetime stands alone, but rather each lifetime builds upon the others in an evolutionary process intended to amass a vast repertoire of experience and to raise our vibration.

Before we incarnated on the planet, we chose the relevant elements of our upcoming life. Free will allows us to make earthly choices in the here and now; we make these choices within the larger choices that have been made before we reincarnated. We can make those choices in a conscious, informed, and purposeful manner or in an unconscious, unaware, and haphazard manner.

Introduction to the Laws of Manifestation: Attraction and Abundance

Within each lifetime, we are actively and dynamically using the Laws of Attraction and Abundance, whether we are consciously aware of it or not. The Manifestation Laws are powerful and compelling. We use them countless times every day. It is in our best interest to know what they are and to begin to comprehend how to use them to harness that power and turn it to our highest good.

Law of Attraction

This Law says that energy exists in a state of pure potential until something or someone acts upon it. All energy is latent possibility, but when the energy of something or someone interacts with it, it is invigorated and begins to transform and transmute. It changes, alters, and creates.

All energy is from Source Energy and is a part of Source Energy. When we generate energy, it connects and interacts with the latent possibility, the pure potential that is within Universal Source Energy. All energy is interconnected and interwoven and forms a great Universal energetic tapestry.

What we think, feel, and how we behave all generate energy. Our energy interacts with the energy in the Universal tapestry. Thoughts and feelings are energy and are heard and felt by the Universal Mind. Behavior augments and increases that energy and is experienced by the Universal Mind.

The energy that is created by what we think, feel, and do plucks a string in the Universal tapestry; we send a message. We inform the Universal Mind that we are making a request, and Source Energy answers in kind. We invite; we attract.

The Law of Abundance simply says that there is a plentiful supply. We are meant to live in a state of abundance, but what does this mean? Abundance refers to the bounty of our material world, but it also pertains to the profusion of experience that is needed for our emotional, social, intellectual, and spiritual growth.

This Law is easily misunderstood. Abundance can mean growth of material resource, monetary gain, big houses, and glamorous vacations; this is generally what we would like it to mean. But it really only speaks to an ample supply. If we are asking for spiritual or intellectual growth, this Law says that there is a plethora of experience available to us to make that happen. However, if we are inadvertently asking for trouble, this Law says that there is plenty of turmoil, disorder, and misfortune as well.

What Is Manifestation: Beginning to Use the Laws

Attraction means pulling toward ourselves that to which we give our attention. Abundance means that there is a plentiful supply. It is in the interest of our highest good to use these Laws in an informed and deliberate manner.

We manifest using these laws. Manifesting means that we are bringing something into definition that has previously been conceptual. We are materializing, or actualizing, or fulfilling. We are making substantive something that has been formerly insubstantial. We do this by sending the energetic vibration of our thoughts, emotions, and actions into Source Energy—into the Universal Mind. We transmit, the Universe receives, and, in turn, transmits; we pluck a string in the Universal tapestry and begin creating our reality.

The point of manifestation is always in the present moment, the here and now. Whatever has happened in the past is past; it is previous to the current moment. If we want to change our story and create a new narrative for ourselves, we start here and now.

We can only create in our own lives. We cannot create in another person's reality because we can only offer the energetic vibration of our own thoughts, emotions, and actions to the Universe. We all have our own journey and are unable to disrupt that which another is making manifest, particularly if there is a significant attachment to the creation. We can suggest, propose and inform, and we can implore, beseech, and threaten, but we cannot alter if alteration is not wanted.

Are we manifesting that which is in our highest good? If we perseverate on the unwanted, we inevitably attract the unwanted; there is an abundant supply. If we attempt to move our attention toward the desired, we will eventually and also inevitably move toward the desired. No one can do it for us. We must love, respect, and honor ourselves enough to begin manifesting that which brings comfort, healing, and thankfulness.

Our thoughts, emotions, and actions are energy, and they have power; they are not idle. We create our reality when we send this energy into the Universe. Our thoughts are central to the process. All manifesting, whether wanted or unwanted, begins with thought.

Thoughts

Thoughts: An Experiment

Physicist Richard Feynman is the originator of the "double slit experiment." Very simply stated, this experiment demonstrates that matter exists in a state of pure potential that is affected by our interaction with it.

The experiment takes place in a stimulus-free environment where electrons are shot onto a wall through a form with two vertical slits. (An electron is a negatively charged elementary particle typically found orbiting the nucleus of an atom.) One would expect that the pattern on the wall would correspond to the vertical slits; we would anticipate the formation of two straight, vertical lines. Instead, the electrons make a wave pattern.

When equipment is assembled to observe and measure this unexpected development, the environment is no longer stimulus free. Someone is interacting with it, observing it, and measuring it. And now the electrons begin to behave as expected. They form vertical slits that correspond to the vertical slits through which they were shot; they behave as we think they should. Expectation, observation, and interaction create the pattern that the electron takes.

The Energetic Possibilities of Thought

Thoughts generate an energetic vibration; thoughts are things. Thoughts begin with our interactions and observations within our environments and are further influenced by our expectations. Our thoughts are built upon our repertoire of experience. Thoughts have vibrational energy, and that energy dramatically affects what we bring into our lives. All manifesting begins with thought.

When we begin to form thoughts (both as babies within each life and as Baby Souls), they are negligible, nominal, or minimal; initially, our thoughts are small. But as we acquire experiences within our situations or circumstances or with people or events, our thoughts form and grow. As we give our attention to them, they gain power.

When we send these powerful thoughts into the Universe, we are telling the Universe that we have observed and interacted with our environment, and this is now what we expect. And because we are cocreators with God, Source Energy obligingly complies.

Changing Our Thoughts, Changing Our Reality

If we want to alter our reality or change our story, we must start with our thoughts. We must move our focus to a positive thought about what it is that is desired and remove our focus from that which is unwanted.

For instance, perhaps we have decided that our current job is unsatisfactory and is causing us stress and distress; the work is boring, our coworkers irritate us, and the boss is ineffective. For some reason, we have decided that we must stay with the current situation. Thinking about or perseverating on all that makes us unhappy is sure to bring us more unhappiness. Instead, we must move our focus to anything we can find that is positive about our circumstances. We start to change our attitude.

An attitude is a state of mind, a positive or negative view of a person, place, thing, or event. Attitudes are based in judgments and can be changed. Changing our attitude begins with a willingness to examine our perceptions and our judgments and to adjust our thoughts. It involves a readiness to scrutinize our part in the story, to use our free will, and to exercise certain, specific control or influence over our thoughts.

A positive attitude is vital to joy and central to overall contentment. Worrying or obsessing about our troubles, even in the most difficult of circumstances, will not make our situation better. Keeping our thoughts anchored in the negative will only invite more distress.

Many circumstances, situations, and events are out of our control. We do not have jurisdiction or management rights over other people. But our thoughts and attitudes are ours, and we can begin to change our story here. Moving our thoughts and attitudes in a positive direction is not necessarily easy, but we start by reaching for the best thought we can imagine and build from there.

Voltaire once wrote, "Life is a shipwreck, but we must not forget to sing in the lifeboats." We live in the human experience, and life *can* be demanding, but it does not have to be a "vale of tears." It takes effort, but a positive attitude, outlook, and thoughts will help us construct a positive life.

Other People's Realities

We cannot create in another person's reality. If other people are causing us distress, we can discuss the situation with them. We can inform, demand, and plead, but we cannot alter their story.

The avenue available to us is to change our thoughts, judgments, and attitudes about that person's thoughts, emotions, and behaviors and the effect they are having on us. We cannot change them; we can only change us.

The more thought we give to the misery we are experiencing at the hands of a particular person, the more misery we invite. The more we can move our thoughts in a positive direction, the more we can create and embrace peace. We can look for all that is harmless and inoffensive about the person in question; we can start with thoughts about that which is benign and begin to build toward that which is beneficial.

Distracting Ourselves from Negative Thoughts

Distraction can be a useful tool if our thoughts and attitudes are mired in the negative. We can reach for the best thought that we can uncover, and when we find ourselves obsessing about our troubles, we can alter the energy by doing something different.

We can change direction and give consideration to a movie, book, a walk outdoors, exercise, meditation, or whatever it is that gives pleasure and removes us from obsessive, negative, cynical thoughts. Coffee with a friend and a good chat might be indicated (but if you spend your friendship time preoccupied with and discussing your troubles, you remain in that energy).

Moving toward Positive Thoughts

To change our realities and narrative, we must first give thought to what we desire. What appearance would our desire take, if we had, right now, all that we want regarding this circumstance, situation, or event? Thoughtfully construct a new reality.

We must try to think generally and not specifically, as we may limit ourselves by making our focus too narrow or too specific. It is best to think about our new construct in terms of our highest good. What would fulfill us in the material world? What would satisfy us emotionally, intellectually, spiritually, and socially?

Think about the elements that would define a perfect job. Think about the attribute and features that would characterize an ideal relationship. Avoid focusing on a particular person or a specific job. Reach for the possibilities.

Emotions

All manifesting, whether wanted or unwanted, begins with thought, but emotion is intertwined with thought and is vital to the creation. Emotions are indicators of whether or not we are in alignment with our Soul's journey to a higher vibration. Positive emotions indicate that we are in harmony with ourselves, are in balance, and are moving in that direction. Negative emotions indicate dissonance and tell us that we are in conflict with our Soul's journey; we have challenges that we need to address.

As we form attitudes, emotion is intricately interwoven with thought. If we are going to change our attitudes, examining our emotions about any given person, situation, or event is vital.

Our emotions are also built upon our repertoire of experience. When we are babies, both within each life and within the context of reincarnation, our emotions are primitive or primal. As we acquire experiences within our situations or circumstances or with people or events, our emotions evolve. They become stronger, more complex, and gain power.

The Informative Power of Emotion

Emotions give us valuable information. They help us mark our progress to the highest expressions of love, trust, joy, and gratitude. For example, feelings of pleasure are precursors or antecedents to feelings of happiness; feelings of happiness are precursors to joy.

We have feelings of pleasure when we enjoy an afternoon with new acquaintances. Sometime later, our acquaintances have become good friends, and we have feelings of happiness when we spend an afternoon with them. At certain special moments during that afternoon, we feel joy.

When we are experiencing positive emotion, we have the feeling that God is indeed in his heaven and all is right with the world (Robert Browning). The decisions that we are making and the direction in which we are going are helping us reach for the higher vibration. We are in harmony with ourselves in mind, body, and Soul, and we are in harmony with the Universal Mind. Positive emotions are confirmation that we are honoring our Soul's direction.

When we are experiencing negative emotions, our Souls are telling us that we are in trouble; we need to change direction. The difficulty may be stemming from our own actions. It may be situations, events, or circumstances that we perceive to be imposed upon us by others.

Allowing Emotion

Suppressing our emotions does not serve us well. When we suppress, repress, or censor our emotions, we miss the message and insights that they can give us. Although it may be difficult, we must allow our emotions to be. If we do not recognize that we are angry, we cannot do anything to alter the situation. If we do not acknowledge that we are sad, that sadness may become despair and pervade the life.

However, wallowing in negative emotion does not serve us well either. We need to identify our negative emotions so that we can get to the cause and begin altering our story. We must have the courage to accept and understand them, but we do not need to make them our life stance or to impose them on others.

Emotions give us the information we need so that we can embrace our highest good. Needless to say, emotion is never an excuse for bad behavior. Emotion is a barometer of our well-being and our journey to higher vibration.

Moving toward Positive Emotions

To change our realities, narrative, and attitudes, we must reach for the most positive feeling that we can imagine. We must modify and adjust our emotions to the best of our ability. If we are feeling despair, we must recognize that emotion and acknowledge the situation, person, or event that is involved. And then we must try to release it.

We release the intense feeling of despair and reach for the next higher feeling. We can reach for sadness or despondency; we can reach for dejection. Eventually, we find that we are able to reach for ennui, or a simpler feeling of tedium. After time, we reach for peace.

Remembering Positive Emotions

It is helpful to remember times and places, persons and events that were emotionally positive—to fill our bodies with the good feelings. Think back to a situation that engendered happiness or a circumstance that was amusing. Remember the contentment of a tender moment in a relationship.

For instance, when I am reaching for euphoria, I remember that last day of each of the three years that I was in high school. On that day, two of my friends and I would clean out our lockers and head for Memorial Park, just the three of us. We would take my transistor radio, lie in the sun on the merry-go-round, listen to music, and talk. We discussed all the things that hopeful teenagers discuss. My thoughts about that day invoke a freewheeling feeling of freedom, contentment, and utter, unadulterated joy. All thanks to Liz, Lynn, and the Beatles.

Emotions: A Partial List

Positive emotions are based in love, trust, joy, and gratitude. Positive emotions include fondness, empathy, compassion, tenderness, amusement, cheerfulness, thankfulness, hope, delight, enjoyment, joviality, satisfaction, enthusiasm, contentment, optimism, eagerness, and relief. These are the kinds of emotion that we are reaching for when we are moving to achieve the higher vibrations.

Negative emotions are based in helplessness, powerlessness, fear, and hatred. They include aggravation, anxiety, rage, hostility, bitterness, resentment, contempt, loathing, jealousy, despair, shame, embarrassment, regret, emptiness, terror, and panic. These are the kinds of emotions that we are releasing as we move to embrace the higher vibration of positive emotion.

Thoughts and Emotions: A Partnership

The Interaction between Thought and Emotion

Emotions are attached to our thoughts; when we think a thought, we also feel something about that thought. For instance, we may feel delight when we think of a sunny day. We may feel satisfaction when we think of our children. We may feel disgust when we think of our job. Thought and emotion are intertwined.

The hypothalamus in the brain transforms thought and the emotion attached to that thought into an amino acid called a neuropeptide. Neuropeptides represent the dominant emotion associated with each particular type of thought. The thought/emotion combination manufactures millions of neuropeptides. They course through our bloodstream and attach themselves to our cells through a specific receptacle designed for this express purpose.

Our cells begin to develop additional receptacles that are exclusively created to capture the neuropeptides that we are sending them. The more of a specific neuropeptide that we send to our cells, the more they want, and so our cells inform our brains to create larger and larger quantities of them.

Each emotion creates a particular neuropeptide. Love creates a unique neuropeptide that is different from the particular neuropeptide that rage creates. Fear has its own neuropeptide. Bitterness, jealousy, contempt, loathing, and despair each have their own neuropeptide, just as gratitude, cheerfulness, hope, contentment, and optimism have their neuropeptide.

If we have feelings of happiness and contentment every time we think of our parents, we make happiness and contentment neuropeptides. If we have feelings of anxiety and regret when we think of our job or vocation, we make anxiety and regret neuropeptides.

So what are we creating? Do we want bodies that are full of receptacles that crave happiness and contentment? Or do we want bodies that crave anxiety and regret? We condition our bodies to crave the neuropeptides that we send them.

Dr. Candace Pert, pharmacologist, has done extensive research regarding cell receptors, neuropeptides, thought, and emotion. She gives a concise, yet simple explanation in the DVD *What the Bleep Do We Know, Down the Rabbit Hole: Quantum Edition. (See References)*

The Alignment of Thought and Emotion

Our thoughts and emotions are interwoven. They are in alignment with each other, and so if we want to create a different scenario for ourselves, we must address both and do so simultaneously.

Changing our emotion is intrinsic to the process of changing our attitude. Attitude is a state of mind and begins with thought, but emotion is an inherent component of the state of mind that we call attitude.

Indeed, recent research indicates that we are much more influenced by the emotion behind the thought than by the thought itself. We are not the rational, logical creatures that we suppose we are, and many of our plans and much of our activity is motivated by emotions of which we are often largely unaware. It is in our best interest to become aware of our emotions and the partnership of thought and emotion. Only then will we be able to begin to make progress toward changing our attitudes and our reality.

Is it easy and quick? No. Progress is incremental, but we will never get to the higher vibration if we do not start and if we do not continue with our effort. If we give up after a few attempts and tell ourselves that it does not work, of course it is not going to work. It requires our ongoing attention.

The Alignment of Thought and Emotion: An Example

Your neighbor has an enormous tree whose branches hang into your yard. Every autumn, when the tree loses its leaves, you spend hours raking. Your neighbor offers no assistance and is uninterested in trimming his tree.

What do you think about this? Do you think your neighbor is an unmitigated and inconsiderate jerk? And do you feel hostility and bitterness when you think of your neighbor? Or do you think your neighbor has a beautiful tree that gives you a splendid display every autumn and that you need the exercise anyway? Do you feel satisfaction and cheerfulness as a result?

Perhaps we are feeling bitter and hostile toward our neighbor with the tree and have a dawning awareness that this attitudinal stance is beginning to become pervasive. We are bringing this thought/feeling combination into additional areas in our life; it is becoming our predominant response to most situations. It is affecting our physical health. Furthermore, it is irritating our loved ones, and they do not want to associate with us. They tolerate us but do not enjoy us.

It will be of great benefit to us if we rearrange our thoughts and feelings about our neighbor, and it will benefit others as well. We can then examine other areas in which bitterness and hostility play a part. We must begin to release the negative thoughts and feelings associated with our neighbor and all else that inspires bitterness and hostility. We must begin to move toward something more positive.

Likely, we will not be able to immediately move our thoughts and feelings into, "I like my neighbor and feel delighted by his tree." We may never go quite this far, but moving up a notch in both feeling and thought is a start. Instead of perseverating on how hateful an old guy he is, we might begin to have some curiosity about our neighbor, think he is an odd fellow, and feel some disappointment in his lack of neighborly reciprocity.

We have to have the better thought and the better feeling together. They must align. It will do us no good if we look at the neighbor, think what a curious fellow he is, and then allow the feelings of hostility and bitterness to well up within us. It will be next to impossible to move ourselves to a more positive emotional place if we continue to look at him and think to ourselves, "I just hate that guy."

Manifestation: Our Thoughts and Feelings

Whether our thoughts and emotions are negative or are positive, they have power and are sending a message to the Universe. The energy that is created by our thoughts and emotions informs the Universal Mind that we are making a request, and Source Energy answers in kind. We invite, and we attract. And there is a plentiful supply.

When we decide that we want to change the story, we must move our thoughts and feelings into the highest possible positive expression. The more we are able to bring them into uniform association with each other, the greater will be our success.

The Role of Our Behaviors and Actions: Their Part in Our Drama

Empowering Our Manifesting by Changing Our Behaviors

If we wish to facilitate a quicker outcome, our actions and behaviors must also align with our stated desire. What we do and how we conduct ourselves is a vital part of our ability to create. Our thoughts and emotions drive our behaviors.

We are often called upon to change our attitude. Changing our attitude is frequently the precursor to changing our behavior. We may need to move out of our comfort zone and challenge ourselves in situations that are awkward or with people and places that are disquieting. We must exercise courage and be brave enough to risk the unknown.

When we perpetuate a pattern of behavior, we also perpetuate the message that we are sending into Source Energy. We continue to send the Universal Mind the message that is built into that behavior. We cannot do the same thing over and over again and expect a different result. Do something dissimilar, atypical, or out of the ordinary. Modify the behavior; change the action. Act as if you are already exactly where you want to be.

How badly do we desire a manifestation of a different reality or a new narrative? Perhaps we would like it if it falls into our laps, but we are not going to do anything to contribute to the process. This will certainly slow the effort. Manifesting our desires will happen more quickly if we put ourselves in the place where change is possible.

We must look at our own involvement in the request. A complacent attitude or apathy does not support the stated desire. We must involve ourselves; we must act as well as think and feel.

If our conduct and actions are contrary to our stated desire, we will indeed sabotage the likelihood of facilitating change. As we send our thoughts and emotions into the Universe, they must align with our desire, but our actions must align as well.

If we say one thing but act in a manner contrary to our verbal communication, we undermine our effort. Behavior informs, so when verbalization and behavior are not synchronized, behavior communicates the actual desire.

Sabotaging Ourselves: Negative Thoughts and Emotions Stimulate Negative Behaviors

We cannot think adverse thoughts and indulge in unhealthy emotions without promoting susceptibility toward regrettable behaviors. That which we nurture, grows. If we foster negative thoughts and emotions, there is a high probability that we will eventually act upon them in some manner.

For instance, we might believe that a friend has taken unfair advantage of us. We had agreed to care for her children in our home until 8:00 p.m. She did not come to get them until midnight and did not call to tell us that she would be delayed. When she did explain her situation, we decided not to believe her.

We indulged in feelings of suspicion and distrust; we nurtured these emotions and allowed them to grow into feelings of bitterness, resentment, and jealousy. We decided we must act. Now we find ourselves engaging in acts of revenge and are gossiping about our (former) friend's bad marriage, incompetent work behaviors, and inadequate parenting.

What are we creating? We are now mired in negative thoughts, emotions, and behaviors. This is neither in our highest good nor in the

129

highest good of our (former) friend. We are generating nasty neuropeptides, creating discord, and are very likely constructing a karmic situation that will need to be addressed, now or later.

Regrettable Behaviors

Regrettable behavior is behavior that does not promote our reach for positive thought and emotion. It interferes with our Soul's evolution toward the higher vibrations of love, joy, and gratitude. It is not in harmony with Source Energy.

When we engage in undesirable behaviors, we are not transforming or transmuting the lower vibrations to the higher vibrations. We are not using power appropriately, and energy is not circulating in the pattern of the number eight; it is not pulling from the lower vibration and bringing it into higher expression. Instead, it is circular, going round and round and never moving into higher expression.

Negative behaviors are unwelcome because they produce a karmic situation that must be addressed at some point in this life or in a future incarnation. They create another link in the karmic chain. Karmic links are most quickly solved and resolved through positive thoughts and emotions and the resultant behaviors; they are remedied by a loving, compassionate, and benevolent approach.

The most obvious regrettable behaviors involve the intentional taking of another human life. But taking life unnecessarily is unacceptable, whether or not it is human life.

If we are asking that something give its life so that ours may be richer, we must be reflective and deliberate in our decision-making.

Taking power over another through physical and sexual assault is also an obviously deplorable action. Taking power over another through verbal, psychological, mental, or emotional manipulation is also improper.

Slanderous speech and gossip are undesirable. Behaviors that arise from greed, avarice, and excess are unwanted. Actions that are motivated by arrogance and pride do not honor the self but put the self above others and are harmful. Hypocritical speech and action is detrimental. Revenge is anti-healing in all directions.

Behavior (or lack of action) that is motivated by negligence or a lack of concern for our own lives and ourselves is unwanted. Emotional listlessness, intellectual indolence, social apathy, and spiritual torpor all contribute to an inability to do our part in our own lives and in the lives of others.

Our behaviors are interwoven with our emotions and thoughts. Our actions, or lack of them, mean something—not just to others, but also to

130

ourselves. Nothing is idle. We either contribute to the higher vibration or we do not. Above all, we do not want to perpetuate a lower vibration.

Crafting Our Request

When we craft our request, we must first determine what we *really* want. Then we reach for the highest thoughts and feelings that are available to us at the moment. We can begin to bring a greater harmony to the situation.

We attempt to feel how we will feel when we get our request; we think the wonderful thoughts that we will have about our lives and ourselves when our application to the Universe is fulfilled. We express gratitude for that which we already have. We modify our behavior. We act; we take our power.

Taking our power is not the same as trying to control. Taking our power means that we are actively, energetically involved; we are bringing personal vitality and drive into our endeavor. Control indicates that we want to dominate and manipulate; we want to force or coerce. We do ourselves a service when we take our power but let go of control and ask for that which is in our highest good. If we are too specific, we may limit amazing possibilities and potentials.

The Vulnerable: Babies and Children

We create our own reality, but we cannot create in another person's reality. All creation begins with thought. At the time of our births (within each lifetime), and in our first few weeks, months, and years of our lives, our repertoire of experience is sparse; we are not cognitive entities or thinking individuals in the way that we later become cognizant and aware.

We have had limited interactions with others, and our observations have been minimal. We are only beginning to have the intellectual ability to form thoughts about those experiences, interactions, and observations, and the thoughts that are beginning to take shape are minimal. Until we can form thoughts, our manifesting abilities are nominal.

At the time of our births, our emotions are primitive; they lack complexity. Our emotions are also built upon our repertoire of experience. It is only as we acquire experiences within our situations or circumstances, or with people or events, that our emotions evolve. We must live more life and have more experiences before we begin to gain emotional intricacy.

Our behaviors are limited and reflect our desire to have our needs met. Our behaviors do not purposefully impinge upon or harm others. We do not invade the space of those around us with the intention to do harm but rather with the request that provision will be made for that which we require.

How then do we explain babies and children who are born into and live in reprehensible situations? How do we explain little ones who are abused or exploited? How do we account for children who are born into poverty, or little ones who are so neglected that they grow up emotionally, intellectually, or physically stunted?

If we create our own reality, how, when, and why is this reality created? These little ones have limited experiences and interactions in the here and now, and they do not have the cognitive abilities to form thoughts about them; their emotions are primal. And they certainly did not behave in a manner that would invite abuse or neglect.

The answer is that they did not create this reality in the current incarnation; it has its origins in past lives. Their repertoire of experience lies in past lives, and these experiences are rooted in what has previously been.

We do not know another person's reincarnational journey. We do not know what karmic issues they are addressing. We do not know what they are here to experience or to learn, and we do not know what they are here to teach. It is not ours to know. Within each incarnation, each of us, babies and children included, are living in the present, balancing the past, and preparing for the future

Babies and children in trouble are *always*, however, ours to serve. When they are young, it is irrelevant whether or not they need or want their experience. They are vulnerable and unable to advocate for their own needs, wants, and desires. Turning away from little ones in distress will create a karmic situation. We may not be able to do for them what we think should be done; that may be a part of their journey and a part of ours. But we must not turn away. The same is true of those who are born with mental and physical compromises and challenges. Again, we may not be able help in a way that we want to help, but we must offer assistance.

We must also understand that, for reasons incomprehensible to us, the journey has been chosen. Other's lives belong to them and not to us. We are not in charge of the outcome. We do the best that we can with what is in front of our face, and we give it our full attention. When our contribution has been made, it has been made and is done. We do not do ourselves or anyone else any good by becoming fixated on and consumed by the troubles in the world. Do your best and walk on.

Part Two: Context

Context refers to relevant circumstances that surround a situation. Context includes the time, place, and people that are involved, both currently and historically. When we manifest, we are creating our realities within certain contexts.

We create within the context of particular families and groups and cultures; we have choices, but so do those around us. We are all interconnected and interrelated. We do not live in isolation, so our created reality is a part of a larger reality that involves our relationships, families, and groups.

We are creating within historical frameworks as well, so our manifestation will also involve the regional history of the area in which we are currently living. The manifestation effort of a frail, elderly Jew living in 1941 Auschwitz will be vastly different from that of a wealthy, robust woman shopping Rodeo Drive in 1993.

We create within the context of our own reincarnational history. What karma are we wishing to balance? What issues do we want to address with other people, or with places, times, or events?

Context: Our Reincarnational History

Our lives (in the present time and place) often seem complicated and involved. When we add our reincarnational history to the history of our current existence, our life's journey becomes increasingly multilayered. At times, it may seem incomprehensible and confusing. If we are bringing issues into the current life that need balancing from previous lives, it becomes more challenging to change our story in the here and now. Sometimes our issues appear to be out of context of our current life.

Each of our lifetimes creates a chapter in our own akashic book, which is a part of the larger akashic record. Each of our lifetimes has its origins in and builds upon preceding lives and prepares us for subsequent lives. Although it may not be understandable to us in the current experience, it is part of the process that will help us raise our vibration; it is in harmony with Universal Law.

This does not mean that we cannot lighten the load and bring more serenity into the existing life. We may not know the reincarnational origins of what we are currently living, but we manifest out of the present moment, so we start here and now. The Universe wants us to live positively in thought, emotion, and behavior. If we are willing to stretch and reach for it, we can improve our attitudes and circumstances.

As we balance karma and move into higher vibration, we will, on occasion, participate in lifetimes that have great challenges. We may involve ourselves in situations that seem interminably severe and may live with people who are unremittingly harsh.

Each lifetime has its roots in past lives. We may not understand why particular conditions and events have been chosen for the life of the here and now. We cannot comprehend it because it is out of context in terms of the present day. It is out of our contemporary framework and would not have been chosen in the current reality.

Nonetheless, on a Soul level it has been chosen, and we must live within the experience. We have the power to choose what we think, feel, and do within that particular experience, however. Our thoughts, emotions, and deeds can exacerbate an already unbalanced karmic situation, or they can heal and balance the previously created karmic chain.

We can change our circumstances. We can reach for the highest thought, the best feeling emotion; we can act as if we are moving in the direction of our stated desire. We can improve the situation. And we can build upon that improvement and continue to enhance and advance until we get closer and closer to that which is desired.

We may not be able to manifest exactly what we think we want (out of our present day definition), but we have the power to change our attitude and then our situation. We have power over our own actions and so can considerably influence what lies ahead.

There is no nobility in suffering and martyrdom, however, so if events can be transformed and transcended, they must be. Many people who define themselves as victims are not. Often people have power that they refuse to take. This is a choice and, as with all choices, it balances or imbalances karma.

Manifesting within Karmic Imbalances

We must be willing to examine and redirect (if necessary) our thoughts, emotions, and actions. We must climb the ladder to the next best thing. And we must keep on; when the going gets rough, we must persist. We must be consistent, and we must continue. We must make it our intention to manifest change, and we must give it our attention.

We cocreate with Source Energy—the Highest Vibration. As we cocreate with this energy, our goal is to increase vibration and move toward love, joy, gratitude, and trust. We want to embrace and reflect that which some call "the Christ Energy" or "the Christ Vibration." We want to direct our attention to our highest good and to the greater good of the Universe.

134

Context: Living with Other People's Realities

Personal Relationships

We do not live in a vacuum. Not only do we live within the context of our own lives and within our own reincarnational history, we live within the context of our relationships, communities, and environments. We live in the context of historical frameworks.

What other people do can significantly affect our personal narrative. We can create in our own lives, but we cannot create in another person's reality if they do not invite us and allow us to do so. The realities of others may affect us in a powerful, sometimes heartrending manner.

Where, when, why, what, and who are all relevant. Where do we live in both time and space? Who have we chosen to take on our journey with us? What is the history and environment of the culture and the people into whose group we have chosen to incarnate?

All events, situations, people, and circumstances carry weight and are significant to our creation. For reasons we may not understand in the here and now, we have chosen to live out our story and to reach for higher vibration within particular contexts.

Creating in the Context of Personal Relationships

Relationships can be long-term and a part of the entirety of our lives, or they can be long-term and endure for many years, but not for our lifetime. They can be short-term, sometimes lasting a few brief years, months, or even hours. Anyone with whom we are in a relationship, however briefly, will affect us in some way, and we will affect him or her.

Into each life, we will bring those who love or support us in some manner. These people may be intimately involved with us; they may be our parents, grandparents, friends, or siblings. They may be teachers, spiritual counselors, or therapists.

They may be people whose relationship to us we perceive to be superficial or casual. This might include community helpers—a policeman, nurse, or emergency medical technician. And they can be people we do not link to ourselves at all—those who are interested in the greater good of the society in which we live.

We may also choose to live with or love those whose realities may significantly challenge us. If we love people who are physically or mentally challenged, ill, or are chemically abusive, their situations will affect us. If we are in relationships with those who are disordered in their personality or character, it will affect us. The closer we are to them, the more intensely we

135

will be affected. We cannot alter their story, and in some situations, they will not do so either.

Sometimes those we love abandon us or disappear in some way. Again, we cannot bring back the disappeared if they do not desire reunification or reconnection. People leave, and that may be part of their journey and ours as well, but it hurts us nonetheless.

When we love people who are significantly challenged, we may need to formulate an imaginative approach if we wish to move ourselves from the lower to the higher vibrations. When we are in relationships with those who are unable or unwilling to help us create a positive experience, we must look exclusively to ourselves for resolution of the situation.

We start with our thoughts and feelings. Are we wallowing in a despondent and miserable quagmire of thinking and feeling? Or are we trying to reach for the most positive thought and emotion? And what are our actions? Are we caring for ourselves in the best possible manner?

Self-honoring and distraction remain significant tools when we are attempting to move ourselves out of negative energy. We can take ourselves to a movie or to a friend's house; we can read a book, do puzzles, write in a journal, paint a picture, meditate, exercise, walk in nature, or collect crystals.

We may need to create a distance between others and ourselves as well.

We do nobody any good by entangling ourselves with their agony, and we may certainly do ourselves harm. We need to sweep in front of our own door and look to our own journey.

Harsh Realities within Personal Relationships

If we are children or vulnerable adults, we may not be able to create that distance and move ourselves out of the situation. Defenseless people are not able to enact their power in a manner that will protect them from physical, mental, or emotional pain. We must offer our assistance.

We do not know why the particular journey has been chosen. We may not be able to influence the outcome. But we must do what we can to help. If we are able to facilitate personal empowerment for the vulnerable, we must do so. And when our contribution to their life narrative has been made, we must walk on.

Harsh Realities: An Example

In 1994, Susan Smith murdered her little boys, ages three and one. She initially told the public that a Black man had stolen her car and that the children were in it at the time. She made tearful pleas for the return of her boys.

These little boys were not responsible for their creation in the current lifetime. They chose the situation and the circumstance before they incarnated; in the context of their existence as Michael and Alexander, they are victims. There was virtually nothing the boys could do to change their story. The little boys could not transform the situation. They could not empower themselves. Intervention belonged to those who had the resources to intercede.

Ms. Smith herself had been profoundly affected by the realities of those around her. At age seven, her biological father died through suicide. Her stepfather sexually molested her, and her biological mother failed to protect her and wanted Susan to keep the family secret. Nonetheless, at the time she murdered her children, she was an adult and was responsible for her choices.

Ms. Smith's biological parents and her stepfather created significant karmic imbalance within her that must be addressed in future lives. In future lives, Ms. Smith must address the karmic imbalance she created with her children. Furthermore, she generated karmic imbalance regarding her false accusation, as she knew full well that placing the blame on a Black man would be ardently embraced by some of the population.

Context: Complex Realities of Groups and Communities

Community also provides a contextual milieu in which we create our reality. This creation also has its roots in previous lives. It has history that comes from the past lives of all who have occupied time and space in this particular environment or setting. It takes place within that historical framework but in the here and now.

It occupies the current time and space, however, and thoughts, emotions, and actions in the current reality expand upon and transform that which is being created. The direction the experience takes depends on what is being manifested now. We have responsibility, each moment, for what is being crafted within our communities and groups.

Individuals come into groups and communities with a repertoire of experience from past life existences. We have lived through many lifetimes, each filled with a rich mixture of thoughts, emotions, and actions. These thoughts, emotions, and actions have built upon each other; in the here and now, they hold significant power.

Personal Responsibility in a Communal Reality

We share the joint karma of our groups and communities; the greater the attachment, the greater the karma. If we support a group, an organization, or a community, we share the karma that is generated by the beliefs or actions within that communal system.

Many communities coalesce around concepts and principles that support the Greater Good. Within these communities, we are able to manifest that which generates health and contributes to positive growth, if that is our choice. We can balance karma and raise our vibration.

However, certain communities, groups, or organizations come together around issues and convictions that do not support the Greater Good. If we are in these groups, we may cause harm to others, either intentionally or unintentionally. We may behave in an exploitive manner or take inappropriate physical, emotional, intellectual, social, or spiritual power over others. We do not balance karma and indeed create another link in our karmic chain.

What is the focus of the communities to which we belong? We cannot participate in or belong to any group and not share the communal karma in some manner. The more we personally contribute, the more karma we balance or generate.

Individuals within groups and communities contribute to the direction that events will take. We are not victims of our situations throughout most of the creation. We contribute to the creation of the experience as a whole. There may come a time, however, when the ability to manifest a change is severely curtailed. In the following example, the power of the thoughts, emotions, and behaviors revolutionized the created situations and circumstances and lead to a catastrophic end.

Personal Responsibility in a Distorted Reality: An Example
Jim Jones was born in Indiana in 1931. He was an intelligent young man and an accelerated learner. He graduated from high school earlier than his classmates and attended college as an honor student.

By 1951, he had embraced the Communist principles of Marx and Lenin and had joined the Communist Party. During that time the United States was in a Cold War with The Soviet Union. The political and governmental system in the United States is a Democracy, whereas the Soviet Union, at that time, was Communist. As a result, Jim Jones suffered societal harassment for his political beliefs. Although his father was reputedly in the Ku Klux Klan, Jones was sympathetic to the Blacks and was an avid integrationist. He held the socialist ideals of communal ownership and self-management and embraced the concept "to each according to his contribution."

During his youth, Jones attended a faith healing; apparently, it was here that he realized the power of evangelical enthusiasm. He decided that he could achieve Marxist principles and create a Marxist society by mobilizing people through religion.

Jones himself was an atheist. In the 1950s, he started the People's Temple (Full Gospel Church) in Indiana so that he could create a Socialist Paradise. He designed an apostolic communal setting that was intended to be a Socialist Eden. In the mid-1960s, he began moving the church to California.

In the mid-1970s, he moved his church headquarters to San Francisco and also began building Jonestown in Guyana, South America. He was now preaching that he was the reincarnation of Jesus, Buddha, Gandhi, and Vladimir Lenin. He was also informing people that he would be a friend, a father, a savior, or a God to any who wanted it. He could meet the need—whatever it was.

Between the mid-1970s and 1978, Jones and his followers fled to South America, as media interest had initiated an extensive investigation of human rights issues regarding the People's Temple practice. Initial complaints involved his personal use of donated church funds. There was increasing alarm that he was using violence and coercion against Temple members, and that people were being held against their will.

The People's Temple in Guyana, South America, was now called an Agricultural Project. Leo Ryan, a congressman from California, went to Guyana to engage in further examination. Governmental officials and staff were included in his contingency as were people from television and newspapers and relatives of some of the Jonestown inhabitants.

When Leo Ryan and his group attempted to leave Guyana, Jim Jones had his armed guards murder them. Of his contingency, Leo Ryan and four others were killed; the remainder escaped. The People's Temple ended then when Jones ordered the 909 Temple members to commit "revolutionary suicide" by consuming cyanide poison. Most died.

Personal Responsibility in a Distorted Reality: When Choices Narrow
Early in the story of the People's Temple, it would have been relatively easy to get out—to leave Jim Jones and the People's Temple. Early in each individual drama, a different narrative could have been created. But Temple followers made choices. No doubt many of them wanted a friend, father, savior, or a God, and Jones was willing to fill the role.

Jim Jones' thoughts, emotions, and actions built upon each other and gained power, and the People's Temple followers' thoughts, emotions, and actions built upon each other and gained power as well. All of the individuals involved contributed to the creation of the experience as a whole. People made choices to follow Jim Jones, to become involved in the People's Temple, and to move to Guyana.

The time came, however, when it was too late to extricate themselves from the situation even if they had so desired. Jim Jones and his cadre of armed guards had taken the inappropriate physical, emotional, intellectual, social, and spiritual control that the Temple followers had offered them.

Individual Accountability in a Communal Reality

In the best of all possible worlds, we would know everything about all groups of personal interest *before* we attached ourselves to them in any way. This is not generally feasible as groups are complex and multifaceted entities. They change; old members exit, and new members enter. The leadership alters, and as leadership transforms, so too does policy and practice.

We remain responsible for our karma, our reach for higher vibration, and ourselves. It is in our best interest to give our full attention to our groups and communities. We must remain conscientious about our individual growth and must maintain personal accountability for our thoughts, emotions, and actions.

It can be vastly seductive when someone else says that they will do it for us. It might be a short-term luxury to be told what to think, how to feel, and what action to take, but it does not benefit our reach for higher vibration in the long-term.

Individual Manifestation in the Context of Place and History

Every time, space, and person carries a history. We manifest out of our personal reincarnational histories and also within the context of the histories and environments in the current incarnation.

Those of us who live in the upper socioeconomic groups in any country will manifest differently than those of us who life in the middle or the lower socioeconomic groups. This is not to say that the middle or lower groups cannot manifest wealth. We can, and we do. However, manifesting wealth will be easier if we live in prosperous countries with good educational systems.

We can manifest peace in troubled situations. We may not be able to attain our entire vision of what we would like it to be, nor should we. Other people are involved, and we cannot create in their realities. We can make gains, however, and we can certainly raise our own vibration. Again, it is easier to do if the trouble is a simple discord in a small group as opposed to deeply entrenched historical violence in a particular area.

Moving toward the greatest good for us all and higher vibration for us individually is not going to happen if we do not start and persevere—even in the most troubled situations. And, of course, the more thoughts, emotions, and actions we add to the effort, the more strength the effort gains and the more swiftly success is achieved.

This is also true for situations that are weighed down by dominance over others, violence, exploitation, hatred, anger, prejudice, and discrimination. The more thought, emotion, and action we add to the effort, the more power it gains.

No matter who we are or where we live, we must try to keep our thoughts, emotions, and actions centered around the common good, love, generosity, compassion, and gratefulness for what we already have. That is what we can do on the world stage. We can contribute to universal peace and goodwill in this way. The more of us that manifest in that direction, the better our world will be.

Section Two: Information, Communication, and Messages

Chapter 7: Meditation and Channeling
- Meditation
  - ❖ Benefits of Meditation
  - ❖ Meditation: Getting Started
  - ❖ Using Visualization to Assist the Meditative State
  - ❖ Using Sound to Assist the Meditative State
    - o Music
    - o Chanting
  - ❖ Using the Kinesthetic Sense to Assist the Meditative State
  - ❖ Completing the Meditation
  - ❖ Guided Meditation
    - o A Meditation for the Body, Mind, and Emotions
    - o Self-Observation Meditation
    - o Past-Life-Regression Meditation
- Channeling
  - ❖ Our Angels and Guides as Intermediaries from Source Energy
  - ❖ The Purpose of Spiritual Communication
  - ❖ Beginning to Communicate: Channeling
    - o Interpreting Information
    - o Metaphorical Message: An Example
  - ❖ Messages for Other People
- Pathways for Receiving Psychic Information
  - ❖ Intuition
    - o Intuition: An Example
  - ❖ Clairsentience
  - ❖ Clairvoyance
  - ❖ Clairaudience
  - ❖ Clairgustance
- How to Increase Psychic Awareness
- Astral Travel
  - ❖ Experiencing Astral Travel
- Psychic Animal Communication

Meditation

Meditation allows a connection to a higher state of consciousness, or a higher vibration. What we are seeking through meditation is an altered state of awareness. Meditation is a contemplative, introspective, and reflective time. It is a time to connect to our inner selves, or Souls. Through the connection to our Souls, we reach for higher vibration.

During meditation, we want to slow the mind and give it an opportunity to take a new direction. We can do this by deliberately turning our attention away from our conscious thoughts and by purposefully directing our awareness to a sound or an object. We can use a real object, such as a flower, flame, or crystal, or a real sound, such as "Aum." Or we can visualize the object or imagine the sound.

Many people believe that they cannot meditate because they cannot still their thoughts. Buddhism compares the mind to a chattering monkey, jumping from one branch to another, and, in our usual waking state, our thoughts do jump from one idea to another. Meditation helps us become aware of the stream of consciousness that passes through our heads; the stream of thoughts never stops, but meditation helps us train the mind so that we can detach from this constant flow and slow it down.

During meditation, we are consciously directing our attention so that our state of awareness is altered. Our brain waves during meditation are different from either the waking or the sleeping state, and both sides of the brain are used when we are in a meditative state.

Benefits of Meditation

Meditation can help us detach from disquieting thoughts. It can give us a space and time to lessen our worries and anxieties. Meditation can calm the emotions and relax the body. In this way, it promotes tranquility and peacefulness and supports general well-being.

Meditation gives us an uncluttered psychological and emotional space; it gives us distance from the immediacy of our everyday existence. During meditation, we are better able to understand our lives more fully. We can more easily see the wholeness of our selves and to examine the various aspects that complete the whole.

Because meditation slows the mind and allows a connection to a higher state of consciousness, it can also be the introduction or the initiation to channeling. Channeling is psychic communication with beings of higher vibration, generally our Guides and Angels. (Channeling will be discussed in more detail later in the chapter).

There is no particular correct or proper way to meditate. There are, however, certain basic practices or procedures that can be useful, and that will assist us in getting into a meditative state. Before I begin, I put myself in a protected space. I ask for guidance from my Spiritual Helpers and ground my own energy to the energy of the earth.

For creating a protected space, I use the following prayer:

I create a protected space of perfect love and perfect trust

> *I clear my mind*
> *I clear my body*
> *I clear my Soul*
> *I clear my Third Eye*
> *White Light is surrounding me*
> *White Light is protecting me*
> *White Light is consuming me*
> *Solving and dissolving all situations for the good of all*
> *My Guides and Angels are with me*
> *I am grateful for the miracles that are happening here and now*
> *I ground to the Earth and open to the Light*

When I ground myself, I visualize roots coming out of the bottoms of my feet and going deep into the earth. Earth is always our ground, and we must always ground ourselves. When we meditate (or channel), we are reaching for higher vibration, but we live here on Earth. Grounding provides the foundation or base from which we will be accessing higher energies. Grounding helps us stay clear and centered; it helps us make sense of our experience.

Ideally, when we decide to meditate, we should:

➤ choose a quiet, pleasant place

➤ choose a time when it is likely that we will be undisturbed and need not hurry

➤ lie down in a comfortable position, or sit quietly maintaining a good posture

➤ close the eyes and relax

➤ breathe *consciously* and from the diaphragm (give attention to your breathing)

➤ take a deep breath in, feeling the abdomen rise

➤ pause and breathe out, relaxing the abdomen

➤ repeat conscious breathing

Relaxation is essential preparation for meditation. Breathe deeply and slowly and relax each individual part of the body. Consciously think of the body; feel the body. We can begin at the head or the feet, it makes no difference at all (I generally begin at the feet, so I will use that as an example):

➤ relax the toes and feet and then the ankles; feel muscles and tendons relax

➤ relax the knees and thighs; feel muscles and tendons relax

➤ relax the arms, hands, and fingers; feel the muscles and tendons relax

➤ breathe into the abdomen and the chest and feel all of the internal organs relax

➤ breathe into the neck and shoulders and feel any tension or strain draining away

➤ bring relaxing, healing energy into the face, lips, eyes, forehead, and scalp

Using Visualization to Assist the Meditative State

Many of us find it helpful to visually and physically concentrate on an object to help move into the meditative state. For some, this is a flower or a candle, but it can also be a crystal, the figure of an Angel, or anything special that helps focus the attention and move into a higher vibration.

Visualizing or imagining pictures in our thoughts can help us get into a reflective, contemplative state as well. Visualization will focus the mind and allow it to take a new direction. In our mind's eye, we can focus on a symbol, flower, flame, or anything that represents our desire to move to a higher vibration. We want to purposefully keep our attention on our chosen object.

Using Sound to Assist the Meditative State

Sound can move us into a meditative state. Aum is a tonal sound; it is the spoken essence of Source Energy and is the most sacred of all syllables. Repeating Aum, aloud or silently, can focus the attention and move us into a state of contemplation and reflection.

Other sounds serve as well. We can choose any sound, word, or short phrase that is comfortable and meaningful to us. A continuous humming sound works for some of us. Others prefer a word, such as *kyrie*, that is slowly and repeatedly intoned. Still others prefer a short phrase, such as "I Am," again slowly and repeatedly spoken.

Music

Many of us find that music raises the vibration and can help achieve or enhance our meditation. There is a great deal of New Age music that has been created for this specific purpose. Other music not created for meditation can be used as well, but use care in the selection. What we hear through music embeds itself in our psyche in an especially powerful manner—more so than does the mere spoken word.

Music that is restful and calm with a positive or life-affirming message is beneficial. Music that gives a negative message, disrespects life, or trivializes the higher concepts, such as gratitude, love, peace, compassion, or joy, should be avoided. Additionally, some music is syncopated in a way that it does not correspond to the heartbeat and so is discordant to the body. This music should also be avoided in meditation.

Chanting

Chanting can help silence thoughts and focus attention. It is a vocalization that moves us into meditation and ingrains a message in the subconscious. Chanting is the continuous recitation of a mantra, which can be a name, word or set of words, or syllables. It is the singing of a prayer.

Chanting is generally melodious and rhythmic. Chanting can be monophonic (having one voice or sound); it can be a simple rhythm, following the straightforward and uncomplicated cadence of a heartbeat. Or it can be complex, either polyrhythmic (having many rhythms) and/or polyphonic (having many voices).

Alleluia and *kyrie eleison* are words from the Christian tradition that are often woven into either simple or complex chants. Alleluia means, "praise God," and kyrie eleison means, "Lord, have mercy." When we chant these words, we are embedding this concept into our subconscious.

An additional example is the Om Mani Padme Hum that can also be used in simple or complex chanting. Om Mani Padme Hum defies literal translation. However, the Dali Lama has advised us that the syllable "Om" refers not only to the pure body and mind of the Buddha, but also to our own impure selves. "Mani" is the jewel and symbolizes our intention to become enlightened and compassionate. "Padme" is the lotus that symbolizes the wisdom that accepts that we are part of a whole, and that we are not selves that are separate from the whole. "Hum," the last syllable, represents the indivisibility of one consciousness. When we chant the Om Mani Padme Hum we are embedding Buddha consciousness into our own subconscious.

Some chants are tonal and have a simple sustained sound. "Aum" is a tonal chant and is the spoken essence, or the primal creative force, of the Universe; it is, therefore, the most sacred of all syllables. All three letters are sounded when using or chanting, "Aum."

Chanting and mantras have been used by most cultures throughout time. The Hindu and Buddhist spiritual traditions are known for their chants, and many of these chants, or at least portions of them, have been adopted and adapted by Western European cultures. African and Native American cultures have extensive chanting histories. When the African and Native American cultures began to interact with European culture, many of their ancient chants evolved into other chants that reflected a combined spiritual expression. The Islamic and the Jewish peoples have well-known chanting histories, and the Christian tradition is rich in chants, with possibly the most well known being the Gregorian Chants.

Chanting can be done alone or in groups; it is a powerful experience either way. We can create our own chants; we can use traditional chants or get music that guides our chants. Whatever our needs, there is a chant that is suitable to us.

Using the Kinesthetic Sense to Assist the Meditative State

As we move our bodies, it is the kinesthetic sense that allows us to locate and recognize our physical self as separate and distinct from the space around us. It is the sense that determines how we locate various parts of our bodies as they connect to our body as a whole. It is a physical sense that relates to motion and balance; it is largely unconscious.

For some of us, meditation is realized through the kinesthetic sense, or through bodily movements, postures, and breathing techniques. Yoga, Tai Chi, and Qi Gong are all kinesthetic activities that can help us achieve meditation. Repetitive kinesthetic activity, such as walking, running, biking, or swimming, encourages a contemplative or reflective state for others.

Dancing is a kinesthetic activity that can lead to a meditative state. Ordinary dancing can do it, but if we combine it with chant or ritual and make a sacred expression out of our dance, it can bring us into a powerful meditative state.

Through kinesthetic meditation of any type, we are able to move into greater health. It opens the channel to Divine Energy and can facilitate physical, emotional, psychological, and spiritual healing. It can help clear emotional blockages and release memories that no longer serve us. Kinesthetic meditation energizes the body and gives us a sense of our connection to Source Energy.

Completing the Meditation

When we are finished with the meditation, we should deliberately and purposefully make it our intention to return to conscious awareness, and we must give ourselves time to return to our usual condition of wakefulness. It is helpful to have a method of return that assists us in moving away from the absorption of the meditation. We can use words, such as, "I return now to my usual waking self, relaxed and refreshed." It is also helpful to shift the body, gently rotate the head, and shake the arms and legs.

Guided Meditation

Meditation can also be guided by someone else and can be done in a group setting. Guided meditation can be very useful, particularly for those who find it difficult to do a self-directed meditation.

When we are leading a guided meditation, we must talk slowly and pause at the end of every line or sentence. This gives the listener time to incorporate the information and to move into the energy of that statement. There are times when a longer pause is appropriate.

Before I begin any meditation, either self-directed or guided, I use the "white light" prayer. Following are examples of guided meditations.

A Meditation for the Body, Mind, and Emotions

➤ And now you are relaxing, you are relaxing, and you are floating

➤ You realize that you are going to an important gathering, a gathering of many people

➤ At this gathering, you will meet others, but most importantly you will meet three vital aspects of yourself

➤ The gathering is held on the top of a mountain

➤ A bird comes to take you to the top of the mountain

➤ This bird is golden

➤ She is a beautiful creature; she is more beautiful than any bird you have ever seen

➤ The golden bird calls your name

➤ She is ready to take you to the top of the mountain, and you fly with her

➤ And now the golden bird lands on that mountain

➤ She leaves you in a still and quiet place right there on the very tip of this mountain

➤ Here are your emotions; your emotions are revealing themselves to you

➤ Notice the form that they are taking

➤ Feel your sorrow (longer pause)

➤ Feel your joy (longer pause)

➤ Remember that they flow through you, and they are not you (longer pause)

➤ And now, just as they emerged, your emotions recede

➤ And now your mind reveals itself to you

➤ Know that you have a mind, but that you are more than your mind

➤ Talk to your mind, listen to your mind, communicate with your mind (longer pause)

➤ And now, just as it materialized, your mind recedes

➢ And now again, another aspect of yourself appears—your physical body

➢ What form is your body taking?

➢ Love the form your body takes

➢ Talk to your body (longer pause)

➢ Know that your body is so important to you, but that you are more than your body (longer pause)

➢ And now, just as your body emerged, it recedes

➢ Suddenly the golden bird appears, and she is ready to carry you off the mountain

➢ You fly with the bird up and back to your usual reality

➢ You return; you are refreshed and filled with energy and vitality

Self-Observation Meditation

➢ And now you are going to a lovely, peaceful meadow

➢ Float down easily and simply

➢ You are alone in the meadow, and the air you breathe is clear, crisp, and cool

➢ The sun shines down on you, and it is a beautiful summer day

➢ See the blue sky above you

➢ See the beautiful color of the flowers that grow in your meadow

➢ Feel the warmth on your body from the sun

➢ Feel the cooling breeze

➢ Feel the grasses as they brush against your body

➢ Take a deep, cleansing breath

➢ Smell the grasses and the clover

➢ Hear the song of the birds

➢ Feel a sense of unity and oneness with all that is

➢ And now you come to a small, quiet lake

➢ You rest beside this lake

➢ You allow your gaze to sweep over the lake

➢ And you see the still, clear water

➢ There, in the blue tranquility of the water

➢ You see a reflection of your face

➢ Your image is mirrored in the water

➢ You observe a dimension of your personality that you know and like (longer pause)

➢ As you watch your image, it moves and begins to change

➢ This change suggests another dimension of your personality (longer pause)

➢ And again you watch your image move and change

- ➤ Still another dimension of your personality expresses itself (longer pause)
- ➤ And now you watch your image change still again
- ➤ You see an image of the you that was you before the you that now bears your name (longer pause)
- ➤ Watch your reflection
- ➤ Watch your reflection and learn
- ➤ Each change is but another part of you
- ➤ Now, become aware of my voice calling you back from the lake
- ➤ Back through the meadow
- ➤ Back to this room
- ➤ Return easily to this room and to your usual waking reality
- ➤ You bring with you a new awareness of yourself and your many dimensions
- ➤ You return; you are refreshed and filled with energy and vitality

Past-Life-Regression Meditation

- ➤ Take a deep breath and relax
- ➤ You are very light and utterly free
- ➤ You are pure and radiant energy
- ➤ Feel yourself unfold and expand
- ➤ Unfold and expand until you fill the spaces around you
- ➤ Until you fill the very room
- ➤ And now I want you to remember
- ➤ Remember that we all carry with us feelings and ideas from other life spaces
- ➤ Understand that some of our feelings and ideas influence us in our current life space
- ➤ By remembering them, we can release them
- ➤ And sometimes the remembering *is* the releasing
- ➤ Realize also that we all carry with us into the current life space potential that is yet to be realized
- ➤ We bring with us potential from other life spaces
- ➤ Remembering this, we can become fuller and richer in our current life space
- ➤ In just a moment, you will move into another life space
- ➤ But right now, I want you to move to the very top of this building
- ➤ Move to the top of the building and look down on the street, remember all that you are seeing
- ➤ Now, float higher and higher, high above the building, high above the city
- ➤ Float high above the earth

- ➢ Enjoy the sensation of freedom and lightness (longer pause)
- ➢ Now I am going to ask you to drift down to Earth again
- ➢ Drift back down but into another life space
- ➢ Return to Earth in another time and another space
- ➢ I am going to count from ten to one
- ➢ When I reach one, you will be in another time and space (count)
- ➢ You are standing on Earth again
- ➢ Look down and become aware of your feet (longer pause)
- ➢ Are you wearing shoes
- ➢ What do your feet, your shoes look like? (longer pause)
- ➢ Look at your legs
- ➢ Look at your arms
- ➢ Look at your body
- ➢ What color is your skin? (longer pause)
- ➢ What do your clothes look like?
- ➢ Are you a man or a woman? (longer pause)
- ➢ Are you outdoors or in a building?
- ➢ Are you alone, or are others with you? (longer pause)
- ➢ Become aware of what you are doing
- ➢ Become fully aware of who you are
- ➢ Where you are
- ➢ What you are doing (longer pause)
- ➢ And now, still in that body and in that life space
- ➢ I am going to ask you to move to a time when you were five years old
- ➢ Move to the place that you lived
- ➢ See it clearly and in detail
- ➢ What do you see?
- ➢ Experience it clearly (longer pause)
- ➢ And now, see the people that live with you
- ➢ See them vividly and clearly
- ➢ Remember your feelings about them
- ➢ Remember your thoughts about them (longer pause)
- ➢ And now see someone that you loved in that lifetime
- ➢ See this person clearly
- ➢ Feel this person's vibration
- ➢ Feel this person powerfully (longer pause)
- ➢ Feel this person's vibration; do you know them in the current life space? (longer pause)
- ➢ And now, move into an important experience in that life space
- ➢ Move into it, and remember it (longer pause)
- ➢ And now, move into another important experience in that life space

151

> ➤ Move into it, and remember it (longer pause)
> ➤ And now, move into another important experience in that life space
> ➤ Move into it, and remember it (longer pause)
> ➤ And now, leave the body of that lifetime behind
> ➤ You have left that body and are moving into a higher consciousness
> ➤ You are moving into a higher consciousness and are able to look at the life you had
> ➤ You are able to look at this past life and know the lessons you learned (longer pause)
> ➤ And now, still looking at this past life
> ➤ Know what you carried from it into the life of the present (longer pause)
> ➤ And now, let go of that past life
> ➤ Let go of that life, but remember the experiences
> ➤ Remember the experiences in a manner that is comfortable for you
> ➤ Leave that life, and travel back to the current reality
> ➤ You travel back to the current time and space and return easily to this room
> ➤ You return to your usual waking reality
> ➤ Your identity and awareness of the current life are restored
> ➤ You return relaxed, refreshed, and filled with energy

Channeling

Channeling is psychic communication that comes from a non-sensory source and is unexplainable in current scientific theory. It is information that is passed from a being that is not in physical form to a being that is in physical form. Information is passed from our Guides and Angels to us. We reach for the higher vibration of our Spiritual Helpers so that they can communicate with us.

Our Angels and Guides as Intermediaries from Source Energy

Channeled messages come to us from a much higher vibration, a vibration where the interconnectedness of all creation is honored and understood. Our Angels and Guides know that we are beings from the Universal Source, and therefore they see us in a more loving light than we are able to see ourselves.

It is important to remember that communication with Guides and Angels comes from the higher vibrations of love and wholeness. It is toward these vibrations that we are evolving. Each time we come to Earth, we come so that we can live the lives we have chosen, learn, expand our repertoire of experience and, by doing so, raise our own vibration.

It is also important to remember that we have free will and can choose to tune in to our Guides and Angels. Or we can choose to give them no attention whatsoever. We can listen to what they have to say and act upon it; but we do not have to. We have free will.

The Purpose of Spiritual Communication

Messages that come to us through channeling are meant to assist us in developing our spiritual selves. The purpose of communication from higher vibrating energy is to help us evolve toward the higher concepts of love, joy, and gratitude; it is to assist us in raising our own vibration.

These messages can help us solve our emotional and relationship concerns, our dilemmas regarding our careers or employment, and other issues of daily life. They will be given to us within the context of our higher good, however. Messages are not meant to give us a quick fix to our problems but rather are to provide information that supports a long-term resolution.

Information from Guides and Angels is meant to support and clarify. Guides and Angels give us information that will help us understand our options in a given situation and to recognize what the consequences of any given choice might be.

Our Spiritual Helpers give information about our part in the drama of our lives. Messages are deeply personal. Guides and Angels will tell us information about other people, but only as it applies to us. Spiritual communication that involves the issues and characters of other individuals is intended to help us make decisions about how we are going to behave within the situation. What we are going to do? How will we take care of ourselves? How will we act toward others?

Information is not to be used as a weapon against anyone else. Its purpose is not to aid or assist *us* so that we can help *them* change. Other people's journeys belong to them. Messages are intended to help us sweep in front of our own doors, so to speak.

At times, our Guides and Angels want us to discover our own answers, so their messages are obscure or ambiguous. They may remain silent on an issue. Our Spiritual Team is always willing to communicate, however, so they may begin giving information on a topic that they deem to be important or relevant to spiritual growth.

Our Spiritual Helpers will not tell us what we want to hear but what we need to hear. Guides and Angels are honest, so if we do not want the answer, we should not ask the question. If the answer is not one that we want to hear, and we keep asking the same question over and over in an attempt to get a different answer, the information becomes nonsensical. If this happens, move on!

Beginning to Communicate: Channeling

Channeling involves opening ourselves up to a flow of energy that vibrates on a higher level. It is beneficial to our effort if we are intentional in our desire to contact our Guides and Angels. Be clear that you desire assistance and information. Ask for contact. Ask for assistance.

Relax and take a few deep breaths. Use the "white light" prayer, and think about what you are saying. Spend a bit of time with each concept within the prayer:

➤ *I create a protected space of perfect love and perfect trust*: We create a sacred space as a statement of intention. We are expecting to communicate with our Guides and Angels and are creating an area in which to do so. Our stated energetic boundaries also protect us from unwanted energies

➤ *I clear my mind, I clear my body, I clear my Soul*: We calm our minds, quiet our emotions, and relax our bodies. We move ourselves into a meditative space where we can communicate with our Spiritual Team.

➤ *I clear my Third Eye*: The Third Eye is the chakra that guides all issues regarding intelligence and intuition; it governs our ability to clearly see the past, present, and future. It helps us trust the inner guidance we are asking to receive.

➤ *White Light is surrounding me, protecting me, consuming me*: White Light is Universal Source Energy. We are requesting the highest vibration that we can manage and asking that it fill and protect us. We are asking for contact with the Universal Mind.

➤ *Solving and dissolving all situations for the good of all*: We are acknowledging that our Guides and Angels know our highest good. We are asking for the wisdom to accept the information we are given, knowing that all situations can be transformed and transmuted.

➤ *My Guides and Angels are with me*: Our Guides and Angels are always with us, but we are asking for a more tangible, or more perceptible, contact. Feel the energy of their presence. Visualize Guides and Angels as embodied beings, and create in the mind a picture of energy moving between them and us. We are acknowledging their presence.

➤ *I am grateful for the miracles that are happening here and now*: We express our gratitude.

➤ *I ground to the earth and open to the Light*: We are asking for contact with high vibration, but we live here on Earth in a human body. Earth is always our ground; being grounded to Earth helps us understand, in terms of our lives here and now, how the information we are being given is relevant.

We are now ready to ask for information regarding a specific issue, or we can ask for a general message. We receive the information from our Guides and Angels in our psychic brain. We then have to move that information to our cognitive brain so that we can interpret it. The information is inevitably altered, at least in part. Because we are in human form, we cannot translate the message in its fullness or entirety. Moreover, we have to put an energetic conceptual communication into words.

If we do not understand the communication or feel that no transmission is forthcoming, we can ask that the information be given in a way that we can understand. Our Spiritual Helpers are willing to work with us. If we do not get the message now, they may give it to us in a different format later if we are sincere about wanting it.

When asking for a channeled message, we may see a picture, hear a word, a phrase, or a song. We may feel an emotion. The message is frequently metaphorical; it is a representation of something, a symbol. Sometimes the message is literal, but it is frequently figurative, and we must call upon our personal repertoire of metaphors and symbols as we interpret the information that is given.

Metaphors are words, pictures, parts of a song, or even feelings that are meant to indicate a resemblance. Metaphors are an analogy between two things or two ideas and are meant to show how these things that are not alike in most aspects are alike in a specific quality or characteristic.

Metaphorical Message: An Example

Susan is a young woman in college and has recently begun to date again following a bad end to a longer-term relationship. Approximately a year ago, Susan had been engaged and was planning her wedding when she discovered that her fiancé was seeing other women. Now Susan has significant issues about trusting her judgment. The experience has shaken her faith in men as well.

Susan is attracted to a recent acquaintance, William. She is unsure about whether or not she dares move forward with this dating experience, however. Susan visits an intuitive reader and asks for a channeled message regarding her dating life in general and William in particular.

Susan explains her situation to the reader and asks if Spiritual Helpers can give her a message regarding her concerns. When Susan asks about William, the reader sees a picture of another man in her mind's eye, or her third eye. This is a man the reader knows well; what the reader understands is that the qualities of the man in the reader's acquaintance reflect certain of William's qualities.

The first several descriptors that come into the reader's mind apply to similar characteristics that William possesses. The reader tells Susan what she is seeing about William. Susan now has information she did not previously possess and can decide whether or not she wishes to pursue a relationship with this man.

Messages for Other People

We must first assume that any messages given to us for someone else are theirs and not ours. We must share them with the person in question, but we must be gentle and respectful when imparting our information. Diplomacy is required.

We must also understand that many people may be offended by intrusion into their lives. Perhaps they have not asked for the information; they indicate that they do not want the information nor do they wish to discuss their circumstances. If this is the situation, it is not our business to chase after them and make sure they listen to what we have to say. They have free will and get to make this decision.

Sometimes the person for whom the message is seemingly intended does not share our philosophy and doubts that we have Spiritual Helpers that might want to communicate with us. In this situation, it might be more helpful to bring the issue into the person's consciousness by asking questions, such as: Is your boss a nice person? Do you feel safe where you are living? Or, how is your health these days?

Messages are private and deeply personal and are not ours to share with anyone other than the person for whom the message was intended. If the person who is the subject of the message refuses the message, perhaps the message is, for some reason, ours. Perhaps we have something to learn, give, or avoid by having this knowledge. In any event, it is not ours to share with uninvolved people.

Pathways for Receiving Psychic Information

There are various ways in which information is received. Most of us have a primary gift and will begin our channeling efforts through this avenue. However, the more we channel, the more we develop not only our primary gift but the other paths to enlightenment as well.

Intuition is the psychic sixth sense of knowing. It is knowing something without knowing how we know it. It is a recognition or awareness of a truth that is not validated by logical or rational thinking. Indeed, it may be contrary to reason, but we know it to be true nonetheless.

Intuition is acknowledging the still, small voice within us and then honoring it by listening to it. It has been called gut instinct, a hunch, a whim, a suspicion, common sense, or God's voice. Intuition is an instinctual, natural impulse, inclination, or urge. It is an instantaneous perception or assessment.

Intuition links us to the synchronicity of the Universe. It is never wrong. Our interpretation of it might be incorrect, but the information itself is never wrong.

Intuition: An Example

We decide in the spur of the moment to take an alternate route home from our job. We have no logical explanation for our decision; we just feel that we should do it, so we do. When we arrive home, a beloved friend, whom we have not seen for several years, is sitting on our front step. She is just about to give up and leave, but we arrive in the nick of time. It is a delightful reunion, and we have a lovely evening together. Later, we find out that there was a massive traffic jam on our customary route, and we would have missed our friend entirely had we taken the usual way.

Clairsentience

Clairsentience is the psychic sixth sense of clear feeling; it can be a bodily feeling but is most often an emotional feeling. Clairsentience is similar to being a psychic emotional sponge. If we have clairsentient abilities, we soak up the emotions of those who are occupying our space.

Clairsentients are also called empathic, or empaths. Empathic is to be differentiated from empathy in that empathy refers to the very human ability to appreciate and understand the perceptions of another person. Empathic abilities are a higher vibration and are a significant expansion of empathy.

As empaths, we have the ability to feel the energy of others around us. We may knowingly or unknowingly allow those energies to penetrate us, or we may accept energies that do not belong to us. This may include bodily pain, but most frequently, it involves emotions of all kinds, including the lower vibrating emotions, such anger, fear, bitterness, and antipathy.

Indications that we are empathically accepting the energies of someone else are:
- Unexpected and unexplained mood changes
- Confusion and lack of focus

- ➤ Feeling drained of personal energy
- ➤ Unwarranted or phantom pain

Clairsentients are often gifted healers. Feeling another person's emotional energy helps our empathic understanding of what is happening with the person who is being healed. Absorbing the other person's energy does not help them or us, however. Feeling the emotional energy of another is meant to give information only.

It is particularly important for the clairsentient to know about and to use appropriate emotional and spiritual boundaries. This will assist us in protecting ourselves from unwanted emotional energy. It is equally important for us to ground to the earth.

Clairvoyance

Clairvoyance is our psychic sixth sense of clear seeing; it is third-eye seeing. Clairvoyance is the ability to look beyond the known physical world and to see into the unseen worlds. As clairvoyants, we get visual messages from Guides and Angels.

Our clairvoyant ability may include getting visual information from past lives. Or we may get a visual message about what is likely to occur in the future. This information is always based on what is happening in the present moment, and free will allows alteration of the situation. Most often, we get visual information about the energy that is surrounding a situation, person, relationship, or event in the here and now.

Clairvoyants may see still pictures, or we may see little movies. The pictures can represent a literal truth, or the message may be metaphoric. Among things that clairvoyants may see are scenes, words, numbers, symbols, people, animals, colors, or spirits. Third-eye seeing includes seeing chakras and auras. Clairvoyant messages may also appear in dreams.

When doing clairvoyant seeing, we may keep our eyes closed, look off into the distance, or look at a specific object. When looking at an object, we are focusing on a picture in our mind's eye, or in the third eye.

Scrying is a form of clairvoyance that entails seeing an image that is cast upon an object. Clairvoyants may use crystal balls, water, or mirrors to scry; when we do so, we are not getting our information from the object, but rather we are using third-eye seeing that projects the picture onto the object.

Additionally, if we are interested in channeling messages from our Guides and Angels, we can pay attention to what we see in our environment. If we are glancing at written material, what stands out on the page? Do we see repeating numbers, or does a specific animal keep making an appearance for us? Are we seeing a certain color wherever we go? Are other people's license plates giving us a visual message? These may be clairvoyant messages as well.

Clairaudience

Clairaudience is our psychic sixth sense of clear hearing. It is hearing voices that are not audible to other people. Clairaudience is the ability to listen to that which is beyond the known natural or material world and to hear messages from Guides and Angels. Those of us with a clairaudient gift hear sounds that are telepathic and are not of the physical realm.

Clairaudient messages may be literal or metaphoric. Many of us receive clairaudient information through music. If the same phrase of a song continues to repeat in our thoughts, we must listen to the words. When we finally acknowledge the message and think about it, that song phrase will recede. (It may be replaced with another song, but the first song will fade away.)

Sometimes the clairaudient message is in the form of a word, or a set of words. For some of us, a little tingle, a pressure in the head, or a ringing sound is a precursor to a clairaudient message. We are also open to clairaudient messages in that state between sleep and wakefulness.

Automatic writing is a form of clairaudience in that it uses words, symbols, or symbolic pictures and does not come from the conscious thoughts of the writer (see Chapter Ten). It is writing without mental censorship or thoughtfulness. Free association, generated in the subconscious, is an important component of automatic writing.

We must give our attention to that which we hear in our physical environment as well. Audible messages can be from other people, from conversations overheard, and from music, television, or movies. And when we are talking to ourselves, pay attention to who is on the "other end."

Clairgustance

Clairgustance is our psychic sixth sense of taste and/or smell and is clear tasting and/or smelling. It is the ability to perceive the essence of a substance without it being in the physical environment. Clairgustance is often connected with loved ones who have passed.

For instance, although there is nothing in the environment that relates in any way to roses, or to the scent of roses, we suddenly get a robust, and clearly identifiable, olfactory sensation of roses. We smell roses. We are powerfully reminded of Grandma, who always smelled of roses, and who has recently crossed to the World of Spirit. Grandma is making a visit. What have we just been thinking, or doing? Grandma's visit is likely related to our immediate thoughts, feelings, or actions. Or, she may be visiting simply to give us comfort.

How to Increase Psychic Awareness

If we want to increase our psychic awareness, we must address it. An increase in psychic ability may come about without our conscious participation. But if we are truly interested in increasing the gift and making the most of it, we must give it our effort. The following practices will benefit an increase in psychic awareness:

➢ We must make it our intention to develop our gifts. Declare our intention, embrace it, and give it daily attention. We must make it our priority.

➢ We must open our awareness to our physical world: to our thoughts, our interactions with others, and all that surrounds us. We must be vigilant and attentive. We must look, listen, and feel with deliberation.

➢ We should meditate on a regular basis. This helps us get into the energy of altered consciousness and aids us in helping our minds—our thoughts and emotions—take a new direction.

➢ We can keep journals of our experiences and dreams. We can pay attention to recurring themes or symbols and write them down for analysis and future use.

➢ And we must practice, practice, and then practice some more. Finding a group of like-minded individuals who want to practice with us can be particularly helpful.

Astral Travel

Astral Travel is an out-of-body experience, or OBE. Astral Travel is a spiritual experience in which the traveler leaves the physical body and travels in the astral body.

The astral body is an intermediate body that lies between the Soul and the physical body. It is not the same as the aura, or the etheric body. The etheric body is an envelope of life energy, whereas the astral body is aligned with and supported by the physical body.

The traveler goes to the astral planes, higher realms, or parallel spiritual spaces. Astral traveling can transcend time and space. An astral traveler may experience various levels of the astral plane and can observe the astral counterparts of the physical world in which the physical body remains. Astral travelers cannot influence, disturb, or affect objects in the physical world, however.

Astral travel is often associated with near-death experiences or in situations of sleep paralysis. It may be part of a drug experience or take place during surgery or a grave illness. Astral travel can also be achieved in deep meditation or in lucid dreaming.

When we experience astral projection, we are frequently lying down, seemingly awake. We begin to feel heavy, almost paralyzed, and then have a vivid sensation of separating from and rising above the physical body. We float above our body and are able to see the existing space our body continues to occupy.

We then travel into other realms and spaces. We may continue to view our current life or have dream-like experiences in other spiritual spaces. Our Guides and Angels may join us and give us information. We may observe past lives. Wherever we go and whatever we do, rest assured that we will return to our physical bodies.

Psychic Animal Communication

Animal communication involves psychic contact, or telepathic communication, with an animal. Telepathy means communicating mind to mind in a manner that is out of the ordinary. Because animals do not have a comparable vocabulary to our own, this communication is generally transmitted through physical or emotional sensation, pictures, or primal thoughts.

Animal communication is a spiritual contact and occurs through an emotional connection to the animal. It requires a loving and gentle attitude toward the animal, one without condescension or pomposity of any kind. If we bring demeaning qualities into our interaction, it will limit our ability to see the animal in its full potential.

It requires a great deal of practice to talk to the animals. Those of us who are interested in developing this skill should begin in a controlled setting or in a situation where the human companion is able to validate our communication with the animal.

Chapter 8: Divination

- What Is Divination?
  - ❖ The Purpose of Psychic Information
  - ❖ Divination: What We Can Expect
  - ❖ Free Will, Environment, and Personality
  - ❖ Our Journey Is Our Own
  - ❖ Searching for the "Right" Answer
  - ❖ Searching for the "Right" Answer: An Example
- Beginning to Work with Divination
- Psychic Readings
  - ❖ Free Will (Again)
  - ❖ Getting and Giving Information
  - ❖ Readings
    - o Carole
    - o Laura
    - o Diana
    - o Rose
    - o Suzanne
- Tarot Cards
  - ❖ Tarot and Ordinary Playing Cards
  - ❖ Doing a Tarot Card Reading
  - ❖ The Layout
    - o Three-Card Spread
    - o Seven-Card Spread
  - ❖ The Cards
    - o Major Arcana
    - o Minor Arcana: Ace through King
  - ❖ The Suits
    - o Wands
    - o Cups
    - o Swords
    - o Pentacles
- Guidance or Oracle Cards
  - ❖ Deck Designs
- Rune Stones
  - ❖ Rune Stone Meanings
- Pendulums
- I Ching
- A Cautionary Word about Drugs and Alcohol

What Is Divination?

Divination comes from the Latin word *divinatio*, which means "projecting" or "predicting," and from the Latin word *divine*, which means "by divine inspiration." Divination, as we practice it today, is divinely inspired forecasting.

Psychic readings, tarot cards, and other systems of divination give us information regarding energies. What are the energies around the current situation? What are our own energies regarding our hopes and fears in this particular experience? What are the energies of the other people involved in this specific event?

And they also give us information about where those energies are likely to take us, depending on our decisions. For instance, if we choose to continue on our current path, we will have several possible outcomes, but one possibility likely predominates. We may choose to stay the course, or we may choose to make a new direction. Divination systems will tell us the probable result of the decision we might choose to make.

The Purpose of Psychic Information

The purpose of psychic information is to help us decide what we will do. How will we think and feel about our situation? Will we embrace negative thoughts and feelings? Will we release them and move on? Will we attempt to take power over others, or allow them to take power over us? Or will we empower ourselves and make an attempt to reach for the highest thought, the most elevated emotion, and the best behavior?

Divination: What We Can Expect

Generally, we do not get new information. Sometimes we suppress information about ourselves, our environment, or other people; we do not allow it into our conscious mind. If this is the situation, our divination is meant to remind us and bring that suppressed knowledge to the forefront of our consciousness so that we can alter the situation if we choose.

Frequently, the message given is simply a confirmation of what we already suppose or know. The information may verify our fears or validate our hopes. It may reinforce our direction or may challenge us to make a new direction. And it will often give us additional information about probable outcomes.

Sometimes we do not want our relationships and circumstances to be what they are, so we ignore what our Spiritual Helpers tell us. Our Guides and Angels love us and want what is best for us; they know the direction in which our highest good lies. We may rebel against the information, and it is our right to do so. But the information is given nonetheless.

Free Will, Environment, and Personality

Our Spiritual Helpers will never tell us what to do, but they will show us what energies surround a situation so that we have a clearer picture of our options. They might help us see the consequences of our choices, but they will not direct those choices. Information that is given to us is intended to clarify and inform.

Nor should anyone who is doing a reading for us tell us what to do; free will and choice is always ours. We can ask for the reader's opinion, and the reader is free to give it, but it should be made clear that it is an opinion. Readers do not know the wholeness of our lives, and it is for us individually to make our decisions.

We must remember that readers have to interpret what they are seeing, hearing, and feeling. The information must be moved from the psychic brain to the rational brain, so it is imperative that we take this into account when having a reading.

Readers are human beings and will be interpreting the information received through their own personal life experiences, beliefs, values, and attitudes. If the information that we are receiving appears to be skewed in some manner, we must ask questions and discuss our concerns with the reader. We are the ones living our lives and making our decisions; it is imperative that we get the best information possible.

Our environment significantly influences our decisions. Periodically, we may be given information that indicates a challenging or difficult outcome if we decide to stay on the present course. Family, religion, community, and culture may persuade us to continue with the current decisions and on the existing path. This is our right to do, and we must remember that much of what we have brought into the current life comes from past life issues. Perhaps we are meant to meet the challenge so that we can learn or so that we can balance karma.

How we make decisions and what we choose to do will vary considerably depending on our personalities and beliefs about ourselves. For instance, who do we think is the boss of our lives? Do we think we are, or do we think someone or something else is? Do we believe we should follow the rules or make the rules? Are we sensitive to our own hurt feelings, or are we concerned about hurting someone else's feelings? How we express our personalities and what we believe about ourselves will alter how we assess and resolve our issues.

Our Journey Is Our Own

We each have our own journey. We cannot nor should we attempt to control other people; we must take power in our own lives and, essentially, only in our own lives. When we get information through any system of divination, we must make choices about how we are going to manage the information and the situation. What we are going to do? How and when are we going to do it?

Sometimes an action on our part is indicated. We must empower ourselves and change direction. At times, no action is required, but a shift in our attitude is implied. We may need to accept that we do not and should not have control over the situation or over another person. Whatever we do, it remains important that we do it in a respectful manner, both to ourselves and to others.

Searching for the "Right" Answer

Our Spiritual Team is going to tell us what is and not what we want to hear. If we choose to ignore the information, that is our right; that is the choice we have made. We cannot control the message, however. It is what it is.

If we information shop, we may start to get gibberish (and this is particularly true if we are doing our own readings). If we want the answer to be different, so we keep asking the same question, we may start to get transmitted material that does not seem to pertain or is incomplete.

Searching for the "Right" Answer: An Example

I did several readings for Lindsey, a young woman whose passion in life was to have the perfect marriage. Lindsey's Numerological Life Path number was one, which meant that she had incarnated with the intention of learning about individuation and independence.

During her first two readings, what her Spiritual Helpers had to say to her was very different from what she wanted to hear. The message was clear: she was to take care of herself, work, play, see friends, and participate in the multiple opportunities that life had to offer her. Lindsey was having none of it, however, and kept going back to the question of when she could expect the arrival of her perfect mate. She was putting her life on hold while she waited for him.

Although Lindsey had a college education, she was not working and was living at home with her parents. She had friends, but she was not spending much time socializing or playing. She was completely focused on finding the perfect mate and creating the perfect marriage.

Eventually, Lindsey found someone. He was attractive, had good social standing and a good job. He also lived a great distance from Lindsey. She did not allow herself time to get to know him and married very quickly. Lindsey now reports that she is living in a situation that is emotionally and verbally abusive. As is not unusual with these situations, in between the bouts of maltreatment, Lindsey's husband is attentive and romantic.

Interestingly, after Lindsey met her husband, at her third and final reading, all that her Guides and Angels showed us was the attentive, romantic part. Lindsey's Spiritual Helpers had previously reminded her of the agenda she had set for herself prior to her current incarnation. Lindsey was determined to ignore it, as she wanted to see what she wanted to see. After several attempts at enlightenment, her Spiritual Helpers allowed it.

Beginning to Work with Divination

Before beginning any divination work, it is essential that a sacred space is created. It is important to clear ourselves of our own agendas, thoughts, and preconceived ideas as well as the energies of others around us, particularly if we have been doing other readings. We then invite Universal Source Energy to enter our space and help us with our channeling. We express gratitude for that which we are about to receive. I use the prayer as follows:

I create a protected space of perfect love and perfect trust
I clear my mind
I clear my body
I clear my Soul
I clear my Third Eye
White Light is surrounding me
White Light is protecting me
White Light is consuming me
Solving and dissolving all situations for the good of all
My Guides and Angels are with me
I am grateful for the miracles that are happening here and now
I ground to the earth and open to the Light

Psychic information can be received through a variety of systems. Intuitive or psychic readings are a common method. At times, the reader will also use tarot cards or guidance cards, rune stones or crystals, or a pendulum. However, cards, stones, crystals, and pendulums can be used personally and by themselves, without benefit of a reader.

There are many systems of divination, and only a few of them will be discussed here. The systems chosen are the systems we are most likely to encounter in our physical world now. Most of the items or objects are readily available in bookstores or specialty shops.

Psychic Readings

Psychic readings are a unique and valuable way to get information about our situations, our life journey, and ourselves. Psychic information is information that is received from our Spiritual Helpers through channeling. This means that our reader is opening to a flow of energy that vibrates on a higher level and is asking to see, hear, feel, and sense that which is not ordinarily experienced. In simple terms, the psychic reader is asking his or her own Spiritual Helpers to have a conversation with the Spiritual Helpers of someone else so that information and insight can be obtained for and given to them.

This information is *always* about the current energy that surrounds a person or a situation. When a reader tells us what is going to happen in our future, that reader is telling us what will likely occur given the direction in which our choices and decisions appear to be moving.

If the reader is experiencing our energy as inert, static, and motionless regarding the situation or experience, the reader will be giving us future information that takes this into account. Simply stated, we are not ready to take any action at this time nor is anyone else around us looking to make a change.

If the reader is experiencing our energy as shifting and realigning in some manner, it then appears that change is likely. We may be ready to move into a different episode in our personal journey, either through our own actions or the actions of someone or something else.

Most often, the reader sees the current energetic circumstance but sees more than one possible outcome. There will be certain directions that look or feel strongest, however, and there will be particular outcomes that are more likely to be chosen. This will be the focus of the reader's discussion.

Free Will (Again)

Again, free will and choice are in operation. We can alter our own outcomes, but we cannot alter the outcomes of another without their participation and consent. Sometimes we go to readers to get magic answers; we want the reader to tell us that a difficult situation, bad circumstance, or a troubling relationship will correct itself without our participation or intervention. Sometimes it will.

But more often, some change in energy is indicated, and because we are the ones asking for the information, it is likely that we are the ones who want the change, so we must make that alteration. We are then cocreating with the Universe. We are reaching for higher vibration.

Getting and Giving Information

When a reader gets information for someone else, it is the responsibility of the reader to give that information to the person to whom it belongs. After a short period of time, sometimes even minutes later, the reader may forget what has been given. Information that is requested from the Universe for someone else belongs to that person; the reader has no reason to continue to be aware of that which has been delivered.

It is essential that the reader is diplomatic, compassionate, and gentle when delivering psychic insight. This is a sacred interaction, and we are asking our Guides and Angels to attend to us. They are sensitive to our needs and desires and concerned for our well-being. As readers, it is our obligation to attempt to emulate these qualities.

It is also vital that privacy is honored, and that the information is not shared with other people. Again, the information that is given is sacrosanct. It would be morally and ethically incorrect to share it with any person other than the person for whom it was intended.

Readings

Psychic readers may get information through clairvoyance, clairaudience, clairsentience, clairgustance or intuition (see Chapter Seven). Generally, more than one psychic sense is in play during a reading.

Psychic readers are similar but not the same. My own Guides and Angels give me information in a way that I can understand, and the symbols and metaphors, the songs and the sayings, are known to me. My Spiritual Helpers know how I am going to translate the information that is given. They know my personal repertoire of experience, so they draw from that.

The following examples are from my own experience. All names and events are slightly altered to protect the privacy of those for whom I do readings:

Carole

Carole has been seeing her boyfriend for several years. Although she identifies him as a good man, she is feeling dissatisfied with the relationship. She wants her Spiritual Helpers to give her information about this situation. Through clear seeing, or clairvoyance, I see a cup of spicy, hot chai tea, and then, still clairvoyantly, I see the Wheel of Fortune card in a tarot deck. Her Guides and Angels are saying that Carole no longer finds comfort and pleasure in the relationship. The wheel has turned.

My Guides and Angels have given me information in a way that I can understand it. I enjoy chai, and I read the tarot, so I am given pictures that are relevant to my own experience.

She asks if the pizzazz will return to the relationship. I see Carole sitting in the grass and hear, through clairaudience, the words, "watching grass grow under her feet." The message is no. It will be what it is now.

Carole and I discuss her possible options. She can stay—he is, after all, a good man—and she can find excitement in other parts of her life. Or, if she is committed to the idea that her man must enliven her life and stimulate her enthusiasm, she might need to look for a relationship elsewhere.

The choice belongs to Carole. What others might do is irrelevant, and if we were to give advice in this situation, we would be giving it out of our own attitudes and values in the current space and time. Moreover, what we might say at age thirty could be different from what we might say at age sixty.

Laura

Laura does not necessarily want a reading, but her friends think she should have this experience and encourage her to sit down with me. Laura is a skeptic, and for me at least, doubters are harder to read. Skeptics are generally not interested in having their present worldview disturbed and so do not allow access. This is perfectly all right as each of us has our own journey and must do it as we do it.

However, as Laura sat down, her Guides and Angels began to vividly show a past life for her. It is my opinion that Laura's Spiritual Helpers opened a door for her in terms of having a different or expanded spiritual philosophy. She can walk through it if she so desires.

The past life that they show for Laura takes places in New York in the early 1900s. She is a young Irish Catholic girl. Although her culture is not accepted by the larger society, it is a sizeable and close-knit group of people. Laura has very little supervision as she lives with her parents, who both work, and an elderly grandmother, who does not have the energy or interest to oversee Laura's activities. As a result, Laura and her group are free to access first the neighborhood and later the city as they wish.

In this previous life, Laura's immediate group includes several girls of her own age, but the larger group consists of the girls' siblings, both male and female. As stated, this is an Irish Catholic culture, and Catholicism is central to their lives.

This was a good life for Laura, and she longs for the freedom and rich experiences that she had here. Although Laura may or may not embrace the concept of reincarnation, she is interested in this life and asks many questions. She tells me that in the life of the here and now, she loves New York City, has been there many times, and returns as often as she can.

Diana

Diana is a fifty-year-old woman with young adult children. She contacts me due to feelings of vulnerability and depression. Diana is taking medication for the depression and is in therapy, but she would like to know what her Guides and Angels have to say about it.

The first thing that we do is to determine Diana's Numerological Life Path number, which is four. Diana would like to build a strong foundation for her life. And then her Spiritual Helpers show a little cartoon general. His army is out of control. The general tries to force his army to do what he wants them to do, but they will not do it; instead, they do what they want to do.

Because they are showing this as a cartoon, the first message is that the level of seriousness here is extreme for the circumstance, and a certain lightening of the energy is indicated. I know that the general is Diana, and that she is seeing the people around her in a hierarchal manner. She believes herself to be the head or leader of this group, and that they are not doing as she thinks they should be doing.

And then the words "let go and let God," which means, essentially, that she is driving herself to distraction by trying to control and to live the lives of those around her. She wants to make them do what she perceives to be "in their own good" (more words from the Guides and Angels). But her people are pushing against her and want to live in their own fashion.

When they do this, Diana responds by self-criticism, self-shaming, and self-punishment. She feels vulnerable because she cannot control the world around her and is depressed because she defines herself as incompetent and just, plain bad.

Then her Guides and Angels show a little girl on a swing; she is all by herself and tries to swing higher and higher. Because I loved to swing as a little girl and continue to love to swing, this has a certain meaning to me. If Diana wants to move away from feelings of depression and vulnerability, she needs to focus on herself and bring pleasure and joy into her life. She needs to swing higher and higher. She cannot control those around her, and even if they are on a path that she defines as destructive, she cannot do anything about it. And so she is to look to her own life, find joy that is hers alone, and is not connected to this group of people. And she is to swing higher and higher. For me, this means playfully both here on Earth and spiritually.

Rose

Rose is a woman in her mid forties. She has come to me because she is dissatisfied with her life and marriage. She describes her life as "mind-numbingly tedious."

Rose became pregnant when she was seventeen and married the baby's father. They had one child, a daughter, who is now an adult. Rose and her husband helped their daughter with her college expenses, and this young woman is now doing well in all aspects of her life.

Rose is also in therapy. The first thing that her Guides and Angels show us is dollar bills and the words, "a whole lot of money." I ask Rose if she is financially comfortable. She says that yes, indeed she is, and that is one of the problems. Her husband has done well for the family, and even though they had a little baby, Rose worked and helped her husband get through college.

Then her Spiritual Helpers show the little Monopoly money man. Making money is a game to her husband, so I ask what he does to make this money. Rose tells me he is in the financial investment world.

And then they show a flower and an eight, and the eight turns on its side. It remains an eight, but it is fallen. The eight is about money and power and, of course, the flower is Rose. Eight in numerology indicates financial independence and making our own way in the material world. It also represents personal power and the gaining and retaining of that power. Rose's eight has fallen; her relationship to her material world and to her personal power are not in balance and have tipped.

What her Guides and Angels are showing is that Rose will find contentment when she balances that eight and takes charge of her life. She would benefit by taking herself out into the world and finding a passion or a vocation. They are not showing marital issues but rather Rose's own stagnation.

Suzanne

Suzanne and her husband have two female children, both adopted from China, who are now nine and twelve. The problem is with Suzanne's relationship to her father-in-law, Jim. Suzanne wants to talk about this relationship and the restoration of family harmony.

Suzanne's husband's family is large and close, and there are many family gatherings. Suzanne tells me that Jim is a "very nice man," but that he treats her children badly. This is a Caucasian, middle-class family, and all of the family is Caucasian except for Suzanne's girls who are, of course, Chinese.

Jim is a lavish gift-giver with the biological grandchildren but very parsimonious with his adopted grandchildren. It is not unusual for Grandpa to give the other grandchildren many gifts over the Christmas holidays but to give his adopted grandchildren nothing at all.

Additionally, the other children have been taken on vacations and to special events, while the adopted children have not. To make matters worse, he has called them "little Chinks" and laughs, pretending that this is a humorous joke.

Now that the girls are older, they are very aware of the different treatment that they receive within the context of the larger family. Suzanne wants to know what to do or to say to educate Jim. She wants to continue to be a part of this close-knit family.

My Spiritual Helpers show me a person that I knew many years ago. Bob was a bigoted person who believed, beyond doubt, that God's chosen were white, middle class and Protestant. They are showing me Bob, so that I can see that Bob's worldview corresponds to the father-in-law.

Then I see Bob's wife, Lois, who personally sacrificed her own philosophy and well-being over and over to mollify and appease Bob. And so they are showing Lois because her energy is similar to Suzanne's.

I tell Suzanne that Jim is Jim, and that my description of him would not lead with the words "nice man." He is a rigid thinker with fixed ideas about race, ethnicity, religion, and class, and that is not going to change. He has no tolerance or affection for those who are not white, Protestant, and middle class. Nothing she can say will alter this situation.

Jim has many positive qualities. According to Suzanne, he works hard and has made a financially stable life for his family. He is generous with his resources, including within the context of the larger, extended family, with the exception of the two family members for whom he holds prejudice.

Had Suzanne not adopted Chinese children, the family may well have been able to let this sleeping, bigoted dog lie. But she did adopt them and so created a situation that now must be addressed in some manner. No magic words are going to change Jim's worldview. Suzanne's daughters are in harm's way in terms of emotional and psychological development.

Suzanne asks about her husband, and they show me Ward Cleaver. Her husband expects her to set the social, psychological, and emotional direction. He is a good man and will follow where she leads.

They also show me a "Ward Cleaver block party," and so I know that, although no one is currently saying anything about the maltreatment of the girls, Suzanne does have a good bit of potential support within the larger family. I cannot tell Suzanne what she should do, but I can give her the information regarding the energies surrounding this situation.

Tarot Cards

The origin of tarot is shrouded in mystery. The first tarot decks, as we have come to know them, are believed to have made their appearance in Europe in the fourteenth century. These decks were based on the four-suited playing card deck but had an additional twenty-two cards, now called the major arcana. Additionally, we know that decks of numbered cards, considered to be mystical, existed in India and the Far East long before the tarot emerged in Europe.

The tarot deck in use today contains seventy-eight cards. The major arcana have twenty-two cards and contain archetypal images that indicate a

Soul direction. The minor arcana have fifty-six cards and represent the path of the Soul direction through events, people, situations, ideas, and behaviors in the physical world. When doing a reading with the tarot, the major arcana cards show us what the Soul wants. The minor arcana show us the way to attain it.

Tarot gives us information about the energies in the environment around us. It gives us metaphoric images that correlate to emotions, thoughts, philosophies, and physical world influences. Tarot describes patterns and rhythms, harmonies and dissonances with those energies.

Tarot and Ordinary Playing Cards

There are four suits in the minor arcana. They correspond to the playing card deck as we now know it:

- ➤ Wands = Clubs
- ➤ Cups = Hearts
- ➤ Swords = Spades
- ➤ Pentacles = Diamonds

In the tarot deck, there are fourteen cards in each suit, ace through ten, plus four court cards: the Page, the Knight, the Queen, and the King. In the playing card deck, there are thirteen cards, ace through ten, and three court cards: Jack, Queen, and King.

We can do readings with the playing card deck, as the meanings of the ace through the ten are similar, or the same, as they are in the tarot. Although the tarot has four court cards, the energies of the Page and the Knight in the tarot can be combined with the Jack in the playing card deck. If we are using playing cards, however, we lose the major arcana.

Doing a Tarot Reading

There are hundreds of Tarot decks available to us, and when choosing a deck, we must pick one that looks and feels right for us, as there is no one right deck. Many people like the more traditional decks, such as the Rider-Waite deck, while others like historically recreated decks, decks with specific themes, or decks that are simply beautiful. Once we have acquired a deck, we clear it of any negative energies (refer to Chapter Three for clearing techniques).

Reading the books or pamphlets that come with the deck is helpful; this will tell us how the artist interprets the energy of each card. However, it is essential to use our intuitive/psychic interpretation as well. What is our initial reaction to that particular card? What do we feel about the card? What else do we see in the card? Do we hear anything when we have drawn the card? What the card says to you will differ from reading to reading. The placement of the card in the layout is crucial.

When doing tarot readings, be sure that the cards are thoroughly shuffled. Cut the deck, and stack it as desired. If we are doing a reading for someone else, that person can cut and stack the deck.

If we are doing readings for many people, we should clear the deck between readings. This can be done by shuffling the deck and, while doing so, stating that it is your intention to clear the deck (this can be done silently).

Some readers do not like others to touch their decks and want the deck wrapped in silk between uses. I do not have these rules for myself and have not found it to hinder me in any way. However, if others are handling my deck, I do clear it when I regain possession.

As we shuffle, cut, stack, and clear our deck, our Guides and Angels are guiding our hands. I have done hundreds of readings throughout the years. I find that the information provided by the tarot deck is always personal, timely, and relevant.

The Layout

A crucial component to our reading is the layout. We must first choose a layout that complements the questions or concerns that we want addressed. The placement of the card is significant. Is the card going to represent where we are in the present moment? Is the card going to represent future energies? Is the card telling us what to avoid, or what to embrace?

There are many simple layouts that are generally perfectly adequate for our inquiry. The three-card layout is one of them. Be sure to identify what each card will mean in each position *before* starting the reading, and be sure to carefully frame the query.

There are countless ways in which we can use the three-card spread. There is no correct method. We can and must create personal questions based on our individual issues. What questions do we want answered?

The following are various uses for the three-card layout:

➢ *Daily Reading:*
1) What are the energetic aspects of the coming day?
2) What should be embraced?
3) What might create difficulty?

➤ *Past, Present, Future Reading:*
1) What was the operational energy in the past regarding (name issue)?
2) What is the current point of manifestation regarding this issue?
3) If I choose this path, where will it likely take me?

➤ *Life Spread:*
1) What direction should I take; what should I embrace?
2) What energies should I welcome into this (name the) relationship?
3) What energies will support me in my current employment?

➤ *Personal Transformation:*
1) What is no longer relevant?
2) What is my point of manifestation for future positive change?
3) What energies should I embrace?

➤ *Relationship Issues:*
1) What is the energy that I bring to the relationship?
2) What is the energy that my partner brings to the relationship?
3) What energy will help us move in a loving direction?

➤ *Current Problem:*
1) What are the energies surrounding my current difficulty?
2) What should I embrace?
3) What should I reject?

There are other, longer, and more complicated spreads. The traditional and most popular perhaps is the Celtic Cross, which is a ten-card spread. We do not need to use layouts that are created by others, however. If the layout or spread does not suit your purposes, create one that does. I personally like a smaller spread, even for more complicated issues.
The following spread is one that I generally use:

Seven-Card Spread

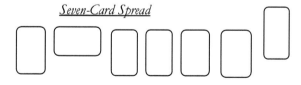

1) What are the current energies surrounding the issue; or what do our Spiritual Helpers wish to address with us today? What is the current atmosphere?
2) What crosses this energy, or what blocks a positive and beneficial flow of energy? What obstacles stand in the way?

175

3) What in the past has contributed to the existing situation?

4) What is the current point of manifestation? What are the possibilities or transformative energies that can come into being?

5) What energies should be welcomed into the life of the here and now?

6) What must be let go?

7) What is the likely result if events and influences continue as indicated?

The Cards

The cards themselves have traditional individual meanings, and it is advantageous to know these meanings. However, we must use our own intuitive/psychic interpretation as well. What we do see? What do we feel?

Some readers shuffle the deck so that some of the cards are reversed or upside down. That is not my practice. I believe the card itself and its position in the layout plus psychic input will tell me what I need to know regarding the energy surrounding the situation. The cards are an energetic indication.

The following are abbreviated meanings of the cards. Each card has multiple meanings and multiple layers within those meanings. Each card has a constructive and an unconstructive expression, depending on the query and the card's placement. For more complete information, please refer to the many resources that devote themselves exclusively to the tarot.

Major Arcana

➢ *The Fool* represents new beginning and endless possibilities; it carries an energy that lives in the moment, is impulsive, unconventional, and unpredictable.

➢ *The Magician* represents discipline and achievement, focus and control; it carries an energy that understands and accomplishes potentials and is able to manifest that which is desired.

➢ *The High Priestess* represents wisdom, intuition, secrets, and mystery; it carries an energy that demands that we look beyond that which is obvious.

➢ *The Empress* represents sensuality, fertility, abundance, and comfort; it is a nurturing, creative energy that is interested in nature, art, and beauty.

➢ *The Emperor* represents stability and responsible leadership; it is a structured, logical energy that often embraces existing dogma, particularly regarding family.

➢ *The Hierophant* represents tradition, convention, and the status quo; it is an energy that embraces acceptance of the world as we know it.

➢ *The Lovers* represent relationships and taking responsibility for choices made within them; it is an energy that desires unity and can be a sensual or romantic energy.

176

➤ *The Chariot* represents the motivation to move forward to victory despite conflict or chaos; it is an energy that embraces self-control and self-protection.

➤ *The Strength Card* represents taking responsibility for your actions and facing reality; it is a compassionate, tolerant energy that desires balance in mind, body, and Soul.

➤ *The Hermit* represents searching the Soul and opening the mind; this is a solitary, often secretive energy that wants knowledge, no matter what the price.

➤ *The Wheel of Fortune* represents an opportunity to change and take a new direction; the energy is unpredictable and uncertain.

➤ *The Justice Card* represents a need to look at truth objectively and to take responsibility for choices made; this energy demands a fair and just outcome.

➤ *The Hanging Man* represents transition, readjustment, and a possible sacrifice; the energy dictates that you do what needs doing, even if others object.

➤ *The Death Card* represents an ending and then the resultant beginning; this energy demands change, as a fear of change can lead to stagnation.

➤ *The Temperance Card* represents perfectly expressed harmony in all things; the energy is diplomatic, cooperative, and moderate.

➤ *The Devil* represents being shackled to unhealthy beliefs and behaviors and the resultant imperfect balance; the energies are obsessive and destructive.

➤ *The Tower* represents unexpected challenges, upheaval, and feelings of oppression; the disruptive energies motivate change, adaptation, and adjustment.

➤ *The Star* represents permission to chart a new course and to realize a dream; the energies are idealistic and visionary.

➤ *The Moon* represents hidden things, self-deception, and losing touch with "reality"; the energy is confusing, and intuition rather than logic is necessary.

➤ *The Sun* represents accomplishment, success, and belief in self; the energies are illuminative and encourage growth.

➤ *The Judgment Card* represents the acceptance of what is, blaming no one; the energies call for reevaluation and revitalization.

➤ *The World* represents accomplishment, completion, and reward; the energies are celebratory and self-confident.

Minor Arcana: Ace through King
➤ *Ace* represents a beginning, a new opportunity, and a new dynamic or fresh vitality; this energy is individual and independent.

➢ *Two* represents balancing within a duality and choices are indicated; this energy is no longer individual as another dynamic has been added.

➢ *Three* represents creativity, growth, and achievement; this energy indicates the combination of two or more dynamics and what has been produced.

➢ *Four* represents structure and stability but can also address issues of stagnation or limitation; this energy embodies the physical world and life on earth.

➢ *Five* represents versatility and diversity; this is an unstable energy that opens opportunity for change.

➢ *Six* represents harmony, cooperation, and communication; this is an idealistic energy that desires equilibrium both in self and in the environment.

➢ *Seven* represents assessment, analysis, reflection, and evaluation; this is often a mystical energy that embraces dreams and illusion.

➢ *Eight* represents action and the power to overcome obstacles; this is an energy filled with movement and desires justice and regeneration.

➢ *Nine* represents bringing something to fruition and the attainment of a goal; the energy is self-confident and courageous.

➢ *Ten* represents completion or the ending and therefore the beginning; its energy seeks understanding and perfection.

➢ *The Page* is light-hearted, eager, and filled with enthusiasm; he is guileless and inexperienced and can be superficial and fickle.

➢ *The Knight* is fearless, energetic, and bold; he is an extremist and can be fanatical and unstable.

➢ *The Queen* is passive, creative, nurturing, generous, and protective; she can be prone to obsessive fixations and behaviors.

➢ *The King* is traditional, powerful, charismatic, and confident; he motivates change, rules his physical world well, but often at the expense of the emotional and psychological.

The Suits

➢ *Wands* are also called rods, staves, staffs, batons, or scepters. This suit embodies new life and vitality and is about creation, passion, inspiration, and initiative. Wands in the constructive expression represent vision and energy and the will to achieve; in the unconstructive expression, they represent restlessness, impulsiveness, and irresponsibility.

➢ *Cups* are also called chalices. This suit embodies relationships, emotion, association, and love and often embraces the idealistic and the romantic. Cups in the constructive expression seek out loving, secure connections within self and with others; in the unconstructive expression, they represent emotional obsession at one end to emotional detachment on the other, either within relationship or within the self.

➢ *Swords* are generally called swords. This suit embodies intellect—the manner in which we think and how we communicate—information, and our philosophies and ideas. In a constructive expression, swords represent a balance between our thinking minds, our intuition, and our feelings; it can also be validation for our current thoughts and ideas. In an unconstructive expression, we rely solely on our rational, logical mind and ignore other avenues of information gathering; it can also indicate that we need to look at our current worldview.

➢ *Pentacles* are also called coins, discs, or stones. This suit embodies Earth, our physical world, material resources, and money; it describes the tangible and the "real." In a constructive expression, pentacles represent a balanced approach to the material world and so a desire to obtain success, status, and wealth without making that the only passion; an unconstructive expression indicates a fixation or obsession with all that is represented by the pentacle.

Guidance or Oracle Cards

Guidance or oracle cards are not tarot cards. Each deck usually has between thirty and sixty cards, as opposed to the tarot deck, which always has seventy-eight cards. Guidance cards as a general rule are not organized by suits or numbers and do not have a major arcana and a minor arcana. They are cards with a positive, life-affirming message and can be used for a variety of purposes.

Guidance cards can be used for daily affirmations or daily messages from our Spiritual Helpers. They can be used in meditation so that we can expand our awareness and understanding of the concepts represented on the card. They can be used for answering questions and for divination.

Each card in the deck has a specific theme, such as "assertiveness," "life purpose," "individuality," "emotional healing," "listening," "wisdom," or "money matters." Each deck generally has a book that gives us details about that card and amplifies and explains the meanings of the particular cards.

If we are using the cards for a daily message, daily affirmation, or for meditation, shuffle the deck, cut the deck if desired, and pull a card. If we are using the deck for answering a question, pose the question, shuffle the deck, cut the deck if desired, and pull a card. Clear the deck between each reading; we can do so by intention and by shuffling our deck. Our Guides and Angels guide our hand and give us the card that is the most useful to us at that particular moment.

If we are using guidance cards for divination or want more detailed information than one card can provide, we must first choose a layout, remembering that the placement of each card is significant. All of the guidance card books with which I am familiar give suggestions and examples for layouts. However, the three-card layout is a good, all-purpose layout. Be sure to identify, however, what each card will mean in each particular position before starting the reading, and be sure to carefully frame the query.

Oracle or guidance cards are easy to use, and there are hundreds of decks available. We must choose one that looks and feels right for us, keeping in mind that we always want to work with the constructive, encouraging, and beneficial, as there are decks that play with the darker energy. We are, however, looking for spiritual enlightenment, personal healing, and expanded knowledge of the self, and so we want to work with the energies that support that particular quest.

Deck Designs include the following:

- *Ascended Masters*
- *Astrology*
- *Angels*
- *Art*
- *Animals*
- *Birds*
- *Bible*
- *Crystals*
- *Color*
- *Celestial Wisdom*
- *Dragons*
- *Egyptian*
- *Faeries*
- *Goddesses*
- *Greek*
- *Guides*
- *Gypsy*
- *Feng Shui*
- *Flowers*
- *I Ching*
- *Kabbalah*
- *Mermaids*
- *Mother Teresa*
- *Native American*
- *Saints*
- *Seashells*
- *Spiritual Archetypes*
- *Trees*
- *Unicorns*
- *Universal Wisdom*
- *Wise Woman*

Rune Stones

The origin of the runes is unknown, but the earliest known runic inscriptions date from approximately 150 CE; however, the runic system may have been in full use as early as 200 BCE. Based on the historical record, it appears that they were in abundant use in the Scandinavian and Germanic cultures early in the Common Era; from here they spread to the Celtic and Anglo-Saxon cultures.

Each of the twenty-four runic characters has a phonetic value, or specific sound, as they represent a system of communication. However, the runes are also based in cultural myth; they represent a concept and have a specific esoteric meaning.

Runes were used for communication, but they were also used for divination. In all cultures in which they were employed, the very name rune (rún or rúna) means "secret" or "mystery." Runes are magical alphabets.

The Elder Futhark is the oldest known runic alphabet. The literal translation of the characters was lost until the mid 1880s, when Sophus Bugge was able to decipher the meanings. Sophus Bugge lived between 1833 and 1907. He was Norwegian, and a language specialist who studied runic inscription and Norse philosophy.

In Scandinavia, the Elder Futhark evolved into the Younger Futhark, which was in use until "modern" times. As the runic system moved across Europe, it evolved still further and within the Anglo-Saxon cultures was known as the Anglo-Saxon Futhorc.

Rune stones, as we now know them, are based in the Elder Futhark and are currently used solely for divination, spiritual communication, and guidance. Each individual character is painted on a stone or a piece of glass, or carved into wood. Each character has an association with something of the earth or with the everyday lives of our ancestors and has a specific, esoteric meaning.

As with tarot, there are many possible layouts, including the daily message, the three-stone layout, the seven-stone layout, and numerous additional combinations. Rune stones generally come with a book that suggests layouts; however, as with tarot or oracle cards, we can certainly devise our own arrangements to meet our individual needs.

The following are abbreviated meanings of the runes. Each rune has multiple meanings and multiple layers within those meanings. For more complete information, please refer to one of the many resources that devote themselves exclusively to the rune stones.

Rune Stone Meanings

➤ ᚠ *Fehu: "cattle."* Fehu energy represents possessions, fortune, prosperity, or riches. It suggests a need to find fulfillment within our lives and to examine our ability to be grateful for that which we have received.

➤ ᚢ *Uruz: "bison."* Uruz energy represents physical and emotional power, vital strength, health, and wisdom. It suggests a need to examine that which no longer serves us and the attendant strength to release it so that we can move toward health.

➢ ᚦ *Thurisaz: "thorn."* Thurisaz energy represents complications, conflicts, defensive strategy, and a will to act. It is a gateway or bridging energy and suggests a need to examine and resolve old conflicts so that peace may prevail.

➢ ᚨ *Ansuz: "mouth."* Ansuz energy represents receiving knowledge and conveying information; it represents signs and signals, a willingness to pay attention to them, and faith in Universal guidance. It suggests a need to acknowledge information and to act.

➢ ᚱ *Ráido: "wagon."* Ráido energy represents a wheel, a chariot, and a journey; this energy can be physical travel, travel through life, or the Soul's journey throughout its incarnations. It suggests a need to allow Spirit to guide us through our journeys.

➢ ᚲ *Kaunaz: "torch."* Kaunaz energy represents fire, or controlled energy; it signifies a desire and resolve to generate, regenerate, and to transform. It suggests a need to look at that which must be finished or "burned away" so that the new may enter.

➢ ᚷ *Gebo: "gift."* Gebo energy represents gifts, generosity, hospitality, connectedness, exchanges, and, perhaps, a sacrifice. It suggests a need for self-approval; the more we are able to recognize ourselves, the greater will be our ability to acknowledge others.

➢ ᚹ *Wunjo: "joy."* Wunjo energy represents harmony, pleasure, delight, hope, well-being, and camaraderie. It suggests a need to acknowledge the principle that joy is our birthright, and it gives us a tacit blessing to pursue abundance.

➢ ᚺ *Hagalaz: "hail."* Hagalaz energy represents uncontrolled forces in nature and in the self; it involves disruption but with protection and brings us to evolution and completion. It suggests a need to acknowledge the stormy energy that forces change in situations that need it.

➢ ᚾ *Nauthiz: "need."* Nauthiz energy represents hardship and lessons, restrictions, constraints, and deliverance. It suggests a need to examine, dispassionately, the shadow side of the self and of life and to release that which cannot be resolved.

➢ ᛁ *Isa: "ice."* Isa energy represents a standstill, a psychological block, or being frozen in place. It suggests a need to concentrate intellectually. It is also an intuitive energy that demands silence so that we can listen to the "still, small voice" within.

➢ ᛃ *Jera: "harvest."* Jera energy represents rewards for previous efforts; it signifies completion, realization, and cyclical prosperity, or a good year. It suggests a need to hold onto our dreams, hopes, and plans so that they can come to fruition.

➤ ᚾ _Eihwaz: "yew tree."_ Eihwaz energy represents defense and the power and will to avert disaster; it is a driving force to endure and to acquire. It suggests the need to see the challenge realistically and then to prepare to overcome it.

➤ ᚲ _Perthro: "casting lots."_ Perthro energy represents mystery and the initiation into secret matters; it helps us see the complex workings of cause and effect. It suggests that we invite Spirit into our lives and allow it to move us to act in our highest good.

➤ ᛉ _Algiz: "elk."_ Algiz energy represents protecting and sheltering our loved ones and ourselves; the antler represents the connection between us and God. It inspires us to ask our Spiritual Helpers to envelop all those we love in radiant energy.

➤ ᛋ _Sowulu: "sun."_ Sowulu energy represents wholeness, the life force, guidance, good circumstances, and future success. It suggests a need to accept and be grateful for our current blessings and for blessings yet to come.

➤ ᛏ _Teiwaz: "sky god."_ Teiwaz energy is warrior energy and represents victory but within the context of justice; it signifies triumph but with an honorable approach to that which has been defeated. It suggests possible self-sacrifice.

➤ ᛒ _Berkana: "birch tree."_ Berkana energy represents birth, growth, new life, and fertility; it is an Earth Mother or Goddess energy. It suggests a need to examine issues of personal growth, creativity, and self-expression.

➤ ᛗ _Ehwaz: "two horses."_ Ehwaz energy represents movement and travel, both in the physical world and in the Spiritual realm; it also signifies harmonious duality, trust, and loyalty. It suggests advancement and progress in partnerships of all kinds.

➤ ᛗ _Mannaz: "humans."_ Mannaz energy is a humanitarian energy that represents the Divine link between humanity and God; it signifies the human race. It suggests a need to use the gift of ourselves to initiate that which will serve the greater good.

➤ ᛚ _Laguz: "water."_ Laguz energy represents life's flow, the primordial waters, vital power, and growth; it signifies our passage to and from life, to and from Source energy. It suggests a Divine Plan and encourages us to release our attachment to outcomes.

➤ ◇ _Inguz: "fertility."_ Inguz energy represents potential, new beginnings, and gestation; it signifies conception and development. It suggests that we have patience and allow that which we have imagined and created to grow in its own time and at its own pace.

➤ ✕ _Dagaz: "day."_ Dagaz energy represents lucidity, light, illumination; it implies that clarity, perceptibility, and visibility will follow periods of darkness or unknowing. It suggests a new day and the ability to move forward with certainty.

➤ ⋈ _Othila: "ancestral."_ Othila energy represents the ancestral home and our predecessors; it is that which we inherit. It suggests a need to look at what has been passed down and determine its further usefulness.

Pendulums

Pendulums are weighted objects, generally crystals, that are suspended from a chain or a cord and are used for divination. Pendulums are personal, and although we can use them for divination for others, they are frequently used for divination for ourselves. As a result, a certain amount of care should be taken with our Pendulum.

We must pick our Pendulums with thoughtful consideration, giving our attention to how it looks but also to how it feels. What is the crystal in use and is it compatible with our needs and desires? Some of us require a crystal that has more grounded energy, while others prefer one with a more substantial spiritual reach (see Chapter Nine for a discussion of crystals and their meanings).

Once we have chosen our Pendulum, it should be cleared in some way. The most important part of clearing, of course, is always intention (for other clearing techniques, however, please refer to Chapter Three). After our Pendulum is cleared, we should sit quietly and hold it in the palm of our hand so that our Pendulum becomes ours and takes on our energetic vibration.

When we use the pendulum, we use our dominant hand; the chain or cord is then wrapped around our index finger but allowed to swing freely. Stabalize the chain or cord with the remaining fingers.

Next we have to determine direction. This is not only personal, it can change over time. When asking yes and no questions, pose questions to the pendulum in which the answer is known to you. This will determine direction. I generally start with saying things like, "My name is Connie," or "My dog's name is Sadie" to determine how "yes" will be presented today. Does the Pendulum swing from side to side, or backward and forward? And then I ask questions in which the answer is "no" to be sure we are synchronizing.

For me, when the Pendulum goes around in circles, it means that no answer will be given today or that we are still in the journey and the outcome is yet to be determined. Sometimes it takes time for the Pendulum to get active. Be patient, watch, and eventually you will get movement.

Now we are ready for divination. We must relax and allow the Pendulum to move as it will and not as we desire; we must let go of our expectations and agendas and prepare ourselves for Universal input. It is essential to bring sincerity and intent into our effort. If we are frivolous, we will get frivolous answers. If we do not like the answers and ask the same questions over and over, we will begin to get gibberish.

We must carefully frame the questions and must not ask that for which we are not willing to receive the answer. Be prepared to explore the answer by precise structuring of additional questions. Generally, one question is not enough, particularily with the "yes and no" method. After each question, ask the Pendulum to stop; I generally simply say, "Stop, please." Wait until it is still before proceeding with other questions.

We must apply our intuition when using the Pendulum; if we do not think that the information is accurate, additional questions should be asked. It is helpful to write down the questions and answers and to keep a journal.

Although it is perfectly all right to stand by the "yes and no" method with the Pendulum, there are other ways in which it can be used. Alphabet charts or wheels can be created so that the Pendulum is able to spell out words. Although somewhat time consuming, this can provide valuable information.

However, I prefer creating wheels that allow the use of metaphoric and/or symbolic constructs in combination with psychic, intuitive interpretation. There are the obvious themes for the wheel, such as astrology with planets, signs, and houses, or numerology and number meanings. Color charts with color meanings can be used or a selection of tarot cards and their meanings. We can also use Angels, animals, trees, flowers, herbs, aromas, and just about anything else that might resonate with us.

We can put a smaller or a larger number of objects on our wheel. If we are creating wheels, however, it is important to have a key of some sort so that we know what the number, animal, or Angel means. Then we can ask for energy surrounding the situation that, combined with intuitive interpretation, will furnish us with a richness that a simple "yes" or "no" will not provide.

When using a wheel, we begin with our Pendulum poised above the center point in the circle. We ask the question, and allow the Pendulum to go as it will.

I Ching

The I Ching is a form of divination in that it gives us information regarding the direction in which we are to search. The I Ching has been in existence for thousands of years and was initially developed as a guide for understanding the workings of the Universe.

There are sixty-four hexagrams, and they are composed of combinations of six stacked horizontal lines. Each line has either yang energy (an unbroken line) or yin energy (a line with a gap in the middle). Each hexagram has a specific meaning.

The hexagram arrangements that are to be used in divination are determined by the throwing of three I Ching coins. The coins have a heads side (yang) and a tails side (yin). Once the hexagrams are determined, we must consult the *Book of Changes* for the explanation and description of the energy.

The *Book of Changes* gives us information on the sixty-four hexagrams. The hexagrams explain concepts such as "innocence," "reduction," "people in the home," "return," "advance," "humility," "happiness," and "observing." The general assessment of the concept is given as well as images that will assist us in further understanding it. And then the principles of the yin and the yang of the concept are explored.

The purpose of I Ching is to help us see how a person of wisdom would resonate to the yin and yang energies in particular circumstances or situations. Yin and yang are abstract terms that do not mean simply male and female but rather refer to qualities such as flexibility or resolve, passivity or activity, stagnation or movement, sorrow or joy.

The I Ching came to the Western part of the planet in the nineteenth century and requires a reflective, introspective patience to be understood. The language of the I Ching or the *Book of Changes* is ambiguous, intangible, metaphorical, allegorical, and symbolic. It is a journey into our personal psychology and challenges us to be better, wiser people within the context of the I Ching concepts.

A Cautionary Word about Drugs and Alcohol

It has been my observation that drugs and alcohol often thin the veils between the physical world and the world of spirit. Drugs and alcohol may disrupt the boundaries in time and space and make those boundaries more permeable. The energies of our past lives along with the histories in our current life appear to be a bit more readily available. The emotions surrounding this historic or past life energy are relatively likely to be genuine (although not always).

However, as we all know, judgment is impaired when people are using. This means that the logical mind is not operating at good capacity and is liable to make incorrect assessment of what is being experienced through the psychic senses. As stated earlier, when doing psychic work, both the psychic brain and the rational brain must work together.

Additionally, using drugs and alcohol also invites negative or lower vibrating energies. If we are attracting entities of lower vibration, we most definitely cannot trust the message. It is always a good idea to create a protected space when involved with divination, and a clear head is essential for setting our intentions.

Chapter 9: Messages, Signs, and Totems

- Communication
  - ❖ What Is a Sign?
  - ❖ Literal Signs
  - ❖ Metaphoric Signs
  - ❖ How Do We Know the Message Is Ours?
  - ❖ Noticing Our Signs and Interpreting Our Messages
    - o Repeating Signs
    - o Signs in Patterns and Combinations
    - o Signs: Where to Find Them
    - o Signs and Our Emotions and Thoughts
  - ❖ Communication: Control and the Search for the "Right" Message
- Totems
- Signs and Totems
- Communication from the Unconscious: Dreams and Writing
  - ❖ Dreams
  - ❖ Lucid Dreams
  - ❖ Automatic Writing
- Collective Metaphoric Meanings
  - ❖ A Brief Summary of Colors
  - ❖ A Brief Summary of Numbers
  - ❖ Animals
  - ❖ Crystals and Gemstones
  - ❖ Trees, Flowers, Herbs, and Plants
  - ❖ Mushrooms
  - ❖ Seashells and Sea Creatures
  - ❖ Symbols

Communication

Our Guides' and Angels' primary function is to help us grow into a higher spiritual vibration. We are human beings living in a human experience, and what happens in our daily lives is important. It is through our individual and collective journeys as human beings that we expand our repertoire of experience and learn to reach for higher vibration. As a result, our Spiritual Helpers are constantly available to us.

Whether or not we wish to acknowledge it consciously, we do recognize the presence of our Spiritual Helpers on a subconscious level. However, the more we open our conscious awareness to Spiritual communication, the more we can maximize our well-being and growth.

Communication from our Spiritual Helpers may guide, reassure, remind, or warn us. Our Spiritual Team may give new information, or they may expand on an issue with which we are currently struggling. Communication may confirm that something or someone is in service to our greater good, or it may warn us that something or someone compromises our well-being and may cause harm.

Our Spiritual Helpers may validate that we are on the best path for our ultimate good, or they may caution us to examine the direction in which we are going. They can support our resolve to continue on the existing path, or they can help us take a new direction, if this is what is indicated. Ultimately, their guidance helps us sustain our overall well-being.

Guides and Angels communicate with us every day of our lives. They transmit messages through various avenues. One manner of communication is through channeled messages, either through our own means or by way of someone else (see Chapter Seven). Another method of communication is through signs.

What Is a Sign?

Signs are messages from our Guides and Angels. Signs are a part of our lives, and we are regularly shown them. Psychic abilities are not necessary for us to interpret our signs. We do need to be attentive and aware, however.

Signs are messages that are conveyed to us through things, animals, or people that we encounter in our physical environment. Signs can come in a variety of expressions or arrangements, but they generally come from something we would expect to see, hear, or experience in our natural or material world.

We can ask for signs. If we are unsure about a person, an event, or a situation in our life, we can ask that we be shown a sign to help us understand the direction or action we should take.

Often our Spiritual Helpers give us signs without our deliberate or conscious request. This does not mean that we do not want the sign but rather that we want it on a Soul level yet perhaps not necessarily on a personality level. However, our Guides and Angels know our Soul's path and will help us stay on it.

Literal Signs

Signs can be literal. For instance, we might be experiencing self-doubt and see a vanity license plate that says, "BTru2U." Or we might be wondering if we should go forward with a certain decision, and then, while we are standing in the grocery line, we overhear someone loudly and forcefully say, "Yes, that is what you should do," just at the moment we are pondering the question. These are literal messages.

Or, while driving our car, we might be wondering if we should go ahead with a certain action. We notice that we are getting all green lights. This is a literal message. Our Guides and Angels are giving us the green light. We can go ahead if we so desire.

Metaphoric Signs

Many signs are metaphoric; they are symbols that are meant to show an analogy between something that we are observing, hearing, or experiencing to something else. Metaphoric signs are more common and plentiful than literal signs. They require more effort both to observe and to interpret.

Many metaphoric signs are personal. If something has always had a certain meaning and significance to us, we must not reject our personal definition. Our Guides and Angels will communicate with us in a way that we can understand. They know what we know, and they know what we believe about a person, an animal, a plant, or a thing. Our Spiritual Team knows our current information base and our present repertoire of experience. They make every effort to talk to us in a way that we can understand.

Guides and Angels may, however, challenge our growth by showing us things that we do not yet know. If the meaning is not special to us, we must do our research. Many metaphoric signs have a general and/or collective meaning. There is a great deal of information about the symbolism of colors, animals, numbers, rocks, and crystals.

We can discover the widespread and commonly held belief and determine whether or not it pertains to us.

In this chapter, I have included certain brief metaphoric descriptions. Additionally, there are numerous books available to us and of course there is the Internet. Additionally, we should not be reluctant to ask others who might be able to enlighten us.

At times, we may be uncertain about whether or not the message is meant for us. If this is so, we can ask that the message be given to us again in a different way—in a way that we can understand.

Remember that our Spiritual Helpers are giving us information about the energy that surrounds a person, place, or circumstance. They are always willing to try again if our own effort to understand is sincere.

We must pay attention to the power of the sign. How big a presence does it have in our attention? Our intuition will help us know whether or not we should notice this sign and its corresponding message.

Noticing Our Signs and Interpreting Our Messages

Signs will often repeat themselves. They may present themselves in the same expressions but in different areas. Or they may present themselves in distinctive combinations or patterns that seem dissimilar yet metaphorically mean a similar thing.

Repeating Signs

Often, signs will repeat. For instance, we begin seeing cows everywhere we look. We go for a drive and have to stop because a herd of cattle is crossing the road. We go home, turn on the TV, and an advertisement featuring a cow catches our eye. For some unknown reason, our coworker four cubicles down makes mooing sounds the next day at work. Our Spiritual Helpers are repeatedly giving a metaphorical message involving a cow. What is the collective metaphoric meaning of a cow? Perhaps we need to slow down and ruminate on something. Are we rushing headlong into a situation without stopping for thought?

Or perhaps we are being encouraged to think differently about an issue that is a currently troublesome. It might be that we are having strong emotions about this situation; we are not using our powers of analysis and logic but have let our emotional agitation interfere with decision-making. On daily walks, we repeatedly find little agates. Agates carry grounding, stabilizing energy. The message is to ground ourselves and center our attention; stabilize ourselves. Use the rational mind. We are scattering our energies by focusing on how we feel and not turning our thoughts to the problem and how to solve it.

Signs in Patterns and Combinations

We may get messages in patterns and combinations. For instance, we might see a movie in which the theme is finding ourselves through joyfully embracing the totality of our lives. Our attention is then called to the number three, and we see it over and over again in various places and in various combinations. And now we notice that we are constantly seeing hummingbirds. The movie, the number three, and the hummingbirds are read together. The movie addresses joy, the number three represents joy and creativity, and the hummingbird represents joy and the good things that are available in life. The message is about joy and our ability to bring sweetness into our lives if we are creative.

We might be suddenly drawn to yellow daffodils. Not only do we want to be near the actual flower, we are drawn to pictures of yellow daffodils. Yellow is the color of conviviality, friendliness, and sharing; it is an optimistic color that inspires warmth and pleasure. Daffodils are affable flowers and indicate graciousness and congeniality. This message is about our social life. Are we having fun and getting together with friends, or are we too busy taking care of our tasks and responsibilities?

Signs: Where to Find Them

Messages can come from conversations that we have with others or conversations overheard. They may come from the printed word; we may find them in books, on posters, or in advertisements. We may read an article that, although it is intended for many, is surely intended for us. They may come from artwork, movies, or music.

Messages may come from real things in our physical world. They can come to us through colors, numbers, animals, rocks and crystals, plants, or seashells. They may come from seeing people who remind us of other people.

Signs and Our Emotions and Thoughts

Our thoughts and feelings will also give us information about our signs and messages. We recognize the sign and then we interpret it through cognitive processes and our base of information. And what do we think and feel about it? Align the thought and the feeling.

What do we think when we see the sign? What thought flashes through the mind? Are we reminded of something else? For instance, when we see hollyhocks, are we reminded of our grandmother, who crossed long ago? And then are we further reminded of a specific incident that took place after we had been in her garden where the hollyhocks grew? What happened? Is something similar happening now? Grandmother might be sending us a loving message and asking that we embrace our similar situation. Or she might be warning us.

What emotions are we feeling? Do we feel peaceful and comfortable, or uncomfortable and anxious? Are we calm and happy, or fearful and angry? The emotions attached to our sign give us invaluable information and help us understand the message.

Align the emotion and the thought. Many things may have happened in and around Grandmother's garden. We must allow our thoughts and memories to inform us of the specific incident. We must feel the emotions regarding the occurrence or event. The combination of thought and emotion will guide us in interpreting our message.

Communication: Control and the Search for the "Right" Message

At times, we do not like the message that we are being given; perhaps it goes against our desires or our perceived needs. And so, although the message has been given, repeated, and delivered in a variety of formats, we continue to pester our Spiritual Team. We want a different answer.

When this happens, our Guides and Angels may remain silent. They stop talking. They might start giving us confusing gibberish so that we cannot make any sense of the message (and indeed, it does not make sense). Sometimes, if we perseverate hard enough and refuse their communication long enough, they may even reflect messages of our desire back to us. We do after all have free will, and if we are going headlong in the "wrong" direction, we get to.

It is sometimes difficult but always critical to remain open to receive the true message. We have free will and can do what we want to do with it. But again, if we do not want the answer, we should not ask the question. It is not the job of our Guides and Angels to serve our requests but rather to give us information that will help get us live our lives and raise our vibration.

Totems

Totems are signs that serve as a distinctive, venerated, and time-honored emblem of a person or group. Totems come from our physical or natural world; they are something that we (or our group) have connected to for the guidance, assistance, support, power, and wisdom that comes from its very essence.

When we think of totems, we often think of animals, particularly mammals. Totems are frequently mammals but can also be birds, reptiles and amphibians, insects and spiders, or fish and other creatures that live in the waters.

Totems can be seashells, or rocks and stones. Totems can come to us from the plant kingdom and can feature any plant including trees, flowers, and herbs. Mushrooms can be totems. There are totem representations that I have not included, but if it comes from the natural world, it is somebody's totem.

Group totems speak to a shared significance, and the totem has a communal collective meaning that may be quite specific to the group. Additionally, these meanings often differ from group to group. Each group defines the collective meaning of their totem.

We all have individual totems as well. Indeed, we may have multiple totems. Our totems can change as we move forward in our journey. As lessons have been learned and experiences have been integrated, vibration has been increased. We are ready for more.

193

As with signs, totems have general or collective meanings. Totem meanings are similar to sign meanings, so the information included later in the chapter applies to both signs and totems. If the collective meaning does not resonate, however, leave it and embrace what is already known.

It may be helpful, however, to research the various meanings given to signs and totems by others, as this can expand our awareness and give us additional information. Again, there are many books, and a great deal has been written on all of the subjects that will be covered in this chapter. Do not hesitate to do additional research, as this is just a cursory examination.

Signs and Totems

Signs generally refer to something that is in the immediate life; they are a shorter-term indicator. Signs may quickly change, alter, and modify as the communication is embraced and understood. Signs can change on a day-to-day basis, and we have thousands of signs throughout the lifetime.

Totems are most often for the longer term and address a life issue. Totems change as well but less frequently. As a life lesson is integrated and the Soul desires something more, the totem can change. Certain totems, however, lend us their power throughout the lifetime.

All creation is made available to us and is given to us in our journey of self-discovery. There is a living wisdom in all that comes from Source Energy, but we must be open to receive it.

Communication from the Unconscious: Dreams and Writing

Dreams

Messages may come through dreams. Everyone dreams; not everyone remembers his or her dreams, but we all dream. Dreams occur in predictable intervals every sixty to ninety minutes. This is so for all human beings and throughout the entire life, from cradle to grave. So again, whether or not we remember our dreams, we dream.

Dreams serve a variety of purposes. Many dreams contain messages that teach us something; they may expand our existing information, or they may give us new information. They may help us process the situations and circumstances of our current lives. We also visit past events and times in our dreams, including past life events and times.

Many of us remember visiting a time, place, or person in our dreams that we do not know from the current life. Yet the dream inspired intense feelings. These can be very pleasant, happy feelings, and we can awake with a longing for that which is no longer in the life. They can also be feelings of terror or rage. If we cannot place these people, times, or events in the current life, they likely came from past life events.

We get messages from our Guides and Angels in our dreams. Dreams about past life issues are the handiwork of our Spiritual Helpers and are meant to help us resolve karma or past life trauma. Our Spiritual Team will send dream messages about issues and concerns in our daily lives as well. If our conscious mind has not been able to allow the message, our Spiritual Helpers may give it to us in a dream.

Sometimes our dreams are recurring dreams, or dreams that repeat. Certain of the details may change, but for the most part, the principal content remains the same. Generally, recurring dreams contain messages that are significant. These dreams repeat so that we are forced to give our attention to them and confront the issues that need to be addressed.

Additionally, loved ones who have crossed find it relatively easy to visit us in our dreams. Sometimes we remember these dreams, and sometimes we do not. But just because we cannot remember the dream or the visit when we awake does not mean that the visit has not happened and that we have not gained something of value as a result.

Dreams are private and subject to personal interpretation. They are personal and unique and often require more than a little thought before they can be understood. We may not comprehend some dreams, particularly repeating dreams, for years.

Sometimes it is difficult to grasp the meaning of our dreams, however, and we would like assistance. There is a vast amount of information available concerning dream symbols and interpretation. This information may be useful, especially if we have no idea what the dream signifies.

Keeping a dream journal will help us understand our dreams. Talking to others may provide insight into the dream or may help us focus on a part of the dream that we have ignored. (Sometimes the dream or parts of the dream are emotionally uncomfortable or even embarrassing, so we want to disregard it. However, that might be the very thing to which we should give our attention).

Lucid Dreams

Lucid dreams are those in which we are aware that we are dreaming. They can occur or begin in two different ways:

➢ The dream starts as a normal, regular dream, and the dreamer, during the course of the dream experience and while remaining asleep, realizes that it is a dream.

➢ The dreamer awakens from the dream but then returns to the dream state with uninterrupted awareness; one moment, the dreamer realizes that he or she are in the waking state, and the next moment, they are back in the dream but now realize that they are dreaming.

Being lucid, or coherent, in a dream is not the same as being in control of the dream. However, the more coherence or rationality we can bring into our dreams, the more likely it is that we can direct their course. If we can direct the course of our dreams, we can ask our Guides and Angels to visit us in the dream state and give us messages that we will remember. We can ask loved ones who have crossed to visit. We can ask for help in processing our daily experiences, or we can ask for information about our daily concerns.

Automatic Writing

Automatic writing is writing that comes to us when we are in an altered state of consciousness. It can come from our Spiritual Helpers, through our intuitive mind, or our subconscious mind. And it can come from loved ones or others who have crossed.

If we are interested in automatic writing, our first step is to relax and move into a calm, meditative state. We can use a pen, pencil, or any writing instrument, or we can use a keyboard. Some prefer a keyboard as the inscription proceeds quickly. Some prefer a writing instrument, as, without it, pictures and symbols are less likely to be created. We must ask for a message and then let it come on its own, without trying to control or force the experience. Often, it takes several attempts to get anything at all.

Once we start writing, we just write. This activity comes from the psychic brain, and when we start reading it and trying to make sense of it, we move into the rational brain and disrupt the flow of information. Automatic writing is spontaneous, unstructured, and unprompted. Sometimes the writer is unaware of what is happening on the page and is in a trance-like state. This is not always so, however, and frequently the writer is very aware and mindful of the experience.

Automatic writing is typically written at a faster pace than is our usual writing; it is often bigger and sprawls across our page. Sometimes the words are joined, unusual spellings may appear, or words that are not commonly used will possibly emerge. At times, pictures and symbols materialize in our writing.

When we are finished and ready to decipher our effort, it is necessary that we inventory our feelings. If we are feeling peaceful and comfortable, we then know that the messages are coming from a source of higher vibration.

If we are feeling anxious or the experience is unnerving in any way, we might want to consider whether or not we wish to proceed. If we have feelings of trepidation or apprehension, we may be in the presence of a lower vibrating energy; this is generally not something that will assist us in our life journey.

Accept and embrace that which is useful. Play with and ponder the material that is interesting or intriguing. Discard the rest.

Collective Metaphoric Meanings

Messages that are given to us through signs and totems have general collective meanings. If the object, animal, or plant does not have a specific individual meaning, it is helpful to look at the collective meaning.

Our Guides and Angels (and Faeries and Star Beings, as well) will send us messages that we can understand. They know if we have access to the collective meanings and will use those objects, animals, plants, or symbols in their communication with us.

Following are certain collective meanings for colors, numbers, animals, crystals, plants, seashells, mushrooms, and certain select symbols.

A Brief Summary of Colors

Colors are easily identifiable and are frequently a significant factor in communication and signs. Color often directs us to a healing issue and sometimes particularly a chakra issue. Color can also help us identify what is needed or wanted in a specific situation or with a certain issue. (Colors were previously discussed in Chapter Two; more detailed information is given there):

  ➤ *Red* is the color of strength, passion, and will.
  ➤ *Orange* is the color of vitality, vigor, warmth, and creativity.
  ➤ *Yellow* is the color of shared experience, optimism, and social ability.
  ➤ *Green* is the color of nature, growth, balance, and healthy change.
  ➤ *Blue* is the color of calm, caring sensitivity.
  ➤ *Indigo* is the color of the seeker.
  ➤ *Violet* is the wisest and most sensitive of colors.
  ➤ *Pink* is the color of unconditional love and compassion.
  ➤ *Brown* is the color grounded to Earth's concerns and is structured and analytical.
  ➤ *Black* is the color of protection and transformation.
  ➤ *White* is the color of purity and truth.
  ➤ *Silver and Gold* are generally associated with the Divine Life Force Energy.

A Brief Summary of Numbers

The numbers one through nine all have universal meaning. These meanings are the basis of numerology. Numbers can be seen almost anywhere, and we can have a particular attachment to a certain number or combination of numbers.

We can notice the numbers on the clock at exactly the same time every day or every night. We can see numbers on road signs and on license plates while driving. Our attention can be drawn to certain numbers on TV or in the movies. Pay attention to patterns, or numbers that repeat.

When we see patterns of numbers, we must look at them individually, but also add them together and reduce them down to a number one through nine. For instance, if we see twenty-three or thirty-two, we look at the individual numbers, two and three, but we also reduce them down: 2+3=5. So each number has its own importance, but the number five is the final destination, so to speak.

The following are the Universal meanings of the numbers (please refer to Numerology in Chapter Ten for a detailed explanation):

  ➤ *One (1)* is about independence, attainment, and individuation; it is about personal will and the courage to be whom and what you are.
  ➤ *Two (2)* is about relationships and cooperation; it is about diplomacy, peacemaking, and adaptability.

➢ *Three (3)* is about the joy of living, creativity, and personal expression; because it is about creation, joy, and manifestation of the self, it is also about sexuality.

➢ *Four (4)* is about work, discipline, construction, and order; it is about the creation of a sound foundation for the life. It is also about constraint and service to others.

➢ *Five (5)* is about progress, change, and the constructive use of freedom; it is also about indulgence or overindulgence in sensuous experiences.

➢ *Six (6)* is about love, responsibility, and balance; it is about service and humanitarianism. It is about taking care of the self in the context of others.

➢ *Seven (7)* is about analyzing and understanding, detachment and wisdom; it is about curiosity and the desire to comprehend the physical world, the metaphysical world, or both.

➢ *Eight (8)* is about power, authority, judgment, and material contentment; it is about achieving balance in the material world and about personal power as opposed to power over others.

➢ *Nine (9)* is about altruism, compassion, selflessness, and forgiveness; it is about a broader understanding of the "Greater Good."

Animals

Animals do not necessarily have universal meaning and can have different meanings for different people. Animals have certain attributes, however, and if the animal does not necessarily have a particular personal meaning, we then must think about what characteristics that animal represents to us.

Or, we can use our resources. There are books as well as tarot or animal guidance cards available for our use. Ted Andrews has done extensive research and has written several books about this subject. His books, as well as his tarot cards, can be found in the New Age section of bookstores.

Angels and Guides can use animals for signs and totems in a variety of ways. We can see an actual animal, see an animal on TV or in the movies, or read about that animal in books. If we are in situations where we are seeing many animals, notice which animal grabs the attention, which animal fascinates, or which animal repels or frightens. Again, pay attention to patterns, or that which repeats.

Animals are complicated creatures with a variety of presentations and habits. All animals have many aspects, qualities, and characteristics and so have multiple meanings. Moreover, they may mean different or additional things to each person. Again, we can trust ourselves to know our own truths, and if we do not have a specific truth regarding any given animal, we can research that animal.

Following are some of the animal meanings that are relevant and useful to me.

Animals as Signs and Totems

➤ *Alligators and Crocodiles* are some of the largest living reptiles. Unlike other reptiles, they are excellent mothers; they help their young hatch from the eggs and carry them to the water and guard them from other predators. They are often thought of as "the Great Mother" and are credited with ancient and elemental creative powers. When they come into our lives, they ask us to nurture and protect all that we have created

➤ *Ants* work in community; they work hard. Perhaps we need to look at our own habits regarding work and community. Are we focusing too much on our individual needs? Are we paying attention to the greater good of the community? Are we doing our part? Are we being lazy?

➤ *Bats* are nocturnal animals; they see particularly well in the night. For human beings, night has long been associated with fear. What are our repressed fears, and how are they affecting our ability to move forward in a healthy direction? Do our fears need to be acutely examined so that we can find our own truth?

➤ *Bears* are very protective of their young. Especially when cubs are involved, bears have the courage to fight if they deem it necessary. Bears hibernate in the winter, living off bodily fat that has been accumulated in the autumn feeding. Are we fiercely protecting that which we have birthed? Are there situations in our lives that we have been avoiding that now require courage to address? Do we need to go deep within and listen to on our own "still, small voice"?

➤ *Bees* are productive little creatures that live in community; they pollinate, fertilize, and then produce honey. Are we being productive? Are we doing our part in our communities, whatever and wherever they are? Are we creating fertile ground for our plans and ideas? Are we enjoying the sweetness in our life?

➤ *Bison* are migratory animals associated with Native Americans and the Old West. Native American cultures hunted the bison. When Native Americans killed the bison, they used the entire carcass in some way; they ate that which was edible and made clothes, tools, and shelters from the rest. European hunters engaged in wholesale slaughter of the bison and often left entire carcasses rotting on the land. Are we fully utilizing that which has been made available to us? Are we grateful for all of the resources in our lives—including our talents and strengths? Are we wasting our time, resources, or energy?

➤ *Blue Jays* are the backyard bullies and will chase other birds away from feeding stations. Are we using our own power appropriately? Is someone bullying us? Are we aware of a situation where someone else is being bullied? Should we help someone discover his or her own power?

➤ *Butterflies and Moths* are creatures that have undergone a process of metamorphosis and have been transformed from one state of being to another. This transformation is profound and occurs on a cellular level. What metamorphosis or transformation is happening, or needs to happen in our lives? Because of the enormity or depth of the transformation, butterflies and moths may represent spiritual or mystical journeying.

➤ *Camels* are feisty animals and can "take the heat"; they can journey for great distances, requiring little water. Do we need to assert ourselves? The journey ahead may be difficult. Should we conserve our resources?

➤ *Cardinals* are self-assured, red birds with a strong call. How strong is our own voice? Are we speaking our truth loudly and clearly?

➤ *Caribou* migrate over three thousand miles in a year. They travel to the northern tundra from their summer feeding grounds so that they can give birth to their young where they are safe from predators. Are we willing to move in a different direction so that we can create? Are we willing to do what we need to do so that we keep our creation safe?

➤ *Cats* are known for their independence, indifference to obedience, and for their distinctive eyes. Do we need to see something more clearly? Do we need to think or act more independently? Certain rules may not be just, moral, or fair; do we need to see them for what they are and address them?

➢ *Caterpillars* become moths or butterflies. Expect transformation in a particular area of the life; there will be a new birth or a new creation of some kind.

➢ *Cheetahs* are known for their speed, flexibility and maneuverability. Do we need to move quickly now? Are we flexible and willing to maneuver?

➢ *Chickadees* are known for their joyful, musical call and for the black cap on their heads. Are we expressing ourselves positively and constructively? Black is the color of protection but also of transformation, so the chickadee's black cap may indicate a need to process our thoughts and make them understandable before we bring them out into the world. Think before speaking.

➢ *Chickens* are fertile creatures that, when able to operate freely and independently, can see the tiniest movement of an insect or find a minuscule speck of grain on the ground. Are we using our senses to discover the details of that which is occurring around us? Are we using this sensory knowledge to feed our inner growth? Are we seizing our opportunities quickly and in a manner that promotes our well-being?

➢ *Condors* rid the environment of that which is lifeless and is no longer useful. They indicate a need to dispose of all that is dangerous to health and a vigorous existence. They signify salvation, deliverance, rebirth, and recovery. Have some of our habits outlived themselves? Are they posing a danger to our well-being?

➢ *Cows* are placid and docile, moving slowly over the landscape as they graze. They chew cud, which is food substance that the cow returns to the mouth from the stomach to chew again. Do we need to slow down and ruminate on the situation?

➢ *Cougars, panthers, mountain lions, or pumas* are stealthy and persistent hunters; they are fierce and solitary. Is it time to go after what it is that we need or want with assertiveness, perhaps even aggression? Is persistence needed? Should we maintain some privacy about that which we are pursuing?

➢ *Coyotes* are legendary in Native American lore. Many Native cultures see the coyote as a trickster or prankster. In much of the coyote myth, the coyote crafts situations so that they look more complex than they in fact are. Are we making a situation more complicated than it is? Are we tricking ourselves into look at the situation unrealistically? Is someone else "pulling the wool over our eyes"?

➢ *Cranes* are birds known for their mating dance and their unique trumpeting call. Cranes mate for life, and when courting, they leap into the air and call to each other. They also have a synchronous unison call that involves complex and specific postures and spatial relationships. Cranes represent connection, love, and trust. Are we in harmony with the ones we love? Are we in harmony with "All That Is"?

➢ *Crickets* are symbols of joy and virtue in certain Chinese cultures; Jiminy Cricket encouraged us to let our conscience be our guide. Jiminy Cricket promoted wishing upon a star as well. Are we following our hearts and being true to our inner voices?

➢ *Crows* are intelligent birds and have been known to discover clever solutions to problems they encounter in their environment. They have a complex language and communicate with each other in ways that are mysterious to those of us who do not understand. Do we need to be clever and use our rational, logical cognitive abilities? Do we need to speak our own truth? What is the transformative, mysterious energy available to us right now?

➢ *Deer* are highly adaptable animals; they have a marvelous ability to be still and perceptive but will leap away from danger. Do we need to be still and perceptive? Do we need to leap away from something? Do we need to adapt something—to make a change somewhere?

➢ *Dogs* are loyal companions and come in a variety of sizes and colors. Who is loyal to us? Are we loyal to ourselves? Are our own loyalties well placed? Are there issues of trustworthiness with someone who may be different from us in some way?

➢ *Dolphins* are playful mammals that live in the water but breathe air. Are we too serious about ourselves? Are we playing enough? Are we drowning in our *emotions*, or are we allowing ourselves room to breathe and think?

➢ *Dragonflies* are marvelous aerialists, moving up or down, backward or forward; they have stunning jewel-like colors. As they move through the air, they often seem the very essence of light itself. Dragonflies remind us to trust the power of Source Energy.

➢ *Ducks* are community oriented, like to have other ducks around them, and will return to areas in which they feel safe and protected. Do we feel safe and protected in our relationships, families, and communities? Are there people close to us who can provide us with physical, psychological, and emotional support and comfort?

➢ *Eagles* represent great power and adaptability. They have exceptional vision and are natural predators. Eagles soar to great heights and are seen as an embodiment of the sun and as messengers from heaven; in this, they symbolize illumination and enlightenment. Are you accepting and expressing your own power, your own visions? Are you prepared to vigorously pursue enlightenment and to adapt to the changes this pursuit is likely to bring to you?

➢ *Elephants* are the largest land animal and represent power and strength. They display affection for each other and are loyal to the herd. Using our own strength and power often requires courage. Are we bravely and appropriately using our powers and strengths? Are we expressing fondness and affection to those we love? Are we demonstrating loyalty to our families and groups?

➤ *Fireflies* are little creatures that light up the night. Are we willing to follow our own light—to chase our hopes and dreams and trust our inspirations?

➤ *Foxes* are particularly skilled at hiding themselves in their surroundings. They have the reputation of being clever and quick. Do we need to be less visible? We are clever and bright; we must use our cunning abilities to facilitate our needs and desires and waste no time!

➤ *Frogs* are highly sensitive to environmental disruption and are a barometer for ecological change; they die back or develop deformities if their environment is toxic. How healthy is our environment? Are we crippling or killing ourselves emotionally, psychologically, or spiritually by participating in something toxic?

➤ *Geese* are known for their migratory behavior, for their calling and their honking. We are being called on a quest. Heed the call.

➤ *Goats* are known for their sure-footedness and their ability to scamper about in rough terrain. Be sure of ourselves; we can undoubtedly manage the emotional, mental, and physical landscape, no matter how difficult it appears at first glance.

➤ *Gorillas* are peaceful and gentle animals that live in large families; they care for each other and show affection. Are we being gentle with those we love? Are we showing the tender care that those we love deserve to have and that we would like to give? Are we discharging our responsibilities to our group?

➤ *Grasshoppers* are capable of tremendous leaps forward. Do we need to thrust ourselves forward with some vigor? Perhaps we are reluctant to take that flying leap as we do not know where we will land.

➤ *Hawks* are raptors with extraordinary vision. Not only are we to open our eyes to all that is around us, but we are to open our psychic eye as well. The hawk represents visionary power and our ability to use it.

➤ *Horses* are noted for graceful movement; they transport people and move goods. We can expect movement or travel in the life. We must be mindful of maintaining our balance as we go forth.

➤ *Hummingbirds* are tiny, beautiful little birds that flit from flower to flower. To many, they are the essence of joy. Is there joy in our life? Is it time to create or embrace joy?

➤ *Iguanas* are some of the largest living lizards. They are tropical herbivores that rely on gut bacteria to digest their food. The newly hatched do not have the bacteria and acquire it by eating adult iguana droppings left by the nest; this prepares them to take their proper place in the iguana world. Iguana warns us that we may have to sort through the waste and wreckage in order to obtain that which has value and discard that which no longer serves.

➤ *Ladybugs* are considered by many to bring good luck.

➤ *Lions* are cats and have a reputation for fierceness, strength, and bravery (hence, the "lion king", or in contradiction, the 'cowardly lion') We are called upon to dare it and do it; call the lion out to lick our hand. We must rely on our own strength, be fierce and brave.

➤ *Moose* are large and seemingly awkward land animals that have the ability to plunge to the very bottom of a lake, stay submerged for up to a minute, and feed on the greens. They are also considered to bring good luck when seen in visions and dreams. Will we take the plunge and go deep into ourselves and into the "mysteries"? Will we allow the moose to bring us mystical, magical gifts? What we find there will nourish us.

➤ *Monkeys and Apes* all use vocalization, body language, and facial expression to communicate; to humans, their communication often seems overstated, with shrill screeching, exaggerated facial expressions, and enthusiastic bodily movements. These animals are not subtle communicators and nor should we be at this time. Are we making ourselves understood? Are our words, facial expressions, and body language in harmony so that we are not giving a mixed message?

➤ *Mice* are sloppy little creatures that leave messes behind wherever they go. They are often fastidious about their own nests, however, and change nests when the nests become unsatisfactory. As a result, they represent fastidiousness and a need for attention to detail. Are we paying meticulous attention to the details in our lives?

➤ *Owls* are historically associated with wisdom and mystery. It is also said that the appearance of the owl announces a visit from a loved one who has crossed. Are we calling on our own psychic abilities, and are we using them wisely?

➤ *Peacocks* are symbols of reincarnation in many cultures. Does our current situation, circumstance, or relationship issue have its roots in a past life imbalance?

➤ *Penguins* are birds that do not fly; instead, they use their wings to swim. Penguins have the unique ability to leap out of the water and land on their feet. As a result, they symbolize the ability to leap out of the body and so represent astral projection and lucid dreaming. Because water corresponds to emotion, penguins also signify the gift of being able to move beyond that which weighs us down emotionally so that we can land on our feet.

➤ *Pigs or Boars* are fierce and territorial animals that will destroy that which is unwanted in the environment; as a result, they can be dangerous to the vulnerable. Are we being too territorial? Are we destroying that which we do not desire without consideration for the vulnerabilities of those around us?

➤ *Rabbits* are creatures that will freeze or flee when danger arrives. Their presence warns us that now is not the time for us to fight, but rather we need to stay still and see what develops. Or, we may need to leave. Rabbits are also known for their procreative tendencies. Are we bringing our own resourceful energies into the world in an appropriate and effective manner?

➢ *Robins* are the harbinger of spring and new growth. We can expect a new beginning or growth in some area.

➢ *Sharks* have incredibly well developed senses and are relentless in the pursuit of their prey. Are we missing things by not using all of our senses? Do we need to be forceful and aggressive in the pursuit of our goals?

➢ *Skunks* are smelly little creatures. Do we need to make a stink and refuse to be unnoticed?

➢ *Snakes* are reptiles that shed their skin and have the ability to move quickly. They represent the shedding of the old and the opportunity for a new beginning. Change may happen quickly, however, and movement on our part might be necessary.

➢ *Spiders* are creatures that weave webs; in legend, they have been said to weave illusion, magic, and destiny. What are we weaving? Are we weaving our destiny? Are we weaving our dreams into reality?

➢ *Squirrels* are particularly known for their autumn gathering in preparation for winter hardships. Are we prepared? Have we husbanded our resources so that we will be able to survive potential hardship?

➢ *Swans* are the largest of the water birds. In the story of the Ugly Duckling, the swan chick is thought to be ugly when assumed to be a duck; however, as the swan matures, it becomes the most beautiful of birds. Swans represent grace, poise, and charm. They also symbolize the inner beauty that increases with maturation.

➢ *Tigers* are sensuous animals with sleek and powerful muscles. In Chinese astrology, the tiger is portrayed as passionate, powerful, and adventurous. The tiger brings new adventures into the life as well as an awakening of the senses. Tiger asks us to take power in our lives and to be prudently mindful of our awakening senses. Embrace our burgeoning sense of adventure.

➢ *Turkeys* are the symbol of Thanksgiving. Are we grateful for the abundance and blessings in our lives? Or are we assuming an attitude of entitlement?

➢ *Turtles* are slow and steady; they remind us to persevere. Through confidence, conviction, and effort, our hard work will be rewarded.

➢ *Walruses* have long, white tusks; they use them to dig for their food but also use them as weapons. Do we need to uncover something hidden? Will this hidden item or object provide sustenance? Or might we need to protect ourselves from that which is currently concealed?

➢ *Whales* are mammals that live in the ocean, are known for their songs and, although they need to breathe air, are able to swim deep into the sea. As a result, whales represent the ability to take our creative constructs to new depths. Furthermore, there is an injunction to sing our own song and to create that which is special and unique to us.

➤ *Wolves* are intelligent, social animals that have a strong sense of loyalty to their group. They live in a hierarchal structure with carefully defined rules and are protective guardians of their young. Are we being loyal to those who deserve our protection? Are we being careful guardians within our group as well as to ourselves? Are we living smart?

➤ *Zebras* are African equids and are in the horse family; they have distinct black and white stripes. As part of the equid family, they represent movement. Black is commonly thought to be the presence of all color, whereas white is the absence of all color; the black and white represents opposites. Zebra asks us to examine the dualities in our emotions, and to let go of fear, anger, and hopelessness and move toward joy and gratitude. It asks us to realize that we are safe and loved.

Crystals and Gemstones

Minerals are a naturally occurring homogeneous solid with a defined chemical composition and a crystalline structure. A gemstone, or stone, is a singular, relatively rare, and precious mineral. A crystal is a mineral in which a collection of atoms is repeated in the same arrangement throughout the entire material. Crystals and stones are appreciated for their density, refraction, and color.

Crystals and stones also have a metaphysical property that comes from their color, shape, and the type or composition of the mineral. Crystals and stones emanate energies that vibrate. These vibrating energies can be used for self-discovery, for healing, and for a more profound connection with the world of Spirit.

Stones and crystals have multiple meanings. They are experienced in much the same way that art and music are experienced. As a result, we may have an individual and unique response to a crystal or a stone. It may have a deep and personal meaning. If the stone does not hold any particular meaning for us, however, we may need to look to someone else's research to help us divine the meaning of its significance.

When we are in the process of choosing our stones and crystals, we must be sure that we are getting our rocks from a reputable source. There are many manmade substitutes that are available to the public, but for healing, self-discovery, or spiritual connection, we generally want to use a naturally occurring rock. We also want a proper identification of our stone and, if possible, its point of origin.

Once we acquire our stone or crystal, we want to clean it and make it our own. Some rocks are friable and crumble easily; some are fragile and readily broken. This means that using water or salt to clean certain rocks will lead to their destruction. There are also some stones that will fade in sunlight. Be sure you know what you have, and clean it accordingly. If in doubt, do your research.

It is usually safe to smudge our rocks. Smudging involves burning plant materials, such as sage, cedar, or sweet grass, or wood, such as palo santo, and passing the smoke over the stone. Use intention while doing so. It is always safe to clean and clear our rocks with intention; release the stone of the energy of others who have owned or handled it and of any negative energy. Purify the stones and crystals by visualizing them surrounded by white light. Then hold them and allow them to attune to your personal energy.

Many of the stones and crystals have more than one color. The structure of the stone is central, but the color of the stone is significant as well. When you are working with stones of different color, give attention to the definition of color and to the chakra correspondence.

Stones can be used for healing, for personal growth and development, and for our journey toward spiritual enlightenment. They are also used as signs and totems.

Following are some of the crystal meanings that are relevant and useful to me:

Crystals and Stones as Signs and Totems

➤ *Agate* is a stabilizing, grounding stone that assists with building self-confidence and improving logical and analytical skills; it also lends courage to the user.

    o Blue Lace Agate is a stone of self-expression and communication; it helps us formulate and clearly articulate our thoughts and feelings.

    o Moss Agate is a stone of emotional stability and peace; it helps us release and heal emotions that are attached to situations that have provoked apprehension, anxiety, or fear. This stone is particularly useful to persons who have addictive behavior patterns.

    o Dendritic Agate encourages attitudes and viewpoints that are based in reality and then the resolve to face the challenges presented. It brings hope of a positive outcome.

    o Fire Agate encourages a brave outlook on life and helps dispel fear. It promotes the concept that life is to be embraced with gusto and assists with passion in all directions, not the least of which is sexual passion.

➤ *Amazonite* promotes a calming peacefulness; it reduces emotional confusion by helping us understand divergent viewpoints and then set appropriate personal boundaries. It improves our ability to perceive Universal truths and to manifest Universal love.

➤ *Amber* is an organic mineral and, strictly speaking, is not a crystal. It is a sunny stone that increases vitality and helps heal sadness and depression. It connects that which we desire on a physical level to our motivation to achieve it; it also connects us to the higher energies and assists us with integrating those energies.

➤ *Amethyst* promotes emotional centering and clarity of mind; it has traditionally been used to overcome addictive behaviors and thought patterns. It calms overactive thoughts, promoting meditation as well as restful sleep. It has a high spiritual vibration that can advance intuitive and psychic abilities and guard against psychic attack.

➤ *Angelite* facilitates contact with our Spiritual Helpers, particularly Angels; it assists us in our journey to obtain Universal truth. It helps us be more compassionate and tolerant with those around us and to speak our truth quietly but consistently. It transforms chaos to harmony and anguish to joy.

➤ *Apatite* is an inspirational stone that encourages serving the highest good of humanity. It is a stone that is open to the future and the past and facilitates our access of information and knowledge for individual as well as collective use.

    ○ Blue Apatite improves psychic awareness.

    ○ Green Apatite opens the heart chakra.

    ○ Gold Apatite facilitates creation and manifestation.

➤ *Aquamarine* was used by ancient sailors as an amulet to protect them from the dangers of the sea. This stone promotes courage and helps us release judgment of others by clarifying our perceptions of their motives and actions, thereby allowing them their own journey while we take responsibility for ours. It is a calming stone that encourages a humanitarian attitude.

➤ *Aventurine* is a stone of prosperity in that it embraces revitalization and transformation; it promotes stable thinking. It encourages forgiveness of both self and others by releasing past perceived injuries. Aventurine supports personal power and pushes against martyr or victim energy; it releases an attachment to the outcome of endeavors while promoting determination and commitment.

➤ *Bloodstone* revitalizes the exhausted, lonely, and disenchanted. It is a good grounding stone while simultaneously connecting us to the Divine; it helps us trust in Universal Source Energy and protects us as we move toward change. It has a transformative quality that assists us in seeing what is the right thing to do and then doing it.

➤ *Calcite* is created in many colors, so each color will affect the function of the stone. It clears negative energy in both the self and the environment. It connects the mind and the emotions, providing a calming effect for both, thereby lending itself to clearer thinking and a reduction of anxiety and nervous tension.

    ○ Clear Calcite is a potent detoxifier that clears energetic blockages.

    ○ Blue Calcite is recuperative; it calms emotions and helps overcome cynicism.

    ○ Green Calcite promotes forgiveness and compassion, helping us release that which no longer serves.

    ○ Gold Calcite assists with meditation and clearer insight to Universal truth.

    ○ Pink Calcite encourages unconditional love; it promotes healing and the release of emotional baggage associated with traumatic experiences.

    ○ Red Calcite increases physical and sexual comfort, as well as overall vitality.

➤ *Carnelian* is a grounding stone and anchors us to the current time and space; it promotes realistic thinking, helps us embrace change, and reduces the apprehension surrounding us when we must make upsetting or alarming decisions. It supports the courage needed to remove ourselves from damaging or abusive situations of any kind.

➤ *Celestite* facilitates the opening of the third eye and the crown chakras; it promotes contact with the angelic realm and invites our Spiritual Helpers into our space. It facilitates feelings of confidence and protection while we work within Divine energies and move toward spiritual enlightenment.

➤ *Chalcedony* absorbs and dissipates negative energies, such as rage, despondency, jealousy, and resentment, and promotes positive energies, such as compassion, joy, generosity, and peace. This stone nurtures the individual and encourages psychic awareness.

➤ *Chiastolite* is a potent protective stone that assists psychic and healing work by preventing psychic attack while promoting spiritual integrity. It alleviates and stabilizes negative thoughts and emotions, dissolves artifice or illusion, and dissipates fears.

➤ *Chrysocolla* governs all aspects of communication, including words, ideas, philosophies, and other sounds, such as music or chanting. It helps reverse destructive and self-defeating emotional agendas and behaviors, such as sarcasm, criticism, and vilification (of self and others). It helps us achieve balance by promoting a positive self-awareness.

➤ *Chrysoprase* is a heart chakra stone and governs love in all of its aspects. It promotes a healthy, non–ego driven love of self. It helps us continue to honor ourselves as we enter into love relationships with others. It elevates our love of nature and of the earth. It advances spiritual love, a love of the Divine, and of truth. It encourages acceptance, hope, and forgiveness and helps those of us who wish to heal abusive or traumatic situations.

➤ *Citrine* is the stone of manifestation and abundance; it stimulates a desire to bring emotional harmony, material bounty, and loving relationships into the life. It encourages us to release old behavior patterns or negative thinking that would prohibit a free flow of beneficial energy. It teaches us that the pleasant, noble, and delightful is our birthright.

➤ *Emerald* is a heart chakra stone that promotes affection, passion, and the love relationships and friendships that are available to us here on Earth. It invites us to experience the love and blessing that is offered to us by Universal Source Energy.

➤ *Fluorite* is a protective stone that deflects psychic manipulation while increasing intuition. It dissipates emotional and psychological incoherence and chaos and helps us organize and center ourselves in these areas. It helps dispel confused thinking patterns, bringing a more constructive application to our thoughts.

➤ *Garnet* comes in several varieties, the most commonly known being red. Red garnet is a root chakra stone and therefore strengthens our instincts, assisting us with courage and the ability to be strong and to survive.

➢ *Hematite* is a grounding stone with protective qualities. It is a root chakra stone that addresses issues of survival by increasing will power, enhancing self-confidence, and promoting concentration. It assists us in triumphing over compulsive tendencies and behaviors and promotes the courage needed to contend with life's challenges.

➢ *Iolite* is a chakra stone that promotes the ability to awaken the third eye chakra. It connects us to Spirit and assists us in seeing, visualizing, or picturing new solutions to old problems. It supports clear thinking and a calm emotional aspect so that we can dispassionately examine life's challenges.

➢ *Iron Pyrite* is a protective stone that blocks negative energies and provides a defensive shield from any lower or harmful vibrations in the area around us.

➢ *Jade* represents wisdom that is acquired through repose and meditation; it is a stone that helps us self-actualize and individuate while realizing that we are spiritual beings living in a human experience.

o Green Jade is a calming stone that promotes health in self and relationships.

o Purple Jade promotes spiritual growth and serenity.

o Red Jade encourages the stabilization of emotional expression.

o Blue Jade promotes calm, clear thinking, and speaking.

o Black Jade is a protective stone that deflects negativity.

➢ *Jasper* is a strong stone that promotes organization, determination, assertiveness, and integrity.

o Red Jasper is a root chakra stone that governs physical strength.

o Orange Jasper is a sacral chakra stone that can help heal sexually negative experiences and promote healthy sexual boundaries.

o Mook Jasper encourages dispassionate examination of old habits and patterns, both personal and ancestral, and promotes the embracing of new experiences.

o Picture Jasper is a stone that honors all that is of the earth and helps us reconnect to our planet's energies. It is also a stone that is in harmony with the akashic record and promotes visualization of past life experiences.

➢ *Kyanite* is a chakra stone of both the throat and the third eye. It assists us in seeing behavior and thought patterns that are self-defeating and then promotes or encourages us to express ourselves in a more honest, integrated manner. It is a spiritually intense stone that intensifies and increases the higher spiritual vibrations.

➢ *Labradorite* is a calming and clarifying stone that assists us in ridding ourselves of psychological, emotional, and past life "junk" that is currently littering our lives. It is an esoteric stone that connects us to the higher realms, assists us in seeing the connectedness in all time and space, and increases our trust in Source Energy and, conjointly, in ourselves.

➤ *Lapis Lazuli* is a chakra stone that stimulates the throat and the third eye chakras. It assists us in speaking our truth clearly, dispassionately, and without compromise. It increases our ability for clear seeing both in the physical world and in the psychic world and helps us integrate our newly observed or perceived truths into our daily lives.

➤ *Malachite* teaches us that all life is choosing, that we cocreate with God and must be responsible for our lives and our choices. It helps us understand that we are not victims or martyrs, but that we have chosen and must now create a responsible direction for ourselves. It encourages self-respect and promotes the construction of healthy psychological, emotional, and physical boundaries.

➤ *Moldavite* has extraterrestrial origins and was formed when a giant meteorite hit Earth in what is now the Czech Republic. It is a stone of exceedingly high vibration. It is a bridge between heaven and earth, so to speak, and greatly enhances and improves our ability to connect to the higher realms. It is not a stone that allows inertia or inaction but will expose that which most needs exposure on all levels, most specifically psychological, emotional, and spiritual. It helps us heal that which has been made known.

➤ *Moonstone* reminds us that all things create themselves in cycles, and that there is a time to plant, a time to nurture that which has been planted, and a time to harvest; everything is in its own time. Moonstone is a chakra stone of the solar plexus and governs emotions, enhancing our ability to acknowledge them and allow them to inform us. It is a stone of the moon and therefore expands and increases intuitive and psychic abilities.

➤ *Obsidian* is a protective stone of great power. It deflects negativity in our environment but reflects back to us our own negative patterns and behaviors. Obsidian shows us our true self.

   o Black Obsidian powerfully reflects back to us the negative aspects of our character so that we may examine, heal, and change old behavior patterns; it also reveals past life concerns that need examination and healing.

   o Snowflake Obsidian reflects back to us our feelings of victimization or martyrdom but with a calm detachment so that we may move into more constructive emotional and behavioral patterns.

   o Mahogany Obsidian increases our sense of our own individual value by reflecting back to us ingrained, negative familial patterns so that they may be dispelled and new emotional and behavioral patterns may be embraced.

   o Rainbow Obsidian reveals past emotional trauma and etheric cording so that we may heal and move into a renewed sense of our Spiritual selves.

- Gold Sheen Obsidian exposes areas in which we are being willful and ego-centered and guides us toward a more balanced expression in which all aspects of self are represented.

➤ *Opal* is a gentle stone that promotes emotional nurturing and grounding. It supports a positive expression of our feelings as well as encourages us to take responsibility for them.

- White Precious Opal amplifies all emotions but promotes the release of negative emotional patterns.
- Black Precious Opal is a powerful stone that amplifies intention, especially as it is attached to potent or intense emotion.
- Fire Opal releases emotional inhibitions and promotes passion, thereby strengthening pleasure; emotional experiences affected by the Fire Opal range from sexual to spiritual.

➤ *Peridot* is a stone of healing and abundance; it teaches us to let go of old hurts and resentments, both in the here and now and in past lives. It asks us to make amends to those we have hurt so that we may move forward with a more joyful expression of our life purpose.

➤ *Pietersite*, also called the "Tempest Stone," grounds us to our etheric body and connects us to our inner voice; it helps us to move through emotional and psychological obstructions and to walk our own path. It promotes the dissolution of encumbrances from past lives that currently hinder us in accessing spiritual truth.

➤ *Quartz* is one of the most plentiful crystals on Earth and is found on every continent. It is thought to be the most potent energy amplifier on the planet, absorbing, organizing, and releasing obstructions in our personal energy and in the energies around us.

- Clear Quartz has the ability to imprint intention and can assist in manifesting goals; it amplifies psychic energy and all emotion.
- Cathedral Quartz holds akashic records.
- Rose Quartz has the gentle, healing energy of unconditional love.
- Smoky Quartz is primarily a grounding or centering stone and can help establish and sustain the energy of the physical body while it aligns with the energies of Universal Light.
- Phantom Quartz has another crystal element embedded within it.
  - Amethyst Phantom helps us remember our Soul's purpose in the current lifetime.
  - Chlorite Phantom helps remove obstructions that impede our Soul's purpose in the current lifetime.
  - Smoky Phantom helps us remember our Soul group's purpose in the current lifetime.

o Rutilated Quartz immerses our own energy in Universal Light. It is the stone of forgiveness and brings joy to the life.

➤ *Rhodochrosite* is a healing stone for emotional, psychological, physical, or sexual trauma. It assists with issues of post-traumatic stress disorder and helps bring joy back into the life.

➤ *Rhodonite* encourages a humanitarian love. It assists in the healing of betrayal and abandonment issues and teaches us that revenge and retaliation are, first and foremost, self-destructive.

➤ *Ruby* is a stone that promotes passion and enthusiasm for life by encouraging the free flow of chi energy throughout the body. This energy is then expressed in a life-affirming manner that supports good health in all directions.

➤ *Sapphire* is a wisdom stone that assists with releasing confusion and bringing peace of mind. It protects us from self-deceptive or catastrophic thinking.

o Blue Sapphire promotes spiritual awareness and encourages us to speak our truth clearly and consistently.

o Green Sapphire is a heart chakra stone that invites loyal and honest friendships and love relationships into the life.

o Yellow Sapphire is a stone of abundance that attracts prosperity; it is also a stone that invigorates the intellect so that all is seen realistically.

o Pink Sapphire is a stone of love and encourages us to forgive others and ourselves for perceived misdeeds.

o White Sapphire is a crown chakra stone that helps open us to the clarity and integrity of Universal Truth.

o Star Sapphire has a five-pointed star in the depths of the stone that indicates an intensification of the energy and an opening of intuition.

➤ *Sardonyx* is a protective stone that helps guard against criminal activity. It intensifies personal vitality and strengthens willpower and self-discipline. This stone invites healthy relationships and promotes stability and joy in connubial relationships.

➤ *Selenite* is an excellent stone for building energy grids, which can be used for spiritual amplification and enlightenment or for protection from outside entities that disturb peace and well-being.

➤ *Serpentine* awakens Kundalini energy, stimulating each chakra from root through crown and thereby opening the path for spiritual enlightenment. (Kundalini is a great reservoir of creative energy, and as it moves through our bodies, our chakras are awakened and our consciousness expanded.)

➤ *Sodalite* is the stone that unites the psychic input of the right-brain with the logical assessment of the left-brain, thereby giving us insight into our attitudinal and behavioral patterns.

➤ *Staurolite* is often called the stone of the Faerie Cross and is said to have been created from the tears of the Faeries when they heard of the death of Jesus of Nazareth. This stone is a talisman that brings good fortune, guards against a tendency to over-commitment or to overwork, and thereby helps relieve stress.

➤ *Steatite (Soapstone)* is a powerful calming stone that promotes positive energy in the environment. It invites the higher vibrations and discourages the lower vibrations. It encourages communication, both sending and receiving, between us and our Angels and Guides. Soapstone helps us broaden our horizons and change with the tides.

➤ *Sugilite* is a powerful protective stone that creates an aura of spiritual light around us. It teaches us to believe in our potentials and helps us understand that we can achieve our dreams.

➤ *Sunstone* is a blessing stone of benevolence and abundance; it provides emotional warmth and encourages self-confidence. It promotes humanitarianism and imparts the leadership abilities needed to bestow blessings on humankind.

➤ *Tiger's Eye* encourages symmetry and assists in balancing polarities or opposites. It helps us to dispassionately see the gifts and talents that are ours to develop and the faults and challenges we might wish to address.

➤ *Topaz* is a stone of good fortune that helps us see ourselves in a loving and multidimensional manner and as we are seen by our Angels and our Guides.

  o Clear Topaz encourages mental clarity and awakens Universal awareness.

  o Blue Topaz is a stone of truth and wisdom, encouraging us to know our own truth and then speak it.

  o Gold Topaz is a stone that asks us to recognize our own talents and aptitudes and then have the will and desire to act upon that information.

➤ *Tourmaline* is a grounding stone that provides a protective shield around the body. It has a strong association with Devic Energy (nature's sacred energy), Earth or Nature energy.

  o Green Tourmaline is a healing stone that promotes vitality.

  o Pink Tourmaline is a stone of unconditional love and encourages faith and trust in love.

  o Red Tourmaline opens our hearts to Universal love and encourages passion in the life.

  o Blue Tourmaline aids psychic awareness and the speaking of our truth.

  o Brown Tourmaline is a grounding stone that helps us love and accept ourselves.

  o Black Tourmaline is a stone of protection and purification.

➢ *Turquoise* is a stone of self-expression, encouraging us to speak our truth. It is a healing stone of wholeness that promotes acceptance of ourselves in our entirety.

➢ *Unakite* is a vision stone that promotes third eye seeing. It helps bring issues from our current past as well as from past lives into the light so that they can be healed.

➢ *Zoisite (with Ruby)* promotes fertility, generation, regeneration, and preservation in all directions. It encourages positive attitudes and emotions and is thereby a powerful healing stone.

Trees, Flowers, Herbs, and Plants

Everything has an energetic vibration, including trees, flowers, herbs, and other plants. Throughout time, many cultures and many people have recognized the spiritual nature of plants and have appreciated their sacred place in the weave of Universal interconnectedness and interrelatedness. In the course of human history and until quite recently, plants were interwoven into people's daily lives; they continue in this role, of course, although we are frequently unaware of it.

Trees have offered protection and shelter and materials for shelter; they have bestowed upon humanity the substances necessary for fire which, in turn, allowed us to cook our food and to keep ourselves warm and alive. Parts of various trees are edible, and other parts have healing properties.

Other plants, including flowers and herbs, have long been included in our diets, have sustained and nurtured us, and have flavored our foods. They have played a proactive role in strengthening us and in preventing disease. The use of herbs and other plants as medicine is in practice now and has been in practice throughout human history. Indeed, many modern pharmaceuticals are based in materials and extracts from the world of plants and trees.

But trees and plants have played an additional role and have featured extensively in myth and legend in all cultures. They have been and are symbols for our passions, beliefs, hopes, and fears. They have been and are emblems, crests, or insignia for both personal and group expression.

Additionally, trees and plants have been used as vehicles for communication and messages from Source Energy. Ancient people and many of us in the current time have understood that by listening to and observing that which God created, we could open ourselves to a higher awareness and raise our vibration. This includes trees, flowers, herbs, and plants.

Trees and other plants do not necessarily have a universal meaning and can have special meanings for different people and groups. Again, we must think of what they mean to us; there are, however, resources to assist us in our search for meaning. Plants and trees have many attributes and so have multiple meanings; as always, we must trust ourselves to know our own truths.

As with stones and crystals, give attention to the color and shape of the tree or plant. If possible, inform yourself about its various uses in the world, both historically and in the present. Is the plant edible or poisonous? Does it have particular healing properties?

Trees and plants can be used for healing, for personal growth and development, and for our journey toward spiritual enlightenment.

Following are some tree meanings that are relevant and useful to me.

➤ *The Apple tree* has a strong association with the Isle of Avalon, the Mystical Island and resting place of King Arthur of Camelot. This tree presides over mystery. It governs the personal harmony that results from a beneficent attitude of goodwill toward others. It represents potent creativity and beauty and cautions against the temptation to use these attributes in an unconstructive manner.

➤ *The Ash tree* is, in various cultures, deemed to be the "Tree of Life." It represents expansiveness, dynamism, and magnificence and promotes a higher awareness. It may at times ask for a departure from personal interest so that the greater good may be served.

➤ *The Aspen tree* represents spiritual ascension brought into focus by a hardship or difficulty of some kind; although a certain amount of struggle is indicated, the Aspen offers spiritual and emotional protection. It is the sacred tree of Hermes and promotes honest self-expression.

➤ *The Beech tree* is a tree of divination; indeed, ancient runes were made from the wood of the Beech. This tree governs the acquisition and preservation of wisdom and promotes the continuation and dissemination of acquired truths and insights.

➤ *The Birch tree* represents new beginnings and the willingness to protect and defend that which has been created. It promotes release of past experiences so that regeneration and renewal can occur. In an unbalanced expression, Birch will reinforce a meek attitude that may hinder desired growth.

➤ *The Cherry tree* represents beauty, purity, and balance; it governs education and the prosperity that can be attained through knowledge. Cherry reinforces our desire for harmony. In an unbalanced expression, this tree will support deception in actions and in speech in a futile effort to avoid disagreement, tension, and the resulting feelings of imbalance.

➤ *The Chestnut tree* supports honest, fair, and independent thinking and action. It promises a new beginning if situations are approached with honor and impartiality.

➤ *The Cottonwood tree* governs our creative center and our need to be fully realized. It promotes an unpretentious desire for recognition and the acknowledgment of our true nature, or genuine self. Cottonwood is the sacred tree of Wakan Tanka, a Native American aspect of God, and represents the holiness of all creation.

➤ *The Cypress tree* is sometimes erroneously called a *cedar*. It is a tree of purification that promotes the release of that which is no longer useful so that new growth is allowed. It facilitates grief and mourning, giving honor to the past and helping us accept what has been and is no longer.

➢ *The Elm* tree is the gateway between our world and the world of Faerie. It governs willpower, dignity, and self-control and teaches us that we reap what we sow and therefore get exactly what we deserve.

➢ *The Fir and Spruce trees* represent our connection to all life. They encourage cooperation and exchange with everything Source Energy has brought into being. These trees promote responsible stewardship of all creation.

➢ *The Gingko tree* represents the primeval life force and is the tree of rebirth and transformation. It governs the reincarnational process and promotes the growth and evolution that takes place over time.

➢ *The Hawthorn tree* represents the unification of male and female energies. It governs the sanctity of sexual joining and promotes honor, propriety, hope, and trust.

➢ *The Hazel tree* is the sacred tree of the Welsh God, Mabon, and promotes youthfulness, good humor, fun, infatuation, and enchantment. It governs peaceful communications that will result in reconciliation.

➢ *The Holly tree* is the sacred tree of Jesus. It has been associated with the "Sword of Truth"; the Holly Tree encourages us to stand for our beliefs, to defend our convictions and principles, and to fight for them.

➢ *The Horse Chestnut (American Buckeye) tree* governs good fortune, luxury, and success. It promotes the manifestation of abundance and encourages generosity.

➢ *The Juniper tree* is a gateway to other dimensions, including the world of the Faerie. The Juniper encourages imagination and creativity and gives us the confidence to pursue our dreams and protection while doing so. It also encourages grounding and centering in reality while pursuing our dreams and inspirations.

➢ *The Larch (Tamarack) tree* promotes unusual and imaginative thinking and doing. It advances audacious and bold action but also encourages overconfidence and impudence.

➢ *The Linden (Basswood)* tree governs conjugal bliss and promotes peace and healing in the connubial or wedded relationship.

➢ *The Magnolia tree* encourages a love of the beauty and dignity that is found in the natural world. It promotes good stewardship of all that God has created and encourages us to participate in the sweet blessings that surround us.

➢ *The Maple tree* promotes personal expansion and risk taking but asks that we do so in a manner that is practical and balanced. *The Sycamore tree* (of the Maple family) adds the component of jollity and merriment.

➢ *The Oak tree* has been sanctified in many cultures. In Norway, it was the sacred tree of Thor, in Greece it was Zeus' hallowed tree, and it has a strong reverential association with the Anglo-Celtic Green Man. It is a strong tree that encourages bravery, valor, autonomy, and sovereignty, but it is also a hospitable tree that governs its sovereign kingdom well.

➤ *The Orange tree* is a generous tree that supports creativity, fecundity, and growth but does so in a pure, innocent, and chaste manner.

➤ *The Palm tree* is a tree of victory and triumph but demands that any action taken must be taken in a dignified and peaceful manner. This tree asks that we trust in the higher Universal vibration, and it will then promote creativity and success.

➤ *The Peach tree* is a gracious, charming tree that brings good fortune, success, and happiness.

➤ *The Pear tree* is a tree that promotes affection. It supports noble governance, wise decisions, good health, and comfort.

➤ *The Pine tree* is a tree of endurance, longevity, and continuity. It is a tree that promotes faith in Source Energy and a hopeful attitude during times of adversity.

➤ *The Plum tree* promotes independent action and honest perseverance.

➤ *The Poplar tree* represents time and the inevitability of change. It is a tree of destiny that promotes courage and provides protection.

➤ *The Redwood tree* asks us to maintain a sense of proportion and encourages perfect balance, perfectly expressed; it discourages extremes in all things and in all directions. The Redwood is a tree of Universal unification and promotes growth through a harmonious expression.

➤ *The Rowan (American Ash) tree* has long had reverential association in what is now the British Isles. It had a strong association with the Druids and was the sacred tree of the Irish Goddess, Brigid. It is a protective tree of magnificent inspiration.

➤ *The Walnut tree* is a tree of confidence. It promotes rational strategic thinking and the logical intellect. In an unbalanced expression, it can also be a tree of deception, as it uses the analytical mind to rationalize unrealistic actions, thoughts, and desires.

➤ *The Willow tree* is a dreaming tree that promotes visions; through visionary revelations, it offers healing for mournful, despondent attitudes and thoughts. It has a modest focus but looks to future and long-term purpose nonetheless. It encourages unpretentious thinking and action.

➤ *The Yew tree* governs change and is a protective tree that transforms through endings and beginnings. It is a tree of rebirth and resurrection.

Flowers, Herbs, and Plants as Signs and Totems

➤ *Anemone* reminds us that we many need to abandon our expectations and move away from our attempt to control outcomes; let it be.

➤ *Aster* reminds us that variety is indeed the spice of life; sharing the gift of beauty blesses the giver as well as the receiver.

221

➢ *Azalea* reminds us to be moderate in our enthusiasms as passion can be fleeting; we do best when maintaining a balanced expression and preserving our own truth.

➢ *Bachelor Buttons* remind us to be true to ourselves and to be virtuous, faithful, and pure in our affections and with our sexual expressions.

➢ *Basil* reminds us that revenge is anti-healing in all directions.

➢ *Bay Leaf (from the Laurel tree)* reminds us that working toward our goals will bring us success and a good reputation.

➢ *Bee Balm (mint family)* reminds us to retain our individuality as we connect with and love others.

➢ *Borage* reminds us to speak our truth diplomatically but with candor and courage.

➢ *Bugloss* reminds us to speak our truth without exaggeration, deceit, or fabrication and to be mindful of how others are communicating with us as well.

➢ *Burdock* reminds us that insistence on getting our own way may lead to isolation and boredom.

➢ *Campanula (Bellflower or Harebell)* reminds us that we can sometimes avoid grief when we are acquiescent and grateful.

➢ *Carnation* reminds us that love and affection are not the same as infatuation and fascination.

   o Pink is an unconditional or unreserved love bond.

   o Red is the color of passion and may indicate high emotion in all directions.

   o Yellow is a reminder to keep our own power in love relationships.

➢ *Catmint* reminds to be robust and generous in our affections.

➢ *Cattail* reminds us that it is within our power to manifest lives that include a larger share of prosperity and peace.

➢ *Chamomile* reminds us to remain calm when facing adversity and approach the situation with initiative and ingenuity.

➢ *Chrysanthemum* reminds us to be optimistic and of good cheer.

   o Red is the color of love.

   o White is the color of truth.

   o Yellow is the color of optimism following disappointments in love.

➢ *Clematis* reminds us that sincerity and integrity in love relationships is essential and that artifice will cause harm.

➢ *Clover* reminds us to think and act creatively within our domestic environments.

   o Red is the color of hard work and industry.

   o White is the color of inclusion, asking that the needs of all be considered.

- o Four-leafed brings love and good fortune.
- ➢ *Cloves* remind us to act in a dignified and self-disciplined manner.
- ➢ *Coltsfoot* reminds us to nurture ourselves and those we love in a balanced manner, allowing others to do for themselves as they are able.
- ➢ *Columbine* reminds us to protect ourselves from the folly and foolishness of other's actions.
  - o Red is the color of survival and self-protection.
  - o Purple is the color of God's help.
- ➢ *Coneflower* reminds us that the answers lie within; we must ground ourselves and listen to our own still, small voice.
- ➢ *Coreopsis* reminds us to be cheerful; it benefits us to be grateful for all that we have.
- ➢ *Cranberry* reminds us to be watchful and to protect ourselves from duplicity and deceit in our relationships.
- ➢ *Crocus* reminds us to be enchanted with the delights of all that is new.
- ➢ *Cyclamen* reminds us that occasionally hesitancy and reticence work in our favor and that sometimes "fools rush in where Angels fear to tread."
- ➢ *Dahlia* reminds us that beauty and elegance are ephemeral.
- ➢ *Daffodil* reminds us that graciousness and good taste are noble attributes.
- ➢ *Daisy* reminds us to be gentle with others and ourselves and to take joy in purity, virtuousness, and innocence.
- ➢ *Dandelion* reminds us that love is our birthright and to allow love to reveal itself in its own time, in its own way, and with its own face.
- ➢ *Day Lily* reminds us not to take our relationships and ourselves so seriously and that playfulness and coquetry are often quite appropriate.
- ➢ *False Indigo* reminds us of the importance of loved ones—family and friends—and just as they are grounded in our love for them, we are grounded in their love for us.
- ➢ *Fennel* reminds us to be strong and worthy of that with which we are gifted.
- ➢ *Forget-me-not* reminds us that it is authentic experience and genuine love that provides a life foundation that will live on in our memory.
- ➢ *Foxglove (Digitalis)* reminds us that if we wish to create anything of beauty, we must be careful, meticulous, and sincere.
- ➢ *Geranium* reminds us that gossip is harmful and to use discretion, civility, and courtesy when communicating either with others or about them.
- ➢ *Goldenrod* reminds us that we deserve a fortunate life, but that we must gain that fortune by cautious and honorable behavior.
- ➢ *Gooseberry* reminds us of the joy found in anticipation.
- ➢ *Hemlock* reminds us to be careful of toxicity in our environments; this includes toxic situations as well as toxic human behaviors.

➢ *Hemp* reminds us that all life is choosing, and that we are full participants in our destiny.

➢ *Hibiscus* reminds us to appreciate delicacy and beauty.

➢ *Holly Hock* reminds us to appreciate the magnificent and bounteous richness that surrounds us.

➢ *Honeysuckle* reminds us to be conscious of the love bonds that tie us to other people and to appreciate the commitments and affections that we enjoy in our relationships.

➢ *Hyacinth* reminds us to play and to enjoy the freewheeling feeling of our bodies.

➢ *Hydrangea* reminds us that although we can and should take pride in our accomplishments, we should refrain from boastfulness or arrogance.

➢ *Iris* reminds us to think before we speak and to deliver our message with wisdom and eloquence.

➢ *Ivy* reminds us to honor our friendships, to allow others their own truth, and to honor those truths even when we do not agree. It reminds us to recall that we are separate but connected.

➢ *Jasmine* reminds us to cheerfully enjoy our sensory experiences but in a balanced, reserved, and modest manner.

➢ *Joe Pye Weed* reminds us that we are strong and hardy and need not be daunted by our situation; we have the wherewithal to impress.

➢ *Jonquil* reminds us that it is not possible to force others to love us in the way that we might demand if we could, but that we can accept the gift of love where it is freely given.

➢ *Lady Slipper* reminds us to appreciate the whimsical and the capricious.

➢ *Lady's Mantle* reminds us to open our hearts and minds to enchantment and inspiration through an awakened intuition.

➢ *Larkspur* reminds us to keep balance in our attachments and be neither fickle nor overzealous.

➢ *Lavender* reminds us to be constant and loyal to those we love so that an atmosphere of distrust can be avoided.

➢ *Lilac* recalls and recreates the purity and innocence of love's beginning.

➢ *Lily* reminds us to honor ourselves and to see ourselves as the pure, dignified, and majestic Souls that we are.

➢ *Lotus* reminds us that our words and thoughts carry a very real power, and that we must be mindful of what we release into the Universe.

➢ *Lupine* reminds us that we must temper the power of our imagination and remain grounded in actuality and authenticity. We must not use the creative mind to invent catastrophe.

➢ *Mallow* reminds us to nurture those we love with gentle tenderness and to see the delicate beauty that resides in them and in the world around them.

➢ *Mandrake* reminds us to act in a responsible, loving, honorable, and reciprocal manner in our sexual lives.

➢ *Marigold* reminds us that all lives carry situations that cause sorrow and despair, but that there remains much in the life that can bring delight, joy, and hope. Good health lies in moving our energy toward the positive.

➢ *Marjoram* reminds us to be patient and polite with those who are either reserved or vacillate in their opinions and actions; their journey is not ours.

➢ *Mint and Peppermint* reminds us to be moderate and warm in our affections. Aggression in love will lead to situations that require comfort and solace for one or both.

➢ *Mistletoe* reminds us that love is a gift and that we must sustain and support each other in challenging times.

➢ *Morning Glory* reminds us that coquetry and flirtation does not make a lasting foundation for love.

➢ *Mountain Bluet and Cornflower* reminds us that true contentment comes from living a virtuous and wholesome life.

➢ *Mullein* reminds us to love with courage and determination.

➢ *Narcissus* reminds us that we, or someone around us, may do well to bring a measure of humility into the situation. Arrogance and conceit do not serve well.

➢ *Nasturtium* reminds us to love our nation and ethnicity with pride and with loyalty but also with balance.

➢ *Oleander* reminds us that beauty and grace have perfection and purpose in and of themselves. It encourages us to protect that which is exquisite.

➢ *Pansy* recalls that which is good about the people and the situations or circumstances around us.

➢ *Peony* reminds us to be moderate in our appearance, and that a gaudy, garish presentation will not make a good impression over time.

➢ *Phlox* reminds us to bring harmony and accord into the current situation.

➢ *Poinsettia* reminds us to celebrate the Divine.

➢ *Poppy* reminds us to be fully engaged in our lives. We miss authentic pleasures and genuine joy when we live disproportionately in fantasy.

➢ *Primrose* reminds us to be steadfast and constant in our love relationships.

➢ *Rhododendron* reminds us to explore life with enthusiasm but in a manner that keeps us out of harm's way.

➢ *Rose* reminds us to love with genuine affection and gentle benevolence.
  o Red is the color of sexuality and desire.
  o Pink is the color of unconditional love.
  o White is the color of purity and innocence.
  o Yellow is the color of power and transformation.

➤ *Rosemary* encourages us to recall in a balanced and realistic manner; neither make heroes of those who are not heroic nor scoundrels of those who blameless.

➤ *Rudbeckia* reminds us to be dispassionately just and fair.

➤ *Rue* reminds us to be merciful.

➤ *St. John's Wort* reminds us that we have power over lower vibrating energies, whether in the environment around us or within ourselves.

➤ *Sage* reminds us to honor the domestic virtues in those people who make our houses our homes.

➤ *Snapdragon* reminds us to do our research, discover the truth, and not presume, suppose, or assume.

➤ *Speedwell* reminds us of the blessedness of faithful friends.

➤ *Spiderwort* reminds us that respect is an essential quality of love and that disrespect and affection are not harmonious.

➤ *Sunflower* reminds us to be honorably the centers of our own Universe.

➤ *Sweet Pea* reminds us that all things have beginnings and endings and when an ending is near to approach it with gallantry and grace.

➤ *Sweet William* reminds us that coarse behavior will not bring a positive result, but propriety and refinement will serve us well.

➤ *Thistle* reminds us that if we are faced with injustice, intolerance, and inequality, defiance and revolt may be in order.

➤ *Tulip* reminds us that good character and reputation are essential elements in successful unions. It asks that we recognize those qualities in ourselves and in each other.

➤ *Valerian* reminds us that sometimes accommodation to another's wishes and desires will, in the end, serve us best. Be calm.

➤ *Violet* reminds us that keeping our approach modest, straightforward, and simple will serve us best at this time.

➤ *Water Lily* reminds us to eloquently speak our truth and to do so from a pure heart and from an examined and truthful perspective.

➤ *Witch Hazel* reminds us that not everything is knowable on a logical level and to embrace the mystery of our lives.

➤ *Wormwood (Mugwort)* reminds us that even when those we love are not present, we can take delight in them and in all else around us.

➤ *Yarrow* reminds us of our own personal power, particularly in times when we are feeling vulnerable. It reminds us to believe in ourselves even though we may be thinking we are unequal to the task ahead.

➤ *Zinnia* reminds us to make new friends and to honor and remember those friends who are currently absent.

Mushrooms

Mushrooms have enjoyed an interesting reputation throughout history and continue to do so in the current time. Whereas many of them are flavorful and healthy, many are also poisonous. Frequently, differentiating between the wholesome mushroom and the deadly variety is difficult, even for the most experienced mushroom aficionado. For those who eat them, an examination under a microscope is often encouraged, as an edible variety may look very similar to a deadly variety. Some of the toxic mushrooms kill quickly, some kill slowly, but they kill nonetheless.

Many of us do not know a great deal about mushrooms, but anyone who spends time in the natural world is sure to encounter them. If we can get beyond our fascination with the toxicity of certain of the mushrooms and our stereotypes about mushrooms in general, we can begin to observe them in a different manner.

Many years ago, a friend introduced me to the world of mushrooms, and I have been enchanted with them ever since. They often have unusual shapes, vibrant colors, and intriguing names and frequently arrange themselves in patterns that capture the imagination.

It is perfectly acceptable to know absolutely nothing about mushrooms and yet be interested in the signs they can give us. If this is the path we choose to take, the shape, color, smell, pattern, and where they are found can give us insight.

For instance, if we find a purple mushroom growing under a pine tree, we might look at the definition for the color purple and the definition for a pine tree. We could then determine that purple is the color of wisdom, whereas the pine is a tree that promotes faith in Source Energy, and so the message is about our relationship to the Divine. Or we might find a club-like mushroom that smells very badly and is growing under an elm tree. The elm governs dignity and self-control, so perhaps this little mushroom is telling us that, right now, we "stink" in this area—maybe we are behaving in an undignified and self-effacing manner. The club shape may tell us that we are bludgeoning others or ourselves.

We can look at one of the definitions included below and choose one that most closely fits the mushroom we are observing. We can do our own research and learn as much about that mushroom as we can. Again, we must trust ourselves. If that mushroom calls forth certain emotions or thoughts, we must honor our own interpretation.

Some of us have found that the names of the mushrooms have an undeniable allure. For those of us who are attracted to this aspect of the mushroom, as well as its shape, color, or pattern, the following definitions might be of interest. Because we are not going to eat them, if we think the mushroom we are observing fits one of the descriptions, a microscopic examination is not necessary and we can just "go with it." Please note that these mushrooms are generally described as they look when in their prime; the color as it is at the time that you are observing is significant as well.

Mushrooms as Signs and Totems

Small, Fragile, Gilled Mushrooms
➤ *Bleeding Mycena:* This is a reddish brown mushroom with a conical or bell shaped cap, one-half to two-inches wide; when the stalk is broken, it oozes a blood-red liquid. The Bleeding Mycena represents that which is broken and in need of healing; you may be allowing something or someone to drain away your life force.

➤ *Clustered Psathyrella:* This is a brownish-colored mushroom with a one- to two-inch-wide conical cap; the ring around the cap edge is frequently a darker shade. It grows in clusters with others of its kind. The Clustered Psathyrella represents our groups, including our families, and encourages us to examine loyalties and to take a more discerning look at family dictates, institutional domination, and social pressure.

➤ *Faerie Ring:* This is a deep brown to light yellow mushroom with a bell cap that can be up to two inches in diameter; when left alone, it grows into a ring with others of its kind. Some Faerie Rings are hundreds of years old. Because these mushrooms are and have been closely associated with the world of Faerie, they represent our relationship to the natural world.

➤ *Golden Trumpet or Fuzzy Foot:* This is a yellow-brown to orange-brown mushroom with a one-quarter to one-inch button cap; they grow in prolific clusters. The Golden Trumpet represents our responsibilities, obligations, and duties within our groups and families and asks us to balance the needs of others with our own needs.

➤ *Hay Maker or Lawn Mower Mushroom:* This is a reddish brown to light brown mushroom with a one-third to $1\frac{1}{4}$-inch conical to bell-shaped cap; it grows in profusion in lawns and meadows. The Hay Maker represents practicality, efficiency, and the ability to make improvements in our environment. It asks that we refrain from that which distracts us from our endeavors and enterprises in our physical, material world.

➤ *Lilac Fiber Head:* This is a mushroom that is lilac at the top of the cone, becoming lighter as it reaches the edges of the cap; the cap is a conical bell shape and is half to $1\frac{1}{2}$ inches in diameter. The Lilac Fiber Head represents our relationship to Source Energy and how we bring our relationship to the Divine into our daily lives and experiences. It reminds us that the Universe is a whole; "as above, so below."

➤ *Mica Cap:* This mushroom is yellow to light brown with deep striations; when it is young, it has shiny particles on the cap. Its cap is cylindrical to bell-shaped with a diameter of one to $2\frac{1}{4}$ inches. The Mica Cap represents our ability to see "behind the veil" and embodies our intuitive and psychic abilities. It asks that we use our psychic mind in harmony with the rational mind.

➤ *Parrot Mushroom*: This sticky mushroom is deep green but fades to yellow-orange to pink; its bell-shaped cap is just over one inch in diameter. The Parrot represents the health of our relationships and asks that we love unconditionally but with balance. It cautions against etheric cording and encourages us to remain our separate, individual selves as we connect with others.

➤ *Sulfur Tuft*: This is an orange to yellow mushroom with green tones; its cap is smoothly rounded, often with a prominent depression in the middle. It is one to $3\frac{1}{4}$ inches in diameter. Sulfur Tuft represents physical pleasures and balance; it reminds us to enjoy the delights available to the body but to do so in moderation so that compulsion and addiction are avoided.

➤ *Velvet Foot or Winter Mushroom*: This is a sticky, reddish-brown to yellow mushroom; its cap is one to $1\frac{1}{2}$ inches in diameter with a long central bump. Velvet Foot represents individuality and cautions us to listen less to others' description of ourselves and to remain true to our personal definition.

➤ *Yellow Unicorn*: This is a bright yellow conical or bell-shaped mushroom; it has a peg at the top of its one-half to $1\frac{1}{2}$-inch cap, which is reminiscent of the unicorn horn. Yellow Unicorn represents purity and innocence and asks that we embrace the joy that can be found in carefree activities and relationships. It reminds us that much exists simply to be enjoyed.

➤ *Yellow or Golden Waxy Cap*: This is an orange to yellow mushroom with a one- to $2\frac{3}{4}$-inch cap; it begins with a button shape and matures into a broad convex with a sunken center. Yellow Waxy Cap represents our social network and abilities and asks that we expand our interests and contacts.

➤ *Witches Hat*: This is a reddish-orange mushroom with a peaked conical cap; it is three-quarters to $1\frac{1}{2}$ inches in diameter. Witches Hat represents our ability to reject two-dimensional stereotypes and institutionalized philosophies. It encourages us to explore the intricacies of our philosophies.

Veiled Mushrooms with Free Gills

➤ *Death Cap*: This mushroom has a smooth, greenish cap and a skirt-like ring at the top of the stalk; it is $2\frac{1}{2}$ to six inches in diameter and is toxic. Death Cap represents compulsive and addictive behaviors in physical pleasures and in relationships. It cautions us to be aware that what may first seem pleasurable and under control may soon take over the life and cause great damage.

➤ *Destroying Angel*: This mushroom is bright white and has a two- to five-inch broad, flat cap that has a small central bump, with a skirt-like ragged ring at the top of the stalk. The Destroying Angel represents the concept of "form versus content"; it is highly toxic and cautions us to remember that all is not always as it seems. People, activities, and organizations may present themselves as healthy and pleasurable, but this may not be so, and closer examination is advisable.

➤ *Fly Agaric*: This mushroom has a rich red to orange cap with scattered patches of white; it is two to ten inches in diameter, and the stalk has spiraling bands near the base and a skirt-like ring at the top. Fly Agaric is poisonous and represents strength, courage, and survival. It asks that we move away from fear, as fear poisons, and remember that our Angels and Guides are available to help us in times of trouble.

➤ *Meadow Mushroom or Pink Bottom*: This mushroom has a one- to four-inch-wide cap that is flat or moderately convex that is white to pale grey-brown; it is generally silky to the touch but may be scaly to some extent. It has a stout stalk with a thin ring. The Meadow Mushroom is a choice edible but often grows in the same habitat as more deadly varieties that have an extremely similar appearance. It, therefore, represents dietary choices and cautions us to remember that we are what we eat and that food is a health choice as much as it is a pleasure.

Veiled Mushrooms with Attached Gills

➤ *Deadly Galerina*: This is a little brown mushroom with a cap that is one to 2½ inches in diameter; the cap edge has fine striations. The stalk has a thin, pale ring. Deadly Galerina is a highly toxic mushroom with an innocent appearance; it represents the danger of superficiality in concepts and philosophies. It asks us to be willing to look beyond the simple presentation and understand the concept or philosophy in its entirety.

➤ *Delicious Lactarius or Orange-Latex Milky*: This mushroom has a broad, convex to sunken cap that is up to five inches in diameter; it is a carroty-orange and frequently has green stains. It has a similarly colored, thick stalk. Delicious Lactarius represents the importance of compassion and generosity in our physical or sexual relationships.

➤ *Honey Mushroom*: This mushroom has a yellow, brown, or red-brown cap that is one to 4½ inches in diameter; it has a whitish stalk that is stained with a ring. Honey Mushroom represents the meaningful experiences that we have in life and embodies our ability to get the most out of them. It asks us to release the experience when it is done but only when it is done and invites us to be willing to move onto new situations and ideas.

➤ *Saffron Parasol or Pungent Mushroom*: This mushroom is yellow-brown to yellow-orange; the one- to two-inch cap is coated with granules and has a tissue-like fringe at the edge of the cap and has a pungent, bitter odor. Saffron Parasol represents awakening to personal power and our ability to change our thoughts and feelings. When experiencing difficult circumstances, it encourages us to turn away from bitterness and desolation and turn toward contentment and thankfulness.

➢ *Scaly Pholiota*: This mushroom has a cap one to four inches in diameter; the cap has a central bump and is covered in yellow-brown scales. The thick stalk is also covered in scales. Scaly Pholiota represents growth and the ability to leave behind that which no longer serves our highest good. It encourages progress and development in all that supports health in mind, body, and spirit.

Mushrooms with Free Gills

➢ *Deer or Fawn Mushroom*: This brown to grayish-brown mushroom has a 1½- to five-inch cap that is flat or with a low, long bump; it is often sticky or wrinkled and has closely set white gills that become pink at maturity. Deer Mushroom represents adaptability and the capacity to be grounded, perceptive, and quiet. It symbolizes the talent for being able to recognize that which might be dangerous and to rise above it.

Mushrooms with Attached Gills

➢ *Almond Scented Russula*: This is a mushroom with a one- to five-inch cap that is yellow-brown to tan; it is usually moist and shiny. It smells like almonds but with a fusty, decaying component and has an unpleasant taste. Almond Scented Russula represents deception. An initial examination would indicate that the situation, relationship, or circumstance might be beneficial. On closer inspection, however, it is unpalatable.

➢ *Anise Clitocybe*: This mushroom has a convex to flat, one- to four-inch cap and comes in a variety of colors, including dull green, bluish-green, bluish-grey, solid blue, or white; the stalk and gills also present in a variety of colors. It has an anise-like odor. Anise Clitocybe represents variety and choice and encourages us to try the untried.

➢ *Blewit or Blue Hat*: This mushroom has a two- to six-inch, broad violet cap that fades to buff or tan as it ages; it has closely set violet gills that may run part way down the stalk. It has a bulbous base and a fragrant odor. Blewit represents clear vision, both in the physical sense and in the psychic sense. It encourages us to observe all that surrounds us in the physical world, but to pay attention to our fantastical visions and our dreams as well. It suggests that we are not bringing our best effort into our observations and encourages heightened awareness.

➢ *Man on Horseback or Canary Trich*: This mushroom has a two- to 4½-inch sticky yellow cap with a brownish center; the gills are closely set and a solid yellow. The stout stock is a pale yellow. Man on Horseback is about movement and change and encourages going forth with optimism. It asks that neither reticence nor mania be a part of your changes but rather to proceed with balance.

➢ *Poison Paxillus*: This poisonous mushroom has a 1½- to five-inch dry, yellowish-brown to dark brown cap; yellowish gills descend to a stalk that is velvety or hairy. Poison Paxillus represents peace and upheaval, contentment and discontent. It desires tranquility and enjoyment but cautions us to be observant and wary of that which will bring agitation and regret.

➢ *Poison Pie*: This poisonous mushroom has a one- to 3½-inch slimy, cream-colored cap with a cinnamon-colored center; it has brownish gills and a strong, radish-like, tart odor. Poison Pie represents Earth's surplus and humankind's actions regarding the devastation of those resources. It warns us as a species to honor the earth; individually, it encourages us to be mindful of our own habits and to amend them where necessary.

➢ *Sickener or Emetic Russula*: This poisonous mushroom has a sticky cap up to 4½ inches wide; it is reddish in color with off-white gills and stalk. Sickener represents thinking before acting and asks that we carefully consider all aspects of our situation before either running away from it or confronting it in an accusatory or belligerent manner.

Boletes

➢ *King Bolete*: This mushroom has a three- to ten-inch cap that is reddish-brown with white to yellowish pores; it has a bulbous stalk that thickens toward the base and is white to brown in color. King Bolete represents good governance and responsible management within intimate groups, but particularly within the family. It carries a generous and fair-minded energy.

➢ *Old Man in the Woods*: This mushroom has a one to six-inch grayish-black cap and is coarse and scaly. The blackish colored stalk is also scaly. Old Man in the Woods represents the wisdom that comes with experience and maturity. It is an astute, perceptive, and penetrating energy that is also protective.

Chanterelles

➢ *Chanterelle*: This mushroom has a one- to six-inch bright yellow to orange cap; the cap's edge is rolled in at first but lifts up with age. Initially, the cap is flat or convex but becomes depressed and vase-shaped upon maturity. Chanterelle represents our ability to enjoy the "spice of life." It encourages new experiences, new directions, and a zest for living.

Toothed Fungi

➢ *Chicken Mushroom*: This mushroom has a large, fan-shaped cap and can grow up to twelve inches wide; the upper surface is bright orange and wrinkled. It is a prolific and edible mushroom that grows without a stalk and is found on the stumps, trunks, and logs of trees. Chicken Mushroom represents our ability to be independent, to operate freely, and to seize our opportunities. It is an inspiring, imaginative energy.

Shelf-like Mushrooms

➢ *Oyster Mushroom*: This mushroom has a grayish-brown to white cap that grows from two to twelve inches wide; the caps generally grow in overlapping tiers. It is edible and is often a staple of hunters and hikers who have extended visits to the woods. It represents responsibility to self and others and encourages the balance that is necessary for the health and well-being of all concerned. The energy is sustaining and conscientious.

Cup-Shaped Mushrooms and Bird's Nest Fungi

➢ *Bird's Nest Fungi*: This fungi looks literally like little eggs in a bird's nest; the "eggs" are in actuality cups that contain the fungi's spore. Bird's Nest Fungi represent creative possibilities. This potential is powered by emotion, and the more passion and enthusiasm we are able to bring into our creation, the more successful it will be. We will quickly move forward if others are critical of our effort as their criticism generates a defensive emotional response on our part and spurs us on.

➢ *Devil's Cup or Devil's Urn*: This mushroom is a large, tough urn-shaped brown cup that is between 1¼ to 3 ¼ inches high and 1 ½ to 2 ½ inches wide. Devil's Cup represents the unhealthy beliefs and behaviors that we hold. There is a compulsive quality to them that is not in balance with our overall health and can result in harm. We may be jeopardizing situations in the beneficial areas that we hold dear.

➢ *Orange Peel*: The inner surface of this mushroom is orange to orange-yellow and is shaped like a shallow cup or a saucer; although it is round, the edges often wave in and out to present an interesting and artistic shape. The cup is ¾ to four inches in diameter. Orange Peel is an edible mushroom and represents generosity, productiveness, and growth. It is a vital, vigorous energy that encourages pushing the boundaries of our creative expression.

Puffballs and Earthstars

➢ *Collared Earthstar*: This mushroom has a star-like shape that is up to 3½ inches wide and has four to eight pointed rays. The color ranges from dark brown through the array of browns and tans to almost white. Collared Earthstar represents a new beginning; its energy signifies the realization of a dream and encourages us to chart a new course. The energies are optimistic, imaginative, and inventive. The number of rays is significant and may give information regarding the best path to take to reach our goal.

➢ *Gem-stuffed Puffball*: This mushroom can be round or can be shaped like a pear or a top; it is white and has both long and short spines covering it. The cup is up to three inches tall and is one to 2½ inches wide. Gem-stuffed Puffball represents change, transformation, and renewal and signifies an amplification of the energies around us as we move into that which needs reform, repair, or alteration.

➤ *Pigskin Poison Puffball*: This brownish-colored mushroom is up to three inches wide and two inches tall, has a rounded form, and is covered in a network of wart-like shapes, fine lines, and cracks. Pigskin Poison Puffball is poisonous and represents the balance in our lives between work and play. It warns that we may not be taking our responsibilities as seriously as we perhaps should; we may be overly involved in escapist thoughts and activities.

Morels, Stinkhorns and Club-Shaped Mushrooms

➤ *Yellow, Blonde, or Honeycomb Morel*: This is a honeycombed, club-shaped blonde to yellow-brown mushroom; the edible cap is between $2\frac{3}{4}$ to $3\frac{1}{2}$ inches tall, and the stalk is one to two inches long. Yellow Morel represents the action and movement in our lives that is necessary to bring us enjoyment; it encourages us to pursue activities that gratify and delight. It signifies the beauty that is to be found in simple pleasures.

➤ *Shaggy Mane*: This club-shaped mushroom is initially white and has fluffy scales; its cap is two to four inches tall. As it matures, it becomes purple and then inky black. Shaggy Mane represents boundaries; it warns us that we should not join or combine that which should not be united. For instance, certain people should not mingle with certain others. We should not drink or text-message and drive. We cannot have an intimate conversation with another if we are watching television. It asks us to give thoughtful consideration to our "multitasking." Which combinations do not serve us or those around us?

➤ *Elegant Stinkhorn*: This is a long, slim, stalk-shaped mushroom that is four to seven inches tall and a half inch wide; the base of the cap is a pinkish-red, and the top is covered in a green slime. It has a disagreeable odor. Elegant Stinkhorn warns us that all is not right in our relationships; something stinks. It asks us to examine the people that we have invited into our lives and to begin to determine whether or not their involvement injures us. What we are allowing? This may be in the area of our sexual lives but can also be in any area where we love. It signifies that unconditional love is "slimed."

Seashells and Sea Creatures

Although I was raised inland and in the middle north of the United States, I was born on the Gulf Coast in Mississippi. As a young adult, I lived in North Carolina for several years and went to the shoreline at every opportunity. I have visited the sea frequently and have spent time on the beaches of the Eastern Seaboard, all around the Gulf Coast, on the Western shores as far north as British Columbia, in Hawaii, Mexico, and the Bahamas. And as with so many of us, seashells and sea creatures have always held a fascination.

For those who live by them, the oceans and seas have been an integral part of their lives. Marine life has nourished and sustained them and offered dietary as well as medicinal provision. The sea has intrigued and beguiled and has been the source of countless stories, myths, and legends.

The ocean, coastline, and creatures that dwell in the deep have been and are symbols for our hopes and fears, our passions and beliefs. Innumerable totems and signs come from the water, and just as our ancestors did, we also listen to and observe the messages that have their origins in the sea and open ourselves to a higher awareness.

Seashells and sea creatures do not necessarily have a universal meaning; different groups and different people may have their own, unique interpretation. Again, we must follow our particular truth and honor the personal significance. If they do not, however, have meaning specific to us, there are resources that can help us to discover the messages that they hold. Maritime creatures have many attributes and multiple meanings; we must trust ourselves to know what is right for us.

Following are meanings for certain of the seashells and sea creatures. These definitions are arranged in broad categories, and within each category, the individual shells or creatures will bring an additional, distinctive energy.

Seashells and Sea Creatures as Signs and Totems

➢ *The Abalone shell* represents creation and integration; it is about the dissolution of old structures and patterns so that a new path for creative opportunity can be constructed. It promotes the generation and production of beauty and reflects it back to the self. That which is within the self reflects and builds upon that which is outside of the self, and conversely, that which is external reflects and builds upon that which is internal.

➢ *The Auger shell* represents both rational thought and intuitive insight; it is about analyzing and understanding the physical world, but is also about comprehending the spiritual world. The Auger encourages us to dig deeper and to uncover that which is concealed; this shell promotes revelation and understanding.

➢ *The Chiton shell* represents defense and is about safeguarding that which is crucial to our health and personal welfare. It promotes the courage to deal with emotional, psychological, and verbal intrusion as well as physical violation.

➢ *The Clam shell* represents sanctuary, recuperation, and reorganization; it is about the need to find peace and calm in a safe environment so that issues and challenges can be given appropriate and thoughtful attention. It promotes an undistracted consideration of the situation.

➢ *The Cockle shell* represents emotions and love; it is about our associations and relationships with others but also about our approach to our selves. It promotes the seeking out of stable and loving connections while honoring our individual needs, wants, and desires and asks for a harmonious balance between the two.

➢ *The Conch shell* represents communication, personal expression, and social abilities; it is about how and what we think and then how we communicate that information. It is about how we convey or share other ideas and philosophies as well. It promotes the gift of speech and asks that we be truthful, sincere, and fair.

➢ *The Coral* represents the construction of a stable foundation and service to others; it is about assuming appropriate responsibilities and completing the tasks associated with them. It promotes consistency, constraint, patience, and loyalty.

➢ *The Cone shell* represents desire and moderation; it is about the thirst for experience that, at its best, inspires us to find the glory in ourselves and to achieve. At its worst, it arouses our appetite for an addictive pursuit of pleasure. The Cone promotes curiosity, diversity, and flexibility and asks for moderation in all things.

➢ *The Cowry shell* represents our physical world, material resources, and money; it is about the desire and ability to obtain success, status, and wealth. It promotes confidence, excellent administrative and executive abilities, and good judgment of people and situations. It asks for a balanced approach so that achievement in the material world does not become an obsession.

➢ *The Limpet shell* represents relationships, commitment, and taking responsibility for choices made; it is about healthy connection that is neither enmeshed nor detached. It promotes unity and asks that we bring our individual selves into our relationships, alliances, and associations.

➢ *The Miter shell* represents the traditional and the conventional; it is about accepting the status quo of the known world. It promotes learning in our established institutions and in the time-honored manner. It asks that we adhere to the high moral standards that we have been taught.

➢ *The Mussel shell* represents balance and responsibility; it is about equilibrium and proportion between the needs of others and the needs of the self. It promotes conscientiousness and a willingness to assist and to serve. It warns that a dictatorial attitude or a stance of martyrdom indicates a grave imbalance.

➤ *The Murex shell* represents analyzing, understanding, and detachment; it is about dispassion and moderation in thought, philosophy, ideas, and communication. It promotes logic, rational intelligence, penetration, and insight and asks that we avoid cynicism or conceit.

➤ *The Nautilus shell* represents spiritual expansion; it is about growth and development in all areas. It promotes emotional, psychological, and physical experience as a pathway to higher consciousness and increased vibration.

➤ *The Sand Dollar* represents the choices that we make as we cocreate with God. In each lifetime, we gather information and experiences through our bodies, minds, emotions, and psyches; based on this input, we make choices. As we reincarnate, we do this over and over. It is through this process that we cocreate with God and ascend spiritually.

➤ *The Scallop shell* represents building a solid foundation in relationships. It is about acknowledging the biology of our body chemistry and hormonal system and truthfully recognizing our emotions. It is about understanding where and in what direction our instincts and emotions want to take us. It is about balancing body chemistry and emotion with thought. It asks that we look at our relationships in their totality so that we can make decisions that support our highest good. Are we allowing our hormones or our emotions to override good sense?

➤ *The Sea Horse* represents specifically male energy that nurtures. It asks women to examine the men around them who are providing male nurture; how are they doing it, when are they doing it, and why? It asks men to observe other men around them and ask the same questions. It also asks men to consider how they themselves are bringing masculine nurture into the lives of those around them.

➤ *The Snail shell* represents material satisfaction and issues of power. It is about achieving and maintaining in the material world and about how much is enough, not enough, or too much. It is also about power and asks that we have appropriate power in our own lives and be responsible for our actions, choices, and outcomes. It also asks that we allow others to take personal power in their own lives and do not take power that is not ours to take. It promotes proficient leadership, good judgment, and consideration for others.

➤ *The Star Fish* represents integration and healing; it is about honoring all parts of the self: the intellect, body, emotions, psyche, and the Soul. It asks us to join our seemingly disparate pieces into a united whole so that we may become truly more than the sum of our parts.

➤ *The Top Shell* represents circular or paradoxical thinking. In an unbalanced expression, it is about rationalizing situations or ideas in a manner that does not serve our highest good. In a balanced expression, it is about the ability to embrace seemingly dissimilar or incongruent thoughts, concepts, ideas, or philosophies as we make an intellectual climb toward what is actual, authentic, or true.

➤ *The Triton shell* represents communication and empathy; it is about the continuum of connection and asks us to examine how we connect to others and how we allow them to connect with us. It promotes balance so that we are neither detached nor merged but have equilibrium in our emotional and etheric boundaries.

➤ *The Tusk shell* represents the intellect; it is about curiosity, inquisitiveness, intellectual flexibility, and the willingness to feed our minds with diverse concepts, principles, and ideas. It promotes balanced thinking while encouraging liveliness of thought.

➤ *The Wentletrap* represents joy and gratitude; it is about the ability to appreciate and to be grateful for the intangible. It is the embracing of the beautiful in all of its aspects and forms, including nature, art, music, the written word, and the blessings of good friends and good times. Joy and gratitude are energies of the highest vibration and help us attract bountiful abundance.

➤ *The Whelk shell* represents the unconscious mind, intuition, and understanding; it is about listening to your Spiritual Helpers as they communicate to you through your own still, small voice and then beginning that climb to understanding. It promotes trust in your intuition.

➤ *The Urchin* represents our relationship to our body and our understanding of our bodies as Temples for the Soul. It is about our physical health, what we put into our bodies, how much exercise and fresh air we give our bodies, and how much we simply love our bodies.

➤ *The Volute shell* represents our unconscious mind and how what is stored there and what processes occur there affect our communications and relationships with others. It is an energy that is rationally unaware but that nonetheless propels our opinions, thoughts, and actions.

Symbols

Symbols are signs or characters that represent something else or something more. The meaning of many symbols has remained constant over time; for others, the meanings have changed. For instance, the Swastika, or variations of it, was an honorable symbol in Egypt, Asia, India, and within the Germanic tribes. It represented such concepts as cosmic regeneration, movement, change, the four directions, or the sun. Sadly, this symbol was hijacked by the Nazis in World War II and now represents racism, intolerance, and genocide. Similarly, the Iron Cross initially signified courage and heroism but also was borrowed by the Nazis and no longer has this noble correspondence.

Symbols can be a part of a sign or totem or can singularly act as signs or totems. Therefore, knowing the symbolic meaning of a shape may be important. For example, crystals can be fashioned into a pyramid, an obelisk, or even a spiral. Certain seashells are in the form of a spiral, while another sea creature styles itself after a star. Plants may be star-shaped, circles, and even hearts. Shape, substance, and structure are all considerations when concerning ourselves with messages, signs, and totems.

Symbols have a general or collective meaning, but they may also have a personal significance that is outside of the commonly held definition. If we do not have an interpretation for any symbol that is individual and distinctive, do the research. What is the widespread and generally accepted characterization?

Symbols in Signs and Totems

➤ *Circles:* Circles have no beginning and no end: they embody wholeness, eternity, and perfection. Circles represent the rates and rhythms of everything that is cyclical: day and night, seasons, ocean tides, and our own bodies. They also commonly represent the sun.

➤ *Spirals:* Spirals are magical symbols that represent cosmic energy. Spirals naturally occur in nature; snails, certain plants, whirlpools, and galaxies all possess spirals. They signify growth, continuity, and expansion in all directions.

➤ *Lines:* A straight, horizontal line represents our base, or our foundations; it also symbolizes Earth itself. A straight, vertical line denotes the self, oneness, and unity with all.

➤ *Squares:* The square is an Earth symbol and can represent ground or grounding; it symbolizes materializing or manifesting that which we wish to embrace or to enfold.

➤ *Triangles:* The triangle has long symbolized divine power and fire; it represents the creative power of three and signifies creation and inspiration, self-expression, success, and prosperity.

➤ *Arrows:* Arrows indicate direction and tell us to look back, forward, up, or down. Back arrows may be asking us to look at something in the past, whereas forward arrows may request a look to the future. Down may indicate we need to ground ourselves and concern ourselves with our earthly lives; up may mean to look to guidance from Spiritual Helpers.

➤ *Obelisks:* Obelisk represents protection and defense; it amplifies energy as we give effort toward manifesting that which we desire.

➤ *Crosses:* The cross has had many meanings throughout history; the most common characterization in the Western world currently corresponds to an honoring of Jesus of Nazareth. This cross represents eternity, divinity, and martyrdom. The Iron Cross traditionally represented heroic bravery but has come to be associated with reward for the Nazi soldier. The Cross of Han is also called the Viking Shield Knot and represents both John the Baptist and the pagan Viking celebration of Midsummer's Eve and fertility.

➤ *Pyramids:* Pyramids collect, focus, and amplify the energy of the triangle.

➤ *Stars:* Stars represent a Divine Gift; they symbolize inspiration and hope as well as truth revealed. The number of points on a star is significant and should be taken into consideration. The seven-pointed star is the symbol of the Gnostic movement in Christianity. The Gnostics embraced knowledge and wisdom; the seven represents analysis and understanding, detachment and wisdom.

➤ *Suns:* The Sun represents our personality, our character, our image of our self, and our creative energies.

➤ *Moons:* The Moon represents our emotions, instincts, and our subconscious. It is highly intuitive and influences our sensitivity, receptivity, and impressionability. The waxing moon indicates its powers are rising, while the waning moon signifies a weakening of its energy.

➤ *Eternity Symbol:* The infinity or eternity symbol represents infinity and eternity. It also represents the reciprocity that is required in perfect balance, perfectly expressed.

➤ *Hearts:* The heart is an ancient symbol; it currently signifies affection, love, or pleasure. In early Greece, curling vines created a heart shape that represented Eros, the god of sexual love; in Rome, it represented Amor. For the early Christians, it characterized the sacred heart of Jesus.

➤ *Ankhs:* The Ankh represents both the physical life and eternal life; it is the symbol for life and its continuity.

➤ *Peace Symbols:* The peace symbol was originally designed in Great Britain as an image representing nuclear disarmament. It has become a worldwide symbol for peace and nonviolence.

➤ *Gender Symbols:* The symbol for Mars and Male or Man is the same. The symbol for Venus and Female or Woman is the same.

➤ *Tao:* This symbol is often used to indicate balance between the male and the female principles. It represents the concept that, within the whole, there are two parts, the Yin and the Yang, that are the contrasting elements in a duality.

➢ *Aum:* Aum is the most sacred of all syllables and is the spoken essence of the Universe; it represents what was, what is, and what is to come.

➢ *Eye of Horus:* This is the all-seeing eye and is a symbol of Universal or Cosmic completeness, unity, and wholeness.

Chapter 10: Personal Metaphysical Blueprints
- ➤ **Part One**
  - Numerology
    - ❖ The Universal Meaning of the Numbers
    - ❖ Numerological Core Information
    - ❖ Progressive Information: Personal Year
    - ❖ Other Numerological Information
  - Astrology
    - ❖ Signs
    - ❖ Houses
    - ❖ Planets
      - o Symbols for the Planets
      - o Energetic Expression of the Planets
  - Cardology (Playing Cards)
    - ❖ Birth or Sun Card Chart
    - ❖ Hearts
    - ❖ Clubs
    - ❖ Diamonds
    - ❖ Spades
    - ❖ Joker
  - Palmistry
    - ❖ Right Palm vs. Left Palm
    - ❖ The Lines on Our Palms
    - ❖ The Three Major Lines on Our Hands
    - ❖ Definition of the Fingers

- ➤ **Part Two**
  - Enneagram
    - ❖ Enneagram Triads
    - ❖ Paths of Integration and Disintegration
    - ❖ Personality Types
  - Graphology
    - ❖ The Importance of Letters
      - o The Personal Pronoun "I"
      - o The Lowercase "t"
    - ❖ Our Page: We Begin to Write
      - o We Choose Our Ink
      - o Our Margins
      - o Line Spacing
      - o Zones

o   The Slope of Our Lines
o   The Size of Our Letters
o   Letter Strokes

Part One

With each incarnation, the Soul returns to Earth to learn lessons that can only be learned in physical form. Our Souls choose to return to Earth at a particular time and in a particular place and choose the names that we will call ourselves. Our Souls choose the environments in which we will function and the people with whom we will surround ourselves. Our Soul's return to Earth is purposeful, and nothing about it is accidental or arbitrary.

To help us comprehend the current journey, the Universe has given us certain tools. These tools can help us to understand and expand our nature and character as well as help us see what energies may be operating for us in the future. These tools can help us recognize what lessons we want to learn while we are in the current incarnation. They can help us learn what we *must* do, what we *want* to do, and how we will show ourselves to the world. People who have studied numerology, astrology, cardology, palmistry, enneagram, and graphology have found that there are particular correlations between the inner dynamics of people and certain observable phenomena.

Numerology charts, astrology charts, and the enneagram, in particular, give us information about our character. Numerology and astrology charts also give us information about what we are here to learn and to do, what areas we have skills upon which we can build, and what our destiny and karmic issues might be. These systems, especially when used in combination, give us our uniquely individual blueprint; it is our personal owner's manual. No one else in the world has this particular combination of energies and expressions.

Numerology is based on the birth name and birth date; astrology is based on the birth date, birth time, and birthplace. The enneagram has a test, or tests, and we must answer a series of questions about ourselves to get our enneagram type.

Cardology utilizes ordinary playing cards that also give us information about character. There are several books available to us that describe and explain this system. Robert Lee Camp, for instance, has done extensive research and has made a considerable effort to help us understand how ordinary playing cards can help us examine our character and assist us in our journey of self-discovery.

Graphology, or the study of handwriting, gives us information about character, as does palmistry, or the study of our hands. Many of these systems, including numerology, astrology, cardology, and palmistry, also give progressive information, or information about what energies will be operating in our future.

A very brief description of these systems will be given in this chapter. All of these systems are a great deal more complicated than is indicated in the abbreviated synopsis that will be given here. If you are interested in any of the described practices investigated in this chapter, there are numerous books that have been written for each system (I have listed some of these books in the reference section; however, there are many additional written resources).

Numerology, astrology, cardology, and palmistry are esoteric systems of self-discovery. They give us information about ourselves, but they can also give us information about future energies. These four systems are not accepted in mainstream society and are often referred to as the pseudosciences.

Loosely defined, science is a systematized gathering of facts or knowledge, using qualitative or quantitative methods. Hard sciences are the sciences that are easily quantified and include biology, chemistry, and mechanical physics. The soft sciences, such as sociology and psychology, are less easily quantified and rely on complementary empirical data in a manner that hard science does not.

Graphology and the enneagram are slowing making their way into greater societal acceptance and stand, in a manner of speaking, between the pseudosciences and the soft sciences. As a result, they will be discussed apart from numerology, astrology, cardology, and palmistry.

Numerology

Numerology is the study of the metaphysical significance of numbers. It has existed throughout most cultures in some form for thousands of years. I will be describing numerology as we currently use it.

Numerology is a system of digit summing, which means that all numbers above nine are reduced to a single digit number: one through nine. Each letter of the alphabet is assigned a number:

➤	1	=	A	J	S
➤	2	=	B	K	T
➤	3	=	C	L	U
➤	4	=	D	M	V
➤	5	=	E	N	W
➤	6	=	F	O	X
➤	7	=	G	P	Y
➤	8	=	H	Q	Z
➤	9	=	I	R	

Each number represents a broad area of human experience and awareness. The numbers indicate specific energies and their potentials.

➢ *One (1)* is about independence, attainment, and individuation. It is about personal will and the courage to be whom and what we are. In a harmonious expression, the one presents as strong-willed and ambitious but also considerate of others. One is about innovative thinking, leadership, and the pioneering spirit. It is about good organizational skills and using those skills to accomplish what needs to be accomplished. If the expression of the one is too assertive, the presentation will be domineering, arrogant, and boastful; the assertive one represents selfishness without regard to the well-being of others. If the one is too passive, the expression will be submissive, dependent, and stubborn; the passive one displays a procrastinating attitude and is fearful of making decisions.

➢ *Two (2)* is about relationships and cooperation. It is about diplomacy and peace-making. In a harmonious expression, the two presents as gentle, diplomatic, and adaptable. The harmonious two can gather information from all sides of an issue and can blend divergent opinions. If the two is too assertive, the expression will be tactless, careless, dishonest, and meddling; the assertive two creates divisiveness instead of harmony. The assertive two also disregards or discounts the details of the larger picture, so harmony is disrupted in this manner as well. If the two is too passive, the expression will be devious, blaming, and sullen. Too much attention is paid to detail and the larger picture is ignored; this creates a situation in which the two is frequently vacillating between various options as new detail is uncovered.

➢ *Three (3)* is about the joy of living, creativity, and personal expression; because it is about creation, joy, and manifestation of the self, it is also about sexuality. In a harmonious expression, the three is creative and artistic. This may confine itself to specific areas, but the ability and need to create is always present. For instance, some people paint or write, while others make beautiful tablescapes or cook tasty and visually appealing food. In the harmonious expression, the three reaches for joy, is sociable, and has the gift of speech. The well-balanced three also possesses intuitive ability. In an assertive expression, the three presents as superficial and extravagant; the assertive three has a wasteful attachment to the material, has gaudy taste, and is impractical. Additionally, the assertive three is vain, engages in hurtful gossip, and may be sexually exploitive. The passive three fails to develop the creative abilities and trivializes the urge to create; the passive three is gloomy and lacks imagination as well as concentration. Additionally, the passive three may express as asexual.

➢ *Four (4)* is about work, discipline, construction, and order; it is about the creation of a sound foundation for the life. It is also about service to others and constraint. In a harmonious expression, the four honestly evaluates the facts and completes the given tasks associated with responsibilities assumed. The harmonious four is organized, consistent, and economical as well as patient and loyal. In an assertive expression, the four presents as intolerant and stubborn, is narrowly focused, and is unable to explore diverse options to problems; issues, situations, and people may be perceived as more limiting than in fact they are. The assertive four lacks sensitivity, is overly serious, and is obsessive about work. The passive four is lazy and resists new ideas and thoughtful examination of issues. The passive four refuses to entertain innovative solutions to current problems and clings stubbornly to the old ways of resolution. This is the disappointed person who continually brings the old solution and expects a new result.

➢ *Five (5)* is about progress, change, and the constructive use of freedom. In a harmonious expression, the five embraces diversity and explores that which is outside of tradition or convention. There is an energetic and progressive attitude that includes curiosity and flexibility; new experiences are desired and there is often a strong need to travel. Assertive fives are restless and irresponsible, ignore rules, and scatter their energies by pursuing too many interests. There is a tendency to overindulge in anything that stimulates the senses, which can lead to abuse or addiction with food, sex, drugs, or alcohol. The passive five wants a rule for everything and is afraid of change. In this expression, the five can be bewildered and uncertain and will have a difficult time learning from experience. The passive five may also be sexually confused.

➢ *Six (6)* is about love, responsibility, and balance; it is about service and humanitarianism. In a harmonious expression, the six seeks out emotional equilibrium between the self and others. There is a fair and conscientious attitude and a willingness to serve humanity. However, the harmonious six also understands the need to provide for and be responsible to the self and balances the needs of the self with the needs of others. In an assertive expression, the six presents as self-righteous and dictatorial and becomes overly involved in the problems and responsibilities of others. The assertive six is conventional in approach, argumentative, and easily upset. The passive six is a martyr and a constant complainer who carries too many burdens, both real and imagined. There is resentment toward family and friends and a reluctance to be of genuine service.

➢ *Seven (7)* is about analyzing and understanding, detachment and wisdom. The seven is curious about and wants to comprehend either the physical world or the mystical world, and very often both. In a harmonious expression, the seven exhibits excellent analytical acumen while being able to remain emotionally aloof; in seeking the deeper truths, the harmonious seven is both technically able and intuitive. In an assertive expression, the seven is intellectually vain or conceited and critical of other's efforts. The assertive seven is eccentric, deceptive, and blames others for failed endeavors or attempts. The passive seven is skeptical, cynical, and secretive; although often able to think about the issues at hand, there is an inability to act. The passive seven is emotionally cold and has feelings of inferiority.

➢ *Eight (8)* is about power, authority, judgment, and material contentment. In a harmonious expression, the eight is confident, successful, and has good executive abilities, administering with consideration for others as well as for the self. The eight is a good judge of character. In the harmonious expression, the eight respects material pleasures and has good judgment regarding how much is too much and how much is not enough. The assertive eight is too ambitious and displays a callous disregard for other people; it is crassly materialistic, loves display, and demands recognition from others. There is an aggressive pursuit of power and an uncompromising desire to gain authority over others. In a passive expression, the eight refuses or is unable to take a leadership position. There is a disrespect of authority and poor judgment regarding others and their motives; as a result, the passive eight may become involved in schemes, conspiracies, and other unproductive machinations. The passive eight is careless regarding money and may display dishonesty in issues regarding financial matters, refusing to take responsibility for the task at hand, or cheating others of time, effort, and shared resources.

➢ *Nine (9)* is about altruism, compassion, selflessness, and forgiveness. In a harmonious expression, the nine desires world harmony, works to build group consciousness, and has a significant understanding of community and the common good; it is compassionate and forgiving toward others. The harmonious nine is frequently creatively gifted and sees, at least in part, artistry as a gift to the world. In an assertive expression, the nine is overly idealistic and lacks tolerance for other people, other cultures, and other viewpoints; there is a belief that there is one right way, and the assertive nine knows what it is. The assertive nine can also be impractical and fickle, repeatedly swapping one cause for another. The passive nine can display a pessimistic attitude toward the future of the world and therefore lean toward depression. It can be aimless, gullible, and easily used by others.

Numerological Core Information

These numbers give us various pieces of information, including what we *must learn*, what we *must do*, what we *want* to do, and how we present ourselves. They help us define our current life journey. They help us understand the karmic issues that we have brought into the life. They help us understand what energies surround us each year.

The following is an abbreviated explanation regarding how you determine some of this information:

➢ *Life Path:* This number is one of the four core numbers in numerology and is, perhaps, the most important piece of the numerology chart. This number indicates in which area the major lesson is to be learned. It describes potentials that are brought into the life and what we may become. It indicates the direction of the life but not the outcome; the outcome is dependent upon how the energy is directed or used. The life path number is gotten from the birth date. For instance, if the birth date is 12/17/1999:

o	(month)	1+2=3
o	(day)	1+7=8
o	(year)	1+9+9+9=28; 2+8=10=1
o	(total)	3+8+1=12; 1+2=3

The life path number is 3

The next three numbers are gotten from the birth name. Each of the names in the complete name is addressed separately. Assign the proper number to each letter, add the numbers, and reduce to a single number, one through nine. For example:

R	O	Y		A	L	L	E	N		S	M	I	T	H				
9	6	7	(4)	1	3	3	5	5	(8)	1	4	9	2	8	(6)		9	all
	6	7	(4)	1			5		(6)			9			(9)		1	vowels
9			(9)		3	3		5	(2)	1	4		2	8	(6)		8	consonants

➤ *Destiny:* This number is the second of the four core numbers and is found by adding all the letters in all of the names together (see example above). This number indicates what must be lived in the current lifetime; this is what we must give of ourselves and what we must bring into the lives of others. This number represents the orientation or point of reference for the current life, or what lifelong principle we must fulfill. *The destiny number for Roy is 9.*

➤ *Soul Urge:* This number is the third of the four core numbers and is found by adding all the vowels in all of the names together (see example above). This number represents our inner longings. It is the heart's desire, or our most intimate and personal yearning. On a deeper, spiritual level, it is what we want to have, be, and do. *The soul urge number for Roy is 1.*

➤ *Personality:* This number is the fourth of the four core numbers and is found by adding all the consonants in all of the names together (see example above). This number is the avenue through which we express our character. It is a personal gatekeeper in that it censors what we tell the world about ourselves. *The personality number for Roy is 8.*

Progressive Information: Personal Year

The only other piece of information that we are going to examine here is the personal year. The personal year is progressive or future information, meaning that it describes the energies that will be encountered in the next year.

Personal years go in order, so if you have a personal year of five this year, it will be six next year.

This number also comes from the birth date, but rather than use the birth year, the current or universal year is used. The universal year is determined by adding the numbers in the current year and reducing them down to a single number.

The universal year has energy and power in and of itself. For our purposes, however, we are only using the universal year in the context of our personal year.

The personal year is the period of time between each birthday; it starts on the date that we have our birthday and is in effect until our next birthday. In our example, the birth date is 12/17 and we are determining the personal year from 12/17/2011 to 12/17/2012:

- o $1+2=3$
- o $1+7=8$
- o $\underline{2+0+1+1=4}$
- o $3+8+4=15=6$

The personal year beginning on 12/17/2011 and ending on 12/17/2012 is 6.

Personal Years

➢ *One:* This is a time for new beginnings, and a time to make new plans and look to the future. Forge ahead with courage.

➢ *Two:* Emotional occurrences are heightened this year. Our success and happiness will depend largely on how much tact and diplomacy we use when relating to others.

➢ *Three:* Now is the time to bring our dreams to reality and to use our creative, imaginative, and inspirational ideas. It is a year for self-improvement.

➢ *Four:* This is a practical year with much work to do, as plans and dreams must be put into concrete form. Now is the time to lay a foundation for future security.

➢ *Five:* This is a year with some uncertainty. Changing conditions and eventful happenings will force us into progress. Generally, this year gives us opportunity for advancement.

➢ *Six:* This is a year for responsibility, obligation, duty, and service; unselfishness and charity should motivate our actions. This is a year for harmony with others.

➢ *Seven:* This is a year for the more intellectual phases of living and for quiet pursuits. It is likely that the year will bring a desire to know more or to specialize in a talent.

> *Eight*: This year brings a desire to improve our financial conditions, and it is necessary to be practical, efficient, and businesslike. We need a plan and a goal from the start.

> *Nine*: This year brings things to a head, and we will realize completion and fulfillment of some of our situations. This year opens the way for new opportunities and interests.

Other Numerological Information

There are many additional pieces of information that can be gotten from the birth date and the birth name using numerology. There are master numbers that express higher potentials and karmic debt numbers that indicate a misapplication of energies and potentials in past lives. There are growth, reality, challenge, and balance numbers. There is additional progressive information, such as cycle and pinnacles numbers. Again, there many books available for further study (I have listed some of these books in the reference section; however, there are many additional written resources).

Astrology

Astrology is the metaphysical study of the heavens and has existed for thousands of years. In the current time, eight planets, the moon, and the sun (and, of course, Earth) are considered to be the foundation of astrology. In astrology, the sun and the moon are referred to as planets.

Pluto is included as a planet. The comet Chiron is often considered to have the importance of a planet. For more information about Chiron, however, please refer to resources that give more detailed information than I will give here. (For instance, *The Astrology Bible* by Judith Hall, and *The Only Astrology Book You'll Ever Need* by Joanna Martine Woolfolk both discuss the comet Chiron.)

The placement of these planets relative to the earth and at the precise time and place of our birth give us our personal astrological information. Because the heavens look different from different places on our own planet, it is important to know where as well as when we were born so that the heavens can be seen from the proper latitude and longitude.

All the planets characterize or express specific defined energies as do the signs and the houses. Where they are at the time and place of our birth and what sign and house they occupy helps define our character, our wants and desires, how we communicate, how we love, what challenges us, and much, much more.

Astrological information is presented in a wheel that depicts the signs and the houses. Our personal astrology chart shows which sign and which house the planets occupy at the time and place of our birth. There are many books that can help us map our personal wheel, and there are also many computer programs that will do it for us.

Because mapping astrological wheels is time consuming and labor intensive, I recommend that a computer program, a book with planetary charts, or a professional astrologer be employed. We only need to get the astrological natal wheel once, as the time and place of our birth does not, obviously, change.

The planets, the houses, and the signs all have specific definitions and specific energies. For instance, if at the time of our birth, the planet Mercury is in the fourth house, there is a distinctly different energy than if Mercury is in the tenth house; or if Mercury is in Libra, there is a distinctly different energy than if Mercury is in Scorpio. Or if Pluto is in Libra and the fourth house, the energies will be unmistakably different than if Mercury were in the same sign and the same house. All of the planets, including the sun and the moon, occupied a particular sign and a particular house at the time we were born.

There are various systems of astrology, including the Placidus system and the Koch system. Here in the Western Hemisphere and among English-speaking astrologers, the Placidus system is the most commonly used. The Placidus system is named after Placidus de Titis, who was a seventeenth century mathematics professor and astrologer. The Koch system is a more complicated version of the Placidus system.

The earth goes around the sun, or completes its rotation, every 365.25 days. It is, therefore, relatively easy to determine sun signs and the time periods for them. Listed below are dates in which the sun was in a particular sign. When we ask each other for sign identification, it is the sun sign to which we refer.

> *Aries:* (♈) March 20–April 19
> *Taurus:* (♉) April 20–May 20
> *Gemini:* (♊) May 21–June 20
> *Cancer:* (♋) June 21–July 22
> *Leo:* (♌) July 23–August 22
> *Virgo:* (♍) August 23–Sept 22
> *Libra:* (♎) Sept 23–Oct 22
> *Scorpio:* (♏) Oct 23–Nov 21
> *Sagittarius:* (♐) Nov 22–Dec 21
> *Capricorn:* (♑) Dec 22–Jan 19
> *Aquarius:* (♒) Jan 20–Feb 18
> *Pisces:* (♓)Feb 19–March 19

The moon is Earth's natural satellite and revolves around the earth every 27.3 days, so the sign and house in which the moon finds itself changes relatively quickly. Mercury completes one revolution around the sun every 87.96 days. It takes Venus 224.68 days to get around the sun, and it takes Mars 686.98 days, or 1.9 years. Jupiter takes 11.862 years, Saturn, 29.456 years, Uranus 84.07 years, Neptune 164.81 years, and Pluto 247.7 years. This is why determining our astrology chart is a complicated business; good resources and/or good astrologers are essential.

The following are brief definitions of the signs, houses, and planets. Once you obtain the astrological wheel, you can begin to determine how these energies influence you.

Signs

➤ *Aries* (the Ram): Aries personalities are gregarious and dynamic and have the potential to be leaders. Indeed, Aries people are often convinced that part of our life purpose is to lead others where they should go. We have impulsive energy and often believe that our wants and desires should be fulfilled for us immediately. Aries can be prone to precipitate displays of temper; we get past it quickly, however, and often cannot understand why others do not. We like action and frequently see an obstacle as a challenge; few challenges are insurmountable. Aries personalities do best when the first impulse can be followed. We are not built for long-term or prolonged experiences and may leave things unfinished. Aries is ruled by Mars.

➤ *Taurus* (the Bull): Taurus personalities are steadfast, reliable, and determined. We are stable, like routine, and are often so averse to change that we may remain in unfavorable situations. We do best when adhering to a preconceived and well-defined plan. Pleasure is important to the Taurus personality, however, and we do want to participate in the enjoyments and delights that life has to offer; indeed, we often insist on the very best. Taurus folk like material possessions, and the acquisition of them can be a driving force in our lives. We can be self-indulgent and stubborn. Taurus is ruled by Venus.

➤ Gemini (the Twins): Gemini personalities are adaptable, versatile, and have a wide variety of interests. We are often full of good ideas; interest wanes quickly, however, and many of those good ideas never see the light of day. We are not meticulous, precise, or enduring. Gemini people have a constant need for intellectual stimulation or we become bored and restless. We like information and, when our curiosity is piqued, will go out and get the answers. Gemini folk often function best when we are doing two or more things at the same time. We often have a quick wit and can be spontaneous, unconventional, and even eccentric. Gemini is ruled by Mercury.

➤ *Cancer* (the Crab): Cancer personalities have a vivid imagination, are shrewd, and have good instincts. We are concerned for and protective of those we love, although we may not show it due to a natural shyness. Indeed, we can get so involved in the care of certain others that boundaries dissolve, and we

253

enmesh with the person for whom we are providing care. Conversely, in an effort to protect ourselves emotionally and psychologically, although we know how to care for others we may choose not to do so. Cancers function best when we are secure. We can be reclusive, secretive, and moody. An unforgiving attitude can result in depression. Cancer is ruled by the moon.

➤ *Leo* (the Lion): Leo personalities are proud, dignified, and self-confident. We are creative and function best when we know what we are doing, are satisfied with our efforts, and are gaining the respect of others. We set high standards for ourselves, stick with the tasks we set, and expect others to do so as well. Behavior can be flamboyant; we are comfortable being the center of attention, and, as a result, others may see us as arrogant. However, Leo people need to know that we are loved and appreciated. Leo is ruled by the sun.

➤ *Virgo* (the Virgin): Virgo personalities are meticulous perfectionists who work hard and pay attention to the detail. We have a place for everything, and everything is in its place; we do not like our order disrupted. On an intellectual and mental level, we are precise and practical, like words, word games, and puzzles, and also like to "have the last word." Virgo folk can be critical and often want to repair or improve that with which we are finding fault. We are prone to catastrophic fantasy, particularly regarding matters of health and hygiene. Virgo is ruled by Mercury.

➤ *Libra* (the Scales): Libra personalities want balance, orderliness, and harmony in life; we are good diplomats and have a fervent preference for fairness and justice. Libra folk like to socialize, and we like conversation: we want to contemplate the world around us and then discuss it. We need periods of solitude and respite from others, however, so that we can renew our vitality and restore the balance that we so very much need for ourselves. Although we are disinclined to live by other's rules, Libras are good at displaying behaviors that please others and are generally charming and courteous. We want partnerships and may be so anxious to be in a relationship that we compromise our own needs and desires. Libra is ruled by Venus.

➤ *Scorpio* (the Scorpion): Scorpio personalities are secretive, difficult to get to know, and this is how we want it. We are fearless and do not feel a need to adhere to social convention; nonetheless, we often resist change. Scorpio folk do best when we can get to the essence of the matter without regard to a diplomatic approach. We are able to combine intuition with logic, which makes us good strategists. We are extremely perceptive and feel things intensely. Scorpio people can be exceptionally self-absorbed and know how to persuade others with just the right words or gestures. Scorpio is ruled by Mars and Pluto.

➤ *Sagittarius* (the Archer): The Sagittarian personalities have limitless enthusiasms and inquiring minds; we want to know why and how things work. We have no time for issues or people we consider to be trivial. Sagittarians need stimulating environments and have a difficult time with routine; we like to travel and like to be around interesting and invigorating people. We can be difficult to satisfy and are always looking to the new and innovative. Sagittarius is ruled by Jupiter.

➢ *Capricorn* (the Goat): Capricorn personalities are sensible, practical, self-disciplined, and able to achieve long-term goals. We like to be the authority figure, the one in charge, and the one to make the rules; we have good leadership ability, so our being in charge generally works well for all involved. We function best, however, when we are focused on achieving a socially valued goal. Capricorn people like tradition and convention. We do not have quick minds and avoid situations where we are required to find the right answer to a complicated question in a short period of time. We are hesitant to show feelings or ask for affection. Capricorn is ruled by Saturn.

➢ *Aquarius* (the Water Bearer): Aquarius personalities are inventive, idealistic, and ingenuous; ideas are important to us. We pride ourselves on being unique and are often unconventional, eccentric, and revolutionary in our thinking. Aquarian people have a fervent desire to make social statements and to help the world. Although we often express as emotionally detached, our inner nature is loyal and loving. In friendships, we need to be with kindred spirits and will detach from those less understanding members of the community. Aquarius is ruled by Saturn and Uranus.

➢ *Pisces* (the Fishes): Pisces personalities are sensitive and are intuitively aware of the emotions of those around us. We are compassionate and concerned for the well-being of others and function best when we are involved in serving the Common Good. We can, however, feel emotionally victimized and see ourselves as martyrs. Pisces folk will often see the world in a romanticized and idealized manner; however, we can also magnify fears and become irrational about them, taking on the mantle of doom. The desire to escape is sometimes strong, and Pisces must be careful of addictive behaviors. Pisces is ruled by Jupiter and Neptune.

Houses

➢ *First house*: This house is the *House of Self* and represents our personality, our physical appearance, the image we have of ourselves, and the image we project to the world. It is about our outlook on life and our physical and mental health.

➢ *Second house*: This house is the *House of Finances and Possessions*. It is about what we want, what we need, and our beliefs about it. It is about money, about physical, tangible property, and about what we value or hold dear. It is about what we will do to get what we want.

➢ *Third house*: This house is the *House of Communication* and governs our success and style in communicating through speech and the written word. It is about our immediate environment and the way we interact with it. It is about siblings, relatives, our attitudes regarding them, and our communication styles with them.

➤ *Fourth house*: This house is the *House of Home and Family* and governs our home life and our relations with our families. It is about our emotional roots and our basic foundation; it is about what makes us feel secure, safe, and comfortable. It is about nurturing, our early memories concerning it, and what effect it continues to have on our lives.

➤ *Fifth house*: This house is the *House of Romance and Creativity* and governs our artistic endeavors, hobbies, and romantic inclinations. The fifth house also governs children, as children are the ultimate creative expression. The fifth house influences the risk taking that is necessary to bring our creative ideas to fruition. It is about play and fun that exists only for itself, about leisure and holidays, and about just plain "feeling fine."

➤ *Sixth house*: This house is the *House of Compassion and Health* and governs the service and the work that we do for others, including charity and volunteer work. The sixth house influences our perceptions and attitudes concerning the obligations that we may have toward others. This house also governs health and hygiene and our habits in these areas. It is about healing, our way of thinking about it, and our approach to it. The sixth house is also about food because, as Hippocrates said, "Thy food shall be thy remedy."

➤ *Seventh house*: This house is the *House of Partnerships and Conflicts* and influences how we experience others as well as the person we become when we are relating to various others. The seventh house governs the type of romantic partner we are likely to attract as well as friends or business partners that we consider to be our equals. It also includes those "equals" that we define as enemies, particularly enemies who have qualities that we ourselves possess but reject and project onto another. This house influences our attitudes toward our children. It also governs contracts and agreements.

➤ *Eighth house*: This house is the *House of Mysticism and Spirituality* and governs our inner priest or priestess. It is about giving up personal control and allowing Spirit to infiltrate our physical, emotional, and intellectual space; it is about ecstasy and letting go. It is also about sex. This house is about endings, letting go of the old, and making a new start; it can also be about physical death. The eighth house governs our jointly held resources, both tangible and intangible, and governs loans, taxes, and inheritance.

➤ *Ninth house*: This house is the *House of Travel and the Pursuit of Knowledge*. It governs our expansion of our selves through education, travel, and spirituality. This house influences our philosophies and how we express our ideas; it affects wisdom and knowledge but also the dogma or propaganda that we may embrace or disseminate. It is the house of higher learning, of publishing, and of broadcasting. Because it is the house of spiritual expansion, it also influences our psychic or intuitive gifts as well as our dreams.

➢ *Tenth house*: This house is the *House of Career and Prominence* and governs our status, reputation, and position in our communities, in our lives, and in our careers. It influences our ambitions and goals as well as the accolades or honors we may receive. It also influences scandal and public disgrace. The tenth house governs our relationship to authority figures, how we act toward them, and how we respond to them.

➢ *Eleventh house*: This house is the *House of Hopes and Aspirations* as well as the *House of Friends*. It governs our associations with the people who genuinely appreciate us for who and what we are, our friends, or our "kindred spirits." It governs abstract thought and influences our search for our personal philosophy. This house governs clubs and unions to which we may belong and the way in which we incorporate our own hopes and dreams into the philosophies of these groups.

➢ *Twelfth house*: This house is the *House of Secrets and Sorrows*. It governs our inner or hidden selves and that which we do not wish the world to see. It influences what psychological troubles we may have and how we deceive ourselves about them. The twelfth house represents the institutions that may negate our individuality, such as corporations, government, military, religions, hospitals, or prisons. It influences our need for sanctuary and retreat, for forgiveness, and for mysticism and faith.

Planets

Symbols for the Planets:

➢ *Sun:* ☉
➢ *Moon:* ☾
➢ *Mercury:* ☿
➢ *Venus:* ♀
➢ *Mars:* ♂

➢ *Jupiter:* ♃
➢ *Saturn:* ♄
➢ *Uranus:* ♅
➢ *Neptune:* ♆
➢ *Pluto:* ♇

Energetic Expression of the Planets

➢ *The Sun* represents our creative center and is the symbol of our ego. The sun sign is the easiest piece of information obtainable in the astrological chart. It is the Sun sign that we refer to when we mention that we are a Libra, an Aries, or a Sagittarius. We are so much more than our sun sign. However, the sun is probably the most important planet in our horoscope and provides us with a rough sketch of our personality, identity, and personal qualities and character. The sun is masculine in nature; it indicates our basic motivation and our need to be recognized.

➤ *The Moon* represents our dreams, emotions, and subconscious. The moon influences and determines our need to give and to receive emotional support. It shapes our innermost desires, needs, fears, and loves. The moon is highly intuitive, represents our inner landscape, and is feminine in nature.

➤ *Mercury* governs communication, reason, and intellect. It determines how we translate information, how we make sense of the world around us, and how we observe, analyze, and think. Mercury influences how we read, write, and speak. Mercury is also the planet that stimulates us to travel and to explore and understand the environments in which we bring ourselves into contact.

➤ *Venus* governs pleasure. It represents our ability to love, appreciate beauty, and enjoy social relationships and occasions. Venus influences what we love, how we love it, and how we attract it; it presides over emotional harmony and peace. Venus influences our appreciation of the arts and music and how we enjoy the physical and material pleasures that are available to us. Venus determines how we give and receive love. Venus is feminine in nature and so affects how we express our sexual selves if we are feminine and how we relate sexually to the feminine if we are masculine.

➤ *Mars* governs willpower, energy, our aggressive behaviors, and sexual drive. Mars is the warrior planet and helps us defend ourselves, stand up for what we think is right or true, protect that which belongs to us, and to meet our challenges with courage. Mars has a competitive energy that influences how we take action and allows us to pursue that which we desire. Mars is masculine in nature and so affects how we express our sexual selves if we are masculine and how we relate sexually to the masculine if we are feminine.

➤ *Jupiter* governs happiness, success, good fortune, and generosity. Our Souls know that abundance is our birthright, and Jupiter wants us to manifest it. Jupiter influences our enthusiasms, joviality and laughter, and how we express our optimism. Indeed, Jupiter often encourages the high life, and extravagance can be part of the expression. Jupiter governs risk taking and influences how we stretch and grow.

➤ *Saturn* governs responsibility, self-control, and maturity. Saturn influences how we address our responsibilities, how we exercise willpower and restraint, and how tenacious we are when we are in pursuit of something we desire. Saturn uncovers limitations and teaches us that we get exactly what we deserve. Saturn has a traditional, conservative energy and values hard work, respectability, and normalcy.

➤ *Uranus* governs change, transformation, and innovation. Uranus influences our ability to think and to act unconventionally and to embrace the unusual or the revolutionary. Uranus is the planet of science and technology and affects our relationship to new inventions and to "fads". Uranus shapes our abilities to be eccentric, impulsive, and unpredictable in a manner that remains within an integrated self-expression.

➤ *Neptune* governs dreams and the imagination and impacts how we interact with reality. Neptune shapes our desire and ability to make things or people appear as we want them to appear; it influences whether or not we are deluding or deceiving ourselves. In this manner, Neptune can offer an escape from reality. Neptune carries an imaginative, sensitive energy and persuades us to find answers through dreams, daydreams, and meditation. Neptune often expresses through the arts and music or through spirituality.

➤ *Pluto* governs change, latent power, and untapped potential. It is the planet of rebirth and transformation. Pluto disposes of that which is no longer useful or necessary and can be intense and ruthless. Pluto often compels change by creating complete upheaval, thereby clearing the way for the new. Pluto influences areas in which we need and desire (on a Soul level) transformation, regeneration, and rejuvenation.

Cardology (Playing Cards)

Cardology is an ancient system that is based on what has evolved into the everyday deck of playing cards. Many believe that this mystical system has its origins thousands of years ago, prior even to the ancient Egyptian dynasties.

Cardology has its foundation in both numerology and astrology. It is mathematically based, hence the numerology, and is believed to originally have been constructed as a way to measure planetary movement. Long ago, we lost much of the knowledge of this system but can continue to get meaningful information from it today. Robert Lee Camp has done extensive research and has expended a great deal of effort to revive this ancient practice. Mr. Camp currently lives in North Carolina and is an astrologer, teacher and author. *Cards of Your Destiny* and *Love Cards* are two of the books he has written on this subject (See References).

Cardology is based on the birthday, and each day is associated with a specific card, which represents or expresses identifiable energies. The birth card, or Sun card, is the card that gives us information about our identity in the current lifetime. Although the birth card describes unique traits, qualities, talents, and potentials in great detail, for the purposes of this book, I will give only the basic meaning of the card. Again, there are many accessible resources if you would like greater detail. (See Birth or Sun Card chart).

Birth or Sun Card Chart

	JAN	FEB	MAR	APR	MAY	JUN	JUL	AUG	SEP	OCT	NOV	DEC
1	K♠	J♠	9♠	7♠	5♠	3♠	A♠	Q♦	10♦	8♦	6♦	4♦
2	Q♠	10♠	8♠	6♠	4♠	2♠	K♦	J♦	9♦	7♦	5♦	3♦
3	J♠	9♠	7♠	5♠	3♠	A♠	Q♦	10♦	8♦	6♦	4♦	2♦
4	10♠	8♠	6♠	4♠	2♠	K♦	J♦	9♦	7♦	5♦	3♦	A♦
5	9♠	7♠	5♠	3♠	A♠	Q♦	10♦	8♦	6♦	4♦	2♦	K♣
6	8♠	6♠	4♠	2♠	K♦	J♦	9♦	7♦	5♦	3♦	A♦	Q♣
7	7♠	5♠	3♠	A♠	Q♦	10♦	8♦	6♦	4♦	2♦	K♣	J♣
8	6♠	4♠	2♠	K♦	J♦	9♦	7♦	5♦	3♦	A♦	Q♣	10♣
9	5♠	3♠	A♠	Q♦	10♦	8♦	6♦	4♦	2♦	K♣	J♣	9♣
10	4♠	2♠	K♦	J♦	9♦	7♦	5♦	3♦	A♦	Q♣	10♣	8♣
11	3♠	A♠	Q♦	10♦	8♦	6♦	4♦	2♦	K♣	J♣	9♣	7♣
12	2♠	K♦	J♦	9♦	7♦	5♦	3♦	A♦	Q♣	10♣	8♣	6♣
13	A♠	Q♦	10♦	8♦	6♦	4♦	2♦	K♣	J♣	9♣	7♣	5♣
14	K♦	J♦	9♦	7♦	5♦	3♦	A♦	Q♣	10♣	8♣	6♣	4♣
15	Q♦	10♦	8♦	6♦	4♦	2♦	K♣	J♣	9♣	7♣	5♣	3♣
16	J♦	9♦	7♦	5♦	3♦	A♦	Q♣	10♣	8♣	6♣	4♣	2♣
17	10♦	8♦	6♦	4♦	2♦	K♣	J♣	9♣	7♣	5♣	3♣	A♣
18	9♦	7♦	5♦	3♦	A♦	Q♣	10♣	8♣	6♣	4♣	2♣	K♥
19	8♦	6♦	4♦	2♦	K♣	J♣	9♣	7♣	5♣	3♣	A♣	Q♥
20	7♦	5♦	3♦	A♦	Q♣	10♣	8♣	6♣	4♣	2♣	K♥	J♥
21	6♦	4♦	2♦	K♣	J♣	9♣	7♣	5♣	3♣	A♣	Q♥	10♥
22	5♦	3♦	A♦	Q♣	10♣	8♣	6♣	4♣	2♣	K♥	J♥	9♥
23	4♦	2♦	K♣	J♣	9♣	7♣	5♣	3♣	A♣	Q♥	10♥	8♥
24	3♦	A♦	Q♣	10♣	8♣	6♣	4♣	2♣	K♥	J♥	9♥	7♥
25	2♦	K♣	J♣	9♣	7♣	5♣	3♣	A♣	Q♥	10♥	8♥	6♥
26	A♦	Q♣	10♣	8♣	6♣	4♣	2♣	K♥	J♥	9♥	7♥	5♥
27	K♣	J♣	9♣	7♣	5♣	3♣	A♣	Q♥	10♥	8♥	6♥	4♥
28	Q♣	10♣	8♣	6♣	4♣	2♣	K♥	J♥	9♥	7♥	5♥	3♥
29	J♣	9♣	7♣	5♣	3♣	A♣	Q♥	10♥	8♥	6♥	4♥	2♥
30	10♣		6♣	4♣	2♣	K♥	J♥	9♥	7♥	5♥	3♥	A♥
31	9♣		5♣		A♣		10♥	8♥		4♥		joker

This suit governs relationships, emotions, associations, and love. It can embrace the idealistic and seek out loving connection with others. In an imbalanced expression, it may either be emotionally obsessive or emotionally detached.

➢ A♥ represents a longing for emotional expression and a desire for new opportunities in the world of love. It is an inventive and creative energy.

➢ 2♥ represents union and our desire to make and preserve our intimate, love relationships. It is an emotionally sensitive energy.

➢ 3♥ represents indecision or experimentation in love relationships. It is a creative, expressive energy that longs for diversity and fun.

➢ 4♥ represents home and family and the desire to create a firm foundation in love. It is a sensible, aware, and grounded energy.

➢ 5♥ represents a romantic, idealistic, and impractical approach to love and to relationships. It is a restless energy that longs for diversity.

➢ 6♥ represents a desire for harmony in relationships. This is a very sensitive, concerned, and gentle energy that can, at times, be too passive.

➢ 7♥ represents challenge and a search for the emotional balance in self and in relationships that will bring wisdom and beauty into the life. This is a receptive energy.

➢ 8♥ represents charisma and charm and the ability to get along with people. This is a very emotionally powerful energy, so care must be taken to act with integrity.

➢ 9♥ represents emotional generosity and an altruistic or humanitarian approach to people. This can be self-sacrificing energy and care must be taken to avoid martyrdom.

➢ 10♥ represents accomplishment and emotional fulfillment, particularly with family and friends. It is a creative, sometimes dramatic energy that longs for expression.

➢ J♥ represents inner nobility and is sometimes called the "Christ Card." It is an emotionally powerful energy that longs to teach others about love.

➢ Q♥ represents a strong need for creativity and may express itself passionately and dramatically. It is a maternal, dynamic energy.

➢ K♥ represents emotional strength through compassion and wisdom. It is both an emotional and an intellectual energy.

Clubs

This suit governs creativity, inspiration, and initiative. It can represent vision and energy and the desire to achieve. In an imbalanced expression, it may be restless, impulsive, and irresponsible.

➢ A♣ represents intellectual curiosity and an eagerness for knowledge and information. This is an inventive and innovative energy.

➢ 2♣ represents a need for mental stimulation but in connection to or association with other people. It is a potently communicative energy.

➢ 3♣ represents shrewd intellectual abilities, a desire to create, and is sometimes called the "Writer's Card." It is an innate, instinctively communicative energy.

➢ 4♣ represents intelligence, discipline, enthusiasm, and an enterprising spirit. It is an outspoken energy that does not suffer fools gladly.

➢ 5♣ represents a versatile, agile mind with a desire for adventure and action. It is a restless energy that longs for variety and diversity.

➢ 6♣ represents balance and responsibility in communication, and there is a need to be truthful and sincere. It is an inspirational energy that waxes and wanes.

➢ 7♣ represents the ability to analyze through intellect and through intuition. This is generally a self-confident energy that can be somewhat inflexible.

➢ 8♣ represents brainpower, both rational and psychic, with a belief that knowledge is power. It is a self-disciplined, organized, and opinionated energy.

➢ 9♣ represents humanitarianism, universal truth, and the collective consciousness. It is an energy that continually demands that the old is released and the new embraced.

➢ 10♣ represents a keen intelligence, a desire for knowledge, and is often called the "Teacher's Card." This is an ambitious energy, full of plans, dreams, and ideas.

➢ J♣ represents self-expression through the intellect. It is an analytical, inspired energy that is quick to understand concepts, philosophies, and ideas.

➢ Q♣ represents a strong intelligence and perceptive intuition. It is a decisive, persuasive energy that values self-reliance and independence.

➢ K♣ represents achievement through intellectualism, analysis, and organization. This is an energy that wants to be in charge and chafes at any subservient position.

Diamonds

This suit governs our physical world, money, and other material resources. It can represent a balanced approach to obtaining success, status, and wealth. In an imbalanced expression, it represents an obsession with status, success, and wealth.

➤ A♦ represents a desire to achieve in the material world and to have status and position. This is an enterprising, innovative, and creative energy.

➤ 2♦ represents material reward through partnerships, relationships, networking, and bargaining. This energy accomplishes through a combination of intuition and logic.

➤ 3♦ represents financial creativity and outstanding social energy. This energy includes good communication skills and an unconventional approach.

➤ 4♦ represents material success through diligence, organization, and hard work. It is a responsible, dependable energy.

➤ 5♦ represents variability in finances and the material world. This is a restless energy, and making and keeping money will not be done in a straightforward manner.

➤ 6♦ represents a need to create environmental harmony and to bring a responsible attitude to our finances and that which we value. This is an acutely perceptive energy.

➤ 7♦ represents an innate and astute sense of value that is enhanced through rational analysis and is often called the spiritual money card. This energy demands that what we get is as important as how it is gotten.

➤ 8♦ represents good fortune and the practical ability to attract abundance and to make money. It is a pragmatic, ambitious, and diligent energy.

➤ 9♦ represents completion as it relates to our values, the material world, and a move to a humanitarian approach. It is a shrewd, practical, and generous energy.

➤ 10♦ represents a desire to excel, success in the material world, and is the "Blessing Card." This is a generous energy that needs moderation and self-discipline.

➤ J♦ represents independent thinking and an expanded awareness of material satisfaction. This is energy with a strong need for personal freedom.

➤ Q♦ represents an embodiment and exemplification of higher values, such as faith, empathy, and compassion. The energy is loving and generous.

➤ K♦ represents business acumen, strong character, and ambition. This is a determined, proud, and unconventional energy that is willing to work hard to succeed.

Spades

This suit governs our philosophies and ideas, how we think and communicate. It can represent balance between our intuitive and rational minds. In an imbalanced expression, it represents either a negative worldview or a sole reliance on logical thinking at the expense of our intuition.

➤ A♠ represents a spiritual quest and finding identity through work and activities. This energy is about change, endings, and the attendant transformation.

➤ 2♠ represents cooperation within partnerships and the need to balance self needs with the needs of others. This is a diplomatic energy that should be in liberal use.

➤ 3♠ represents creativity, self-expression, and is often called the "Artists Card." The energy is inspirational, idealistic, and is associated with unique inner vision.

➤ 4♠ represents stability, security, and satisfaction in general but particularly in work. This is an ambitious, organized energy that is driven by a desire for material comfort.

➤ 5♠ represents restlessness that motivates change in work, home, lifestyle, and health. This is an edgy energy that seeks out divergent experiences and people.

➤ 6♠ represents a need for balance in work, family, and other responsibilities. This is a dreamy energy that longs to know the deeper mysteries of life.

➤ 7♠ represents intuition, introspection, and reflection. This is a mystical energy that helps balance behaviors that are self-defeating or negative.

➤ 8♠ represents success in the material world through organization, determination, and diligence. The energy here is of power and strong convictions.

➤ 9♠ represents diligence and determination to overcome challenges. This is emotionally sensitive energy that must be harnessed to disallow delay and disillusionment.

➤ 10♠ represents significant achievement and profound satisfaction through ambition and hard work. This is creative energy with an expansive vision.

➤ J♠ represents entry into esoteric wisdom and is called the "Spiritual Initiate Card." This is creative energy, and its expression will depend on values, maturity, and willingness.

➤ Q♠ represents self-mastery and shrewd insight into human affairs. This is diligent, clever energy that embraces hard work and desires accomplishment and recognition.

➤ K♠ represents immense potential for achievement if inspiration is followed and the common and the mundane is transcended. This is an independent, enduring energy.

Joker

> *Joker* is represented by zero and is a law unto itself. It is an unorthodox, nonconformist energy, and is a mystery and an enigma. Joker operates by a different set of rules; it can be or personify any card in the deck. It is eternal energy that is fascinating, intelligent, and creative.

Palmistry

Palmistry is the metaphysical study of our hands. Evidence of the practice of palmistry has been found in ancient Chinese, Indian, and Egyptian cultures. The Greek philosopher Aristotle wrote a book about palmistry. The tenets put forward in his book have not changed significantly since the time of that writing. Aristotle described the correlation between the shape of our hands and fingers and the lines and mounds found in the palms of our hands with certain observable or predictable characteristics or phenomenon.

Right Palm vs. Left Palm

There is some discussion regarding what information is to be found on which palm, and there are several ways of approaching this issue. Traditional palmists believe that the left palm reveals potentials or destinies, while the right palm reveals how we have used that potential and what we have accomplished. Some palmists believe that the dominant hand reveals potentials, whereas the non-dominant hand reveals how successfully we have accomplished those potentials. So if we are left-handed, the left hand reveals potential and the right hand reveals accomplishment.

Many modern palmists tend to consider the left palm as the palm that represents our personal and private life; it governs right-brain function, such as creative ability, imagination, emotion, and intuition. The right palm represents our public life; it governs left-brain function, such as reason, logic, language, science, math, and the material world.

The Lines on Our Palms

A palm with many lines indicates a person who is very open to the energies, emotions, and anxieties of others. A palm with fewer lines indicates a person who is well defended emotionally and is inclined to tend to personal business, paying little heed to the lives of others.

Strong lines indicate a strong sense of purpose. Weak lines indicate a weak sense of purpose. Interrupted lines indicate a questioning or hesitant approach, while lines that are uninterrupted indicate a more straightforward approach.

Thick lines mean that a tremendous amount of energy is available and is likely being utilized. Faint lines mean a lack of energy. Straight lines infer straightforwardness and all that this implies, such as directness, practicality, and consistency. Curved lines indicate flexibility and the ability to use unconventional or alternative tactics.

The Three Major Lines on Our Hands

➤ *The Life Line*, or Vitality Line, runs approximately from mid-palm and around the thumb. It is to be read from the thumb and going down toward the wrist. The Life Line represents the vigor and enthusiasm that we bring into our lives. It is represents stamina and how much effort and energy we are willing to expend to get what we want.

➤ *The Head Line* crosses mid-palm and is to be read from thumb to little finger. The Head Line indicates the characteristics and quality of our mind and intellectual inquisitiveness. It is about how we receive and process information, and how we articulate philosophies, ideas, and concepts. It is about our mental abilities and aptitude.

➤ *The Heart Line* starts beneath the little finger, moves across the upper palm, and generally ends at the base of the index or middle finger. The Heart Line represents our emotional approach to life and our personal feelings for those around us. It is about how we begin and end relationships. It is also about our sexual selves and what we need and want in the sexual arena.

Definition of the Fingers

➤ *The First Finger* is called the index finger and is associated with the planet Jupiter. The first finger represents our leadership abilities and our confidence in ourselves; it represents how we express our enthusiasms, interests, and relationship to success. If the first finger is long (rising above the nail base of the middle finger), we have confidence in our capacity to take a leadership role and take pride in our achievements. If the first finger is short, we lack confidence in our ability to make assessments and decisions. We lean toward the traditional and conservative.

➤ *The Second Finger* is called the middle finger and is associated with the planet Saturn. The second finger represents our relationship to our logical mind and the interplay between logic and emotion; it represents our ability to exercise restraint and take responsibility. If the second finger is long, we have an excellent ability to concentrate and to grasp information presented to us; we are able to think clearly and in a contained, controlled manner, even in the face of strong emotion. If our second finger is short (is a similar length to or shorter than the ring finger), we do not have a pronounced sense of responsibility, are not risk takers, and tend to play it safe. If the middle finger is curved. we may find it hard to let go and move on; there is a tendency to collect things, perhaps even to hoard.

➤ *The Third Finger* is called the ring finger and is associated with the Sun. The third finger represents our social self and our need to be accepted. It represents our personality and our relationship to personal growth. The third finger should be a similar length as the index finger. If the ring finger is longer than the index finger, we express ourselves in a social, joyful, and creative manner. If it is shorter, we are likely to be too inner directed or self-involved. If we have three or more Venus (vertical) lines at the base of the ring finger, we are able to see situations and issues from several perspectives and may have more than one career or love interest.

➤ *The Fourth Finger* is called the little finger and is associated with Mercury. The fourth finger represents our communication abilities and how we interpret the world around us. It represents how we understand the environments in which we find ourselves, including family environment. If our fourth finger is long (reaching to the first joint from the top of the ring finger), we are good communicators and clear thinkers. If the little finger bends away from the hand, we have an inclination toward deceitfulness. Vertical lines at the base of the little finger indicate an ability to think rationally and to make sound decisions.

➤ *The Thumb* is associated with Uranus and represents our ability to be true to ourselves and to be flexible in our attitudes. It represents how we think and our ability to be unconventional within the context of society. A long thumb (reaches to the middle joint of the index finger) indicates that we have a strong sense of ourselves and confidence about our place in the world. A short thumb (does not reach to the base of the index finger) indicates poor boundaries, an inability to think atypically, and dependence on others' opinions. A small space between the thumb and the side of the hand indicates inflexible thinking and an inability to think alternatively. A pronounced "waist" at the base of the thumb means that we are curious and engaged in life.

The shape of our hands, fingers, and fingernails also give us important information but will not be discussed here. If we want additional information, there are many resources devoted specifically to palmistry that can give us what we need or want. (I have listed some of these books in the reference section; however, there are many additional written resources).

Again, free will plays an important role. Choices made will physically alter the hands. Life's memories are written on our hands, and age and experience will alter them.

Part Two

The enneagram and graphology are slowing making their way into greater societal and cultural acceptance. The enneagram has been used in corporate settings, and graphology has been used both in corporate settings and within the legal system. Both the enneagram and graphology help us understand our character.

Our enneagram number is found through answering a series of questions. I will only give very brief information about the enneagram in this chapter; it will not include any questions or tests. The information given here is intended to pique your curiosity. For the questions and tests, please refer to any of the numerous books that have been written exclusively about the enneagram. (I have listed some of these books in the reference section; however, there are many additional written resources).

Graphology concerns itself with our handwriting. There are particular correlations between every aspect of our handwriting and our inner personal dynamics. Again, I will just give abbreviated information, and again, there are countless books and other resources available for a more extensive understanding of graphology. (I have listed some of these books in the reference section; however, there are many additional written resources).

Enneagram

The enneagram is thought to go back to ancient Babylon. It was ostensibly developed by the Sufis, a religious order of Muslim mystics, but then lost at some point in history. In the 1920s, Ivan Gurdjieff, a psychologist who lived in Paris at the time, discovered it and began to disseminate the information; how and where he unearthed the enneagram remains unknown.

The enneagram is a vehicle of self-discovery and can facilitate our understanding of our personality and character. Its purpose is to aid us in a deep, introspective look at the very core or essence of our innermost selves. The enneagram shows us how we perceive ourselves not how others perceive us. To find our personality type, there are tests that can be taken. However, by simply reading the descriptors of the nine types, we may be able to identify ourselves.

Ennea is the Greek word for the number nine, and *gram* is Greek for drawing. Enneagram, then, means a drawing with nine points. Within the nine points, there are three centers, or triads.

Enneagram Triads

➢ *Heart triad* people are concerned with emotions and relationships. We believe that understanding people is the most important goal, and we do it

‎ aware of people and their needs and trust that our
can make them feel valuable. We like interacting with
‎ seen in a positive light. We are sensitive to the
‎l when faced with a challenging situation, we attempt
‎nding what those around us are feeling and what they
‎ıt amount of time and energy are spent on personal
‎ers two, three, and four are in the heart triad.
‎le are thinkers and are calculating and deliberate. We
‎ty and look for the objective viewpoint. We collect
‎tion and believe that it is valuable and worthwhile;
‎en a challenging situation arises, we remain
‎nalyze it, and then decide whether or not we will
‎ınt to know the rule. We communicate through
‎selves as firmly grounded in reality. The numbers
‎ı the head triad.

➤ *Instinct triad* people are physically energetic and are concerned with survival and safety. We like to have influence and power. In challenging situations, we tend to take control and will adopt a firm stance. We make demands on others but make just as many demands on ourselves. We often compare ourselves with others just to see if we are doing well. We like to improve. It is important for us to know who is right and who is wrong because we like to be on the right side of any issue. Our reputation is important to us. Rearranging, changing, and improving things are regular activities for us. The numbers eight, nine, and one are in the instinct triad.

Wings are the numbers that are located on either side of our personality number. We have access to both wings, but one is generally dominant. For example, if your basic personality type is one, your wings are nine and two; if your basic personality type is four, your wings are three and five. The wings will complement or challenge the energy of your basic personality type.

Paths of Integration and Disintegration

We also have paths of integration and disintegration. The path of integration is a path of conscious choice, and moving in an integrated direction takes effort. The path of disintegration is the path of least resistance. It is the path we take when we are under stress or duress and are not expressing our best traits.

When we are on the path of integration, we are moving toward the positive qualities of our integration number; when we are on the path of disintegration, we are moving toward the negative qualities of our disintegration number:

Type	Integration	Disintegration
One	Seven	Four
Two	Four	Eight
Three	Six	Nine
Four	One	Two
Five	Eight	Seven
Six	Nine	Three
Seven	Five	One
Eight	Two	Five
Nine	Three	Six

The Enneagram initially focused on the negative aspect of our personality traits. However, in the past thirty to forty years, there has been a significant shift to include the positive personality traits and to give added attention to them. Ultimately, the goal is to move around the enneagram and integrate all of the positive expressions of all of the numbers. The enneagram is a system of self-development and transcendence.

Personality Types

➢ *One: The Perfectionist.* At our best, we are organized, efficient, practical, and realistic; we work hard and are able to accomplish a great deal. We are committed to justice and the truth, are honest and ethical, and like others to be so as well. We are self-disciplined, have high standards, and work hard to make life better for those around us. At our worst, we are critical, argumentative, and uncompromising. Our primary negative expression is anger.

➢ *Two: The Helper.* At our best, we are generous, nurturing, and sensitive to the needs and wants of those around us. We relate well to others and are good listeners. We like to have fun, are playful and enthusiastic, and enjoy good humor. We are adaptable and energetic. At our worst, we are insincere and emotionally needy, controlling and possessive. Our primary negative expression is pride.

➢ *Three: The Achiever.* At our best, we are self-confident, optimistic, and energetic. We set goals and have the self-direction and motivation to achieve them. We are industrious and bring a practical but frequently competitive energy into our jobs, even into our relationships. We like to win. At our worst, we are controlling and dishonest, self-absorbed, defensive, and impatient with people and situations around us. Our primary negative expression is deceit.

➢ *Four: The Individualist.* At our best, we are artistic and creative with a refined sense of the romantic. We are introspective and idealistic. Although we like to express ourselves, we also tend to be introverts. We like answers and can be quite intense in our search for them. We are intuitive, sensitive, and compassionate when relating to others. At our worst, we are emotionally needy, jealous, and moody; we are self-absorbed, self-righteous, and critical of others. Our primary negative expression is envy.

➢ *Five: The Observer.* At our best, we analytical, objective, and insightful. We like to relate one-to-one, are private about our lives and our selves, and are introverted and self-contained. We are curious and are often just a bit eccentric. We persevere at that which we think is important. At our worst, we are emotionally withdrawn, negative, suspicious, and argumentative. Our primary negative expression is greed.

➢ *Six: The Questioner.* At our best, we are responsible, reliable, dutiful, and loyal. We care about those around us and are compassionate, helpful, and trustworthy. We like good humor and are quite witty. We like to know the boundaries and limitations of that which is around us. At our worst, we are suspicious, controlling, inflexible, and sarcastic. Our primary negative expression is fear.

➢ *Seven: The Adventurer.* At our best, we are lively, energetic, and optimistic. We delight in ideas, our own and others', and are imaginative, quick, and spontaneous. We are charming, social, and like to have fun. We are productive and can accomplish a great deal in a short time. At our worst, we are distracted, defensive, self-absorbed, and opinionated. Our primary negative expression is gluttony.

➢ *Eight: The Leader.* At our best, we are courageous, confident, and able to command authority in difficult situations. We are straightforward with others, are protective of those we love, and are faithful and loyal. We have a tendency to be intense, assertive, and forceful. At our worst, we are arrogant, combative, possessive, and demanding. Our primary negative expression is lust.

➢ *Nine: The Peacemaker.* At our best, we are patient, peaceful, and pleasant. We are generous, supportive, and reassuring with others. Due to our vast capacity for empathy, we generally know what those around us need. We are able to see many sides of any issue, have good diplomatic skills, and are good mediators. At our worst, we are stubborn, unassertive, defensive, and are too willing to accommodate. Our primary negative expression is sloth.

Graphology

Graphology is the study of the shapes and patterns in individual handwriting. It reveals the expression of our personality and is an indicator of our behaviors. Interestingly, if we make it our intention to expend the effort to change certain aspects of our handwriting, we can also change aspects of the correlating behaviors.

The American Psychological Association has issued a statement indicating that graphology can be a reliable tool for determining character traits, such as risk for substance abuse, emotional stability, and tendencies regarding honesty. Graphology is taught in major universities in Germany, Israel, and France.

The first known documentation of graphology appeared in 1622 when an Italian physician and university professor, Camillo Baldi, wrote a treatise entitled, *A Method to Recognize the Nature and Quality of a Writer from his Letters*. However, interest in the correlation between handwriting and human behavior and personality is as ancient as writing itself. Confucius, who lived between 551 BCE and 479 BCE, cautioned his followers to "beware of the man whose writing sways like a reed in the wind."

In 1985, a German, William Preyer, conducted a series of experiments and established handwriting analysis as "brain writing." He discovered that fundamental similarities existed in the writer's handwriting idiosyncrasies, even when writers used the opposite hand, their mouth, or their feet. Handwriting is a centrally organized function of our brain.

There are hundreds of books written regarding graphology, and only an abbreviated description will be given here. Graphology is complicated and multifaceted, and the manner in which each individual letter is written is significant. People form letters in numerous ways, and each letter indicates a personality trait or behavior. For the level of detail needed in regard to individual letters, however, books specifically devoted to graphology are indicated.

The Importance of Letters

The Personal Pronoun "I"

The personal pronoun "I" has considerable significance, as it reveals how we see ourselves and how we project our image into the world. The "I" represents our ego. It describes our personality, identity, and character. Following is an extremely brief explanation of the personal pronoun "I."

If the "I" is made as a straight standing line (I) with connected bars across the top and the bottom, we are good rational thinkers. We are capable, constructive, and confident. If the "I" is one straight line, we are aware of our own value, have a strong ego, and are independent. If we form the "I" in an unfinished manner, we have a poorly formed ego and may not like other people.

If we have a large upper loop, we may be somewhat vain and like to talk about ourselves. If we cross the upper loop, we may be self-rejecting. A pointed upper loop indicates a keen mind.

When the other letters are straight but our "I" leans left, we are likely a self-critical introvert. Right-leaning "I" indicates extroversion, but if our "I" is extremely right slanted, we may be self-absorbed.

The Lowercase "t"

With lowercase "t," the stem, the height of the stem, and the bar are important. If we have a looped stem, we are articulate and talkative and do not necessarily find it important to conform to the desires of others. A pointed and separated stem indicates stubbornness and duplicity. A long stem signifies an intellectual inclination, while a short stem points to a more conventional nature. A stem that is spread out suggests indolence.

If we make our bar above the stem, we are comfortable living in the world of our imagination. If our bar is high but on the stem, we are ambitious and idealistic. If our bar is low on the stem, we doubt our abilities and are underachievers. A long, sharp bar indicates sarcasm, while a short bar indicates timidity. A bar with a downstroke suggests bossiness, while a bar with an upstroke represents optimism. An undulating bar implies a certain level of frivolousness, gaiety, and a love of fun.

Our Page: We Begin to Write

In graphology, the blank page is our world. The manner in which we place our message on the page indicates how we look at our world, how we approach it, how we respond to it, and how we interact with it. As we mature and change, so too does our handwriting. An analysis of handwriting indicates character and behavior at the present time. Changing our handwriting can help us alter traits or mannerisms that we wish to change.

We Choose Our Ink

The color of the ink that we choose is meaningful. Blue ink signifies a happy, friendly attitude, whereas black ink reveals a more conventional, efficient approach. Red ink reveals an exaggerated sense of self, a sensual nature, and a desire to be the center of attention. Green or other colored inks are often used by young people and illustrate a desire to be different.

Our Margins
Margins indicate our unconscious attitudes toward space and how we use it. Upper, lower, right, and left margins are all examined when analyzing handwriting. For instance, if our upper margin is wide, we likely have a more formal and reserved aspect to our character. If it is narrow, we tend toward a more informal and direct approach.

A wide lower margin is indicative of superficiality and aloofness in our dealings with others, while a narrow margin signifies a lack of reserve and over-familiarity with others.

Left margins designate self-esteem and the esteem we desire from others. Right margins indicate the distance we desire between others and ourselves.

Line Spacing
Spacing between lines, letters, and words is significant. The amount of space we allow between lines indicates the distance we wish to keep between awareness of our emotions and ourselves. Spacing between words signifies how much space we desire between others and ourselves. Spacing between letters in words reveals our tendency toward introversion or extroversion.

Zones
As we write a line of script, there are three visible zones: the upper, the middle, and the lower. For instance, in the upper zone is the top of the written "d" or "b," in the lower zone is the bottom of the "f" or "g,"and the "o" and "r" are in the middle.

The upper zone reveals our degree of intellect, abstract thought, and imagination. It indicates our spiritual aspirations as well. This zone is future oriented.

The middle zone represents the present. It signifies everyday concerns, daily goals, and habits.

The lower zone looks to the past and reveals our relationship to our material world. It indicates the strength or weakness of our desire for material possessions. It also represents our sexuality and biological drives.

The Slope of Our Lines
The slope of our lines is also central to our understanding of our selves through the analysis of our handwriting. An upward sloping line indicates optimism and joy. It signifies an affectionate nature. An upward sloping line reveals the ability to confront and manage adverse situations and circumstances.

A downward sloping line signifies physical fatigue or a weariness of life in general. It indicates discouragement and disappointment. A downward sloping line very often reveals depression.

A steady line reveals self-control and reliability. The steady line indicates a logical, reasonable approach and an ability to be emotionally dispassionate.

Arches in our line slopes designate an enthusiastic start but a quick loss of interest in many of our enterprises. Concaves in the slope of our lines specify a slower start but an increasing amount of enthusiasm.

The Size of Our Letters

The size, or the height and width, of our letters indicate our creative abilities, our degree of self-esteem, and living space issues. Average-sized letters are indicative of adaptability and represent a reasonable and logical approach to situations and issues. They signify a composed and polite personality.

If we write with large letters, we are generally quite comfortable being the center of attention. We are self-confident and ambitious. Large letters signify a forceful personality and a tendency to monopolize conversations.

Small letters indicate the ability to understand the importance of detail. Small letters represent a rational, analytical mind. They epitomize the resourceful academician.

Varied letters—some average, some small or large—reveal a vivacious, excitable personality. Moodiness and quick temper are also indicated, however.

Letter Strokes

Letter strokes are how we begin, connect, or end our letters. They indicate social attitudes and represent how we assess new situations and how we adjust to them. They represent our unconscious or authentic selves.

If the beginning of our letter is long and below the baseline, we have a need to succeed. If it is absent, we want to start something without delay. If the beginning starts in the upper zone, we are idealistic.

If the ending of our letter is long and stretches outward, we are generous. If it reaches upward, we like credit for what we have accomplished. If our letter ends on an exceptionally high note, we are seekers of knowledge. If it is blunt and does not extend outward, we are candid and decisive.

If we connect our letters evenly, we are logical and systematic. If our letter connectors are disconnected, we are imaginative, creative, and nonconformists.

References

Adler, Margot. *Drawing Down the Moon: Witches, Druids, Goddess-Worshippers, and Other Pagans in America.* Boston: Beacon Press, 1979.

Amend, Karen and Ruiz, Mary S. *Hand Writing Analysis: The Complete Basic Book.* California: Newcastle Publishing Co Inc, 1986.

Andrews, Ted. *Animal Speak: The Spiritual & Magical Powers of Creatures Great and Small.* Minnesota: Llewellyn Publications, 1993.

Andrews, Ted. *Animal-Wise: The Spirit Language and Signs of Nature.* Tennessee: Dragonhawk Publishing, 1999.

Andrews, Ted. *How to Heal with Color (How to Series).* Minnesota: Llewellyn Publications, 2006.

Ashley, Leonard R N. *The Complete Book of Numerology.* New Jersey: Barricade Books, 2005.

Avery, Kevin Quinn DMS. *The Numbers of Life: The Hidden Power in Numerology.* New York: Doubleday & Company Inc, 1977.

Barnstone, Willis and Meyer, Marvin. *The Gnostic Bible: Gnostic Texts of Mystical Wisdom from the Ancient and Medieval Worlds.* Boston and London: New Seeds Books, 2006.

Bartlett, Sarah. *The Tarot Bible: The Definitive Guide to the Cards and Spreads.* New York: Sterling Publishing Co, 2006.

Birkbeck, Lyn. *The Watkins Astrology Handbook: The Practical System of DIY Astrology.* London: Watkins Publishing, 2006.

Blum, Ralph. *Rune Play: A Method of Self Counseling and a Year-Round Rune Casting Recordbook.* New York: St Martin's Press, 1985.

Bly, Carol. *Changing the Bully Who Rules the World: Reading and Thinking About Ethics.* Minnesota: Milkweed Editions, 1996.

Bolen, Jean Shinoda MD. *Goddesses in Every Woman: A New Psychology of Women.* New York: Harper Colophon, 1985.

Briere, John PH.D and Scott, Catherine M.D. *Principles of Trauma Therapy: A Guide to Symptoms, Evaluation and Treatment.* California: Sage Publications Inc, 2006.

Buchman, Dian Dincin. *Herbal Medicine: The Natural Way to Get Well and Stay Well.* New Jersey: Wing Books, 1994.

Buess, Lynn M. *Numerology for the New Age.* California: DeVorss & Company, 1982.

Byrd, Anita. *Handwriting Analysis.* New York: Arco Publishing, 1982.

Camp, Robert Lee. *Cards of your Destiny: What Your Birthday Reveals About You and Your Past, Present and Future.* Illinois: Sourcebooks, Inc, 2004.

Camp, Robert Lee. *Love Cards, 2E: What Your Birthday Reveals About You and Your Personal Relationships.* Illinois: Sourcebooks Inc, 2004.

Cheung, Theresa. *The Element Encyclopedia of the Psychic World: The Ultimate A-Z of Spirits, Mysteries, and the Paranormal.* London: Harper Element, 2006

Chocron, Daya Sarai. *The Healing Power of Shells: Gifts of the Sea.* Great Britain: Earthdancer Books, 2005.

Cleary, Thomas. *I Ching, the Book of Changes.* Boston & London: Shambhala, 1992.

Clifford, Frank C. *Palm Reading Deck of Cards.* New York: Metro Books, 2008.

Conway, Flo and Siegelman, Jim. *Holy Terror: The Fundamentalist War on America's Freedoms in Religion, Politics and Our Private Lives.* New York: Dell Publishing Co Inc, 1982, 1984.

Decoz, Hans and Monte, Tom. *Numerology.* New York: Perigee Book, 1994.

De Sainte Colombe, Paul. *Grapho-Therapeutics: Pen and Pencil Therapy.* California: Paul de Ste. Colombe Center, 1980.

Driggs, John H. *Soulless: When Someone You Love Doesn't Have a Conscience.* © 2005. Presented Century College, MN: December 7, 2007.

Duke, James A PH.D. *The Green Pharmacy Herbal Handbook: Your Comprehensive Reference to the Best Herbs for Healing.* USA: Rodale/Reach, 2000.

Dunn, Teri. *100 Favorite Perennials.* New York: Metro Books, 1998.

Erlandsen, Kristin. *Real Estate Feng Shui: From "For Sale" to "Sold" in 9 Easy Steps.* Minnesota: Peaceful Places Publishing, 2010.

Fairchild, Dennis. *The Fortune Telling Handbook.* Philadelphia, London: Running Press, 2003.

Frankl, Viktor E. *Man's Search for Meaning.* Boston: Beacon Press, 2006.

Gardner, Joy. *Healing Yourself.* Washington: Healing Yourself Publishing, 1980.

Gardner, Ruth. *Instant Handwriting Analysis: a Key to Personal Success.* Minnesota: Llewellyn Publications, 1989.

Gerulskris-Estes, Susan. *The Book of Tarot: Illustrated With the Morgan-Greer Tarot.* Connecticut: U S Games Systems Inc, 1981.

Gettings, Fred. *The Arkana Dictionary of Astrology.* London: The Penguin Group, 1985.

Ginsburg, Herbert and Opper, Sylvia. *Piaget's Theory of Intellectual Development.* New Jersey: Prentice-Hall Inc, 1969.

Goodwin, Matthew Oliver. *Numerology: The Complete Guide, Volume 1, The Personality Reading.* California: Newcastle Publishing Co, 1981.

Goodwyn, Melba. *Ghost Worlds: A Guide to Poltergeists, Portals, Ecto-Mist, and Spirit Behavior.* Minnesota: Llewellyn Publications, 2007.

Gray, Susan. *The Woman's Book of Runes.* New York: Barnes & Noble, 1999.

Green, Jane Nugent. *You and Your Private I: Personality and the Written Self Image.* Minnesota: Llewellyn Publications, 1983.

Greenaway, Kate. *Language of Flowers*. New York: Dover Publications, 1992.
Greene, Brian. *The Elegant Universe: Super Strings, Hidden Dimensions, and the Quest for the Ultimate Theory*. New York, Vintage Books: 2003.
Hageneder, Fred. *The Meaning of Trees: Botany, History, Healing, Lore*. California: Chronicle Books, 2005.
Hall, Judy. *The Astrology Bible The: Definitive Guide to the Zodiac*. New York: Sterling Publishing Co, 2005.
Hall, Judy. *The Crystal Bible*. Ohio: Walking Stick Press, 2003.
Hanson, Michelle. *Ocean Oracle: What Seashells Reveal About our True Nature*. Oregon: Beyond Worlds Publishing, 2007.
Harding, Esther M. *Woman's Mysteries: Ancient and Modern*. New York: Harper Colophon, 1971.
Hay, Louise. *Heal Your Body: The Mental Causes for Physical Illness and the Metaphysical Way to Overcome Them*. California: Hay House, 1984 (expanded, revised 1988)
Hicks, Esther and Jerry. *Ask and it is Given: Learning to Manifest Your Desires*. California: Hay House, 2004.
Hicks, Esther and Jerry. *The Law of Attraction: The Basics of the Teachings of Abraham*. California: Hay House, 2006.
Hicks, Esther and Jerry. *The Astonishing Power of Emotions*. California: Hay House, 2007.
Hine, Lewis. *Lewis Hine: Photographs of Child Labor in the New South*, Mississippi: University Press of Mississippi, 1986.
Hoffman, David. *The New Holistic Herbal*. New York: Barnes and Noble Books, 1990.
Hoopes, Margaret M and Harper, James M. *Birth Order Roles and Sibling Patterns in Individual and Family Therapy*. Maryland: Aspen Publishers Inc, 1987.
Hurley, Kathleen V and Dobson, Theodore E. *What's My Type?* California: Harper Collins Publisher, 1991.
International Society for the Study of Trauma and Dissociation, and Midwest Society for the Study of Trauma and Dissociation. *Advances in the Integrated Treatment of Trauma: Processing, Affect Regulation and Mindfulness*. Presented: Briere, John PH.D. Bloomington, MN: May 2, 2008.
Institute for Natural Resources. *His Brain, Her Brain*. Concord, California: © 2007.
Isaacs, Alan (edit). *Dictionary of Physics*. London: Constable & Robinson Ltd, 2003.
Jamison, Kay Redfield. *An Unquiet Mind: A Memoir of Moods and Madness*. New York: Vintage Books, 1996.
Jeffers, Sharon. *Cards of Destiny: A Birthday Book and Daily Divination Guide*. California: Crossing Press, 2006.

Jones, Roger S. *Physics for the Rest of Us: Ten Basic Ideas of Twentieth Century Physics That Everyone Should Know…and How They Have Shaped Our Culture and Consciousness.* New York: Barnes & Noble, 1999.

Jordan, Juno Dr. *Many Things on Numerology: Controversies and Questions.* California: DeVorss & Company, 1981.

Jordan, Juno Dr. *Numerology: the Romance in Your Name.* California DeVorss & Company, 1965.

Jordan, Juno Dr. *Your Right Action Number.* California; DeVorss & Company, 1983.

Katsaros, Peter. *National Audubon Society Pocket Guide to Familiar Mushrooms.* New York: Alfred A. Knopf, 2008.

Keyes, Ken Jr.. *The Hundredth Monkey.* Oregon: Vision Books, 1983.

Laing, R D. *The Politics of the Family and Other Essays.* New York: Vintage Books, 1972.

Lehner, Ernst and Johanna. *Folklore and Symbolism of Flowers, Plants and Trees (Dover Pictorial Archive).* New York: Dover Publications, 2003.

Lincoff, Gary H. *National Audubon Society Field Guide to Mushrooms.* New York: Alfred A. Knopf, 1981.

Linden, Anne'. *Boundaries in Human Relationships: How to be Separate and Connected.* Connecticut: Crown House Publishing Ltd, 2008.

Mariechild, Diane. *Mother Wit: a Feminist Guide to Psychic Development.* New York: The Crossing Press, 1981.

Marthaler, Dennis and Marilyn. *Illness, Thoughts and Change.* Minneapolis Minnesota: Published: Marthaler, Dennis and Marilyn, 1982.

Matthews, Rupert; Emerson, Richard; Harwood, Jeremy; Selsdon, Esther; McCulloch, Victoria; Devereux, Paul. *Unseen World The: Science, Theories and Phenomena Behind Paranormal Events.* New York: Reader's Digest Book, Essential Works, Ltd., 2008.

McCabe, James D. *The Language and Sentiment of Flowers.* Massachusetts: Applewood Books, 2003.

Merrill, Francis E. *Society and Culture: An Introduction to Sociology.* Englewood Cliffs, New Jersey: Prentice-Hall Inc., 1965.

Miller, Stephen M. Ohio: Barbour Publishing Inc, 2007.

Mills, C Wright. *The Power Elite.* New York: Oxford University Press, 1968.

Mindell, Earl R.PH, PH.D. *Earl Mindell's Herb Bible.* New York: Fireside, 1992.

Moore, Barbara. *The Gilded Tarot Companion.* Minnesota: Llewellyn Publications, 2007.

Morag, Hali. *Runes (Complete Guides Series).* Israel: Astrolog Publishing Company, 2003.

Mottana, Annibale and Crespi, Rodolfo and Liborio, Giuseppe. *Guide to Rocks and Minerals.* New York: Simon & Schuster, 1977.

Mussen, Paul Henry and Conger, John Janeway and Kagan, Jerome. *Child Development and Personality.* New York: Harper & Row, 1969.

New Covenant: New Testament. (New Revised Standard Version Bible). Iowa: World Bible Publishers Inc, 1989.

Ozaniec, Naomi. *101 Essential Tips Everyday Meditation.* New York: Dorling Kindersley Limited, 1997, 2003.

O'Connell, Mark and Airey, Raje. *The Complete Encyclopedia of Signs and Symbols: Identification, Analysis and Interpretation of the Visual Codes and the Subconscious Language that Shapes and Describes our Thoughts and Emotions.* U K: 2006.

Oliver, Evelyn Dorothy and Lewis, James R.. *Angels A to Z.* Michigan: Visible Ink Press, 2008.

Pagels, Elaine. *The Gnostic Gospels.* New York: Vintage Books, 1979 .

Palmer, Helen and Brown, Paul B. *The Enneagram Advantage: Putting the Nine Personality Types to Work in the Office.* New York: Three Rivers Press, 1997.

PESI. Presented: Warner, Colleen Dr. *The Boss is Out: Helping Students with Executive Dysfunction.* Wisconsin: PESI LLC,© 2008.

Peshkin, Alan. *God's Choice: the Total World of a Fundamental Christian School.* Chicago: University of Chicago Press, 1986.

Rehder, Harald A. *National Audubon Society Field Guide to Shells.* New York: Alfred A Knopf, 1981.

Riske, Kris Brandt. *The Complete Book of Astrology: The Easy Way to Learn Astrology.* Minnesota, Llewellyn Publications, 2008.

Riso, Don Richard. *Personality Types: Using the Enneagram for Self-Discovery.* Boston: Houghton Mifflin Company, 1987.

Riso, Don Richard. *Discovering Your Personality Type: The New Enneagram Questionnaire.* Boston: Houghton Mifflin Company, 1995.

Rogers-Gallagher, Kim. *Astrology for the Light Side of the Brain.* California: ACS Publications, 1995.

Royal, Penny C. *Herbally Yours: A Comprehensive Herbal Handbook Simple Enough for the Herbal Student, Complete Enough for the Herbal Practitioner.* Utah: BiWorld Publishers, 1981.

Sacks, Oliver. *An Anthropologist on Mars: Seven Paradoxical Tales.* New York: Vintage Books, 1995.

Schaef, Anne Wilson. *Women's Reality: An Emerging Female System.* Minnesota: Winston Press, 1981.

Simmons, Robert and Ahsian, Naisha. *The Book of Stones: Who They Are And What They Teach*. Vermont: Heaven & Earth Publishing LLC, 2005.

Simpson, Liz. *The Book of Chakra Healing*. New York: Sterling Publishing Co Inc, 1999.

Slater, Lauren. *Welcome to My Country*. New York: Random House, 1996.

Snyder, Leon. *Flowers for Northern Gardens*. Minnesota: University of Minnesota Press, 1983.

Starchild, Zera. *The Aquarian Runes: The Ancient Art of Runecasting Enters the Aquarian Age*. California: Doorway Publications & Books, 1993.

Stephens, Jose and Warwick-Smith, Simon. *The Michael Handbook: A Channeled System for Self Understanding*. California: Warwick Press, 1990.

Stern, Kenneth S. *A Force upon the Plain: The American Militia Movement and the Politics of Hate*. New York: Simon & Schuster, 1996.

Stone, Nannette. *The Little Black Book of Tarot,*. New York: Peter Pauper Press Inc, 2005.

Sullivan, Geri and Crawford, Saffi. *The Power of Playing Cards: An Ancient System for Understanding Yourself, Your Destiny and Your Relationships*. New York: Fireside, 2004 .

Thorsson, Edred. *Futhark: a Handbook of Rune Magic*. Maine: Samuel Weiser, Inc, 1985.

Titlow, Budd. *Seashells Jewels from the Sea*. Minnesota: Voyageur Press, 2007

Tyler, Varro E. PH.D. *The Honest Herbal: A Sensible Guide to the Use of Herbs and Related Remedies*. New York: Pharmaceutical Products Press, 1993.

Virtue, Doreen. *Chakra Clearing*. California: Hay House Inc, 2004.

Wanless, James PH.D. *Voyager Tarot: Intuition Cards for the 21st Century*. Massachusetts: Fair Winds Press, 1998.

Weinstein, Marion. *Positive Magic: Ancient Metaphysical Techniques for Modern Lives*. New Jersey: New Page Books, 2002.

Woolfolk, Martine Joanna. *The Only Astrology Book You'll Ever Need*. Maryland: Taylor Trade Publishing, 2006.

Young, Ellin Dodge and Schuler, Carol Ann. *The Vibes Book: A Game of Self Analysis*. New York: Noble Offset Printers, 1979.

Zim, Herbert S and Ingle, Lester. *Seashores*. New York: Golden Press, 1955.

Zim, Herbert S and Shaffer, Paul R. *Rock and Minerals: A Guide to Minerals, Gems, and Rocks (Golden Press #24499)*. New York: Golden Press, 1957.

Movies

What the Bleep Do We Know, Dir. William Arntz, Co-Dir. Betsy Chasse and Mark Vicente, Roadside Attractions, 2004, DVD, *What the Bleep Do We Know, Down the Rabbit Hole: Quantum Edition*, Fox Home Entertainment, 2006

CPSIA information can be obtained at www.ICGtesting.com
Printed in the USA
BVOW060205260412

288709BV00005B/30/P

9 781452 546285